Practical Composition in Photography

The Practical Photography Series

Practical Composition in Photography Axel Brück
Practical Exposure in Photography Leonard Gaunt
Practical Effects in Photography Carl Bernard & Karen No
Practical Wildlife Photography Ken Preston-Mafham

Axel Brück

Practical Composition in Photography

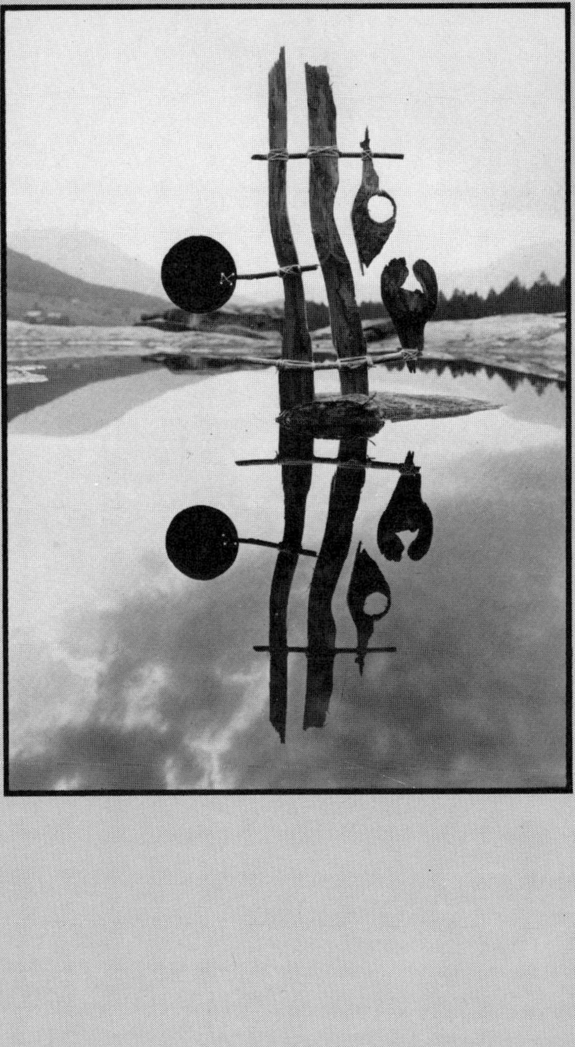

Focal Press London & Boston

Focal Press
is an imprint of the Butterworth Group
which has principal offices in
London, Boston, Durban, Singapore, Sydney, Toronto, Wellington

First published 1981
Reprinted 1982

British Library Cataloguing in Publication Data

Brück, Axel
Practical composition in photography. –
(Practical series).
1. Composition (Photography)
I. Title
770′.28 TR179 80–40–759

ISBN 0–240–51060–7

Printed and bound in Great Britain by A. Wheaton & Co., Exeter

Contents

1 Composition: Its Meanings and Implications

If you look up the word 'composition' in a dictionary, you will probably find a definition like this: 'C.: well thought-out arrangement'. This suggests that we are going to deal with arrangements in photography (well thought-out or not). But such a definition is not really very helpful and in this book I will be demonstrating that there is much more to the term 'composition' than is at first apparent. Indeed, even the definition quoted above contains much more information than is immediately obvious and we really should look at it more closely. Although I do not wish to bore you with a purely theoretical discussion, we should be clear and agreed upon what we are talking about before becoming involved with the application of composition to photography. By necessity, and because I believe that you are much more interested in the practical side of things, I will be brief. So do not skip the following page or two, for even a cursory impression of the principle of the thing will give you a firmer grasp and better understanding of our discussion.

Now, to return to the definition quoted above. It consists of two parts dealing with entirely different concepts.

Arrangement of pictorial elements

The first part which we will deal with concerns the term 'arrangement'. This word implies that there are elements which are arranged by someone. This someone of course is you as the photographer. Thus there remains the question: What are the elements (of composition) which you arrange when creating a photograph? We will of course go very carefully into these elements in the following chapters, but it should be noted here that everything – let me repeat *everything* – which goes into the making of a photograph is to be regarded as an element of composition.

This needs some explaining. Usually, when someone is talking about composition, he is exclusively concerned with the so-called pictorial elements and their arrangement. This means that he deals with lines, diagonals, triangles, planes of different values, etc. But this is an inadmissible simplification because everything which contributes to the overall appearance of a photograph is an element of composition, from the things enumerated above to the type of paper used and even the surroundings in which the photograph is presented. These factors naturally affect the subject matter of a photograph in that it advances from an element of the environment to an element of composition due to the photographer's decision to represent it in the photograph and to do so in a certain way.

Although an almost unlimited number of viewpoints is possible with this kind of subject, the frontal one shows its organisation most clearly. The parallel lines between the different parts of the picture stress its simplicity.

The first picture (*1*) I have chosen for this book is an example of this last point. It shows the edge of a field of reeds (knowing next to nothing about plants I at least believe them to be that), rendered in an extremely simple configuration. The picture is divided into three sections (from top to bottom): the empty (white) sky, the reeds and the ground. The section depicting the reeds is further divided into three sections characterised by the following properties: the top section, containing few stems and the blooms; the middle part, consisting of a mass of criss-crossing stems and the bottom part, where fewer stems run almost parallel to each other in front of a dark background. These, then, are the main picture elements.

Having kept in mind our argument that composition is a form of arrangement, you should now be able to evaluate the things thus described. You might have been tempted to dismiss them as a simple description of some properties of the subject matter. If you really still think so, you should look again. Walking along the edge of a field of reeds, as I did when taking this photograph, I discovered that there is enormous variety in the way these plants can grow. But even if you chose this same spot to take a picture you would still have a large number of ways in which to realise your photograph.

When you decide to take a picture of any one part of a subject and to render it in a certain way, you have transformed the properties of your subject into elements of composition by your decision, which leads to a fundamental principle of composition: when you take a picture of something, you do not depict reality. By choosing to isolate a segment of reality in the frame of your photograph and by arranging the elements of this segment of reality through the properties of the photographic process and by your choice of viewpoint, moment of exposure, etc., you re-arrange reality: you compose a photograph. If this were not so, the term 'composition' would be entirely without meaning. If taking a photograph meant nothing more than depicting reality, then there could be no question of arranging anything. On the other hand, if you *do* arrange something, there can be no talk of 'just depicting reality'.

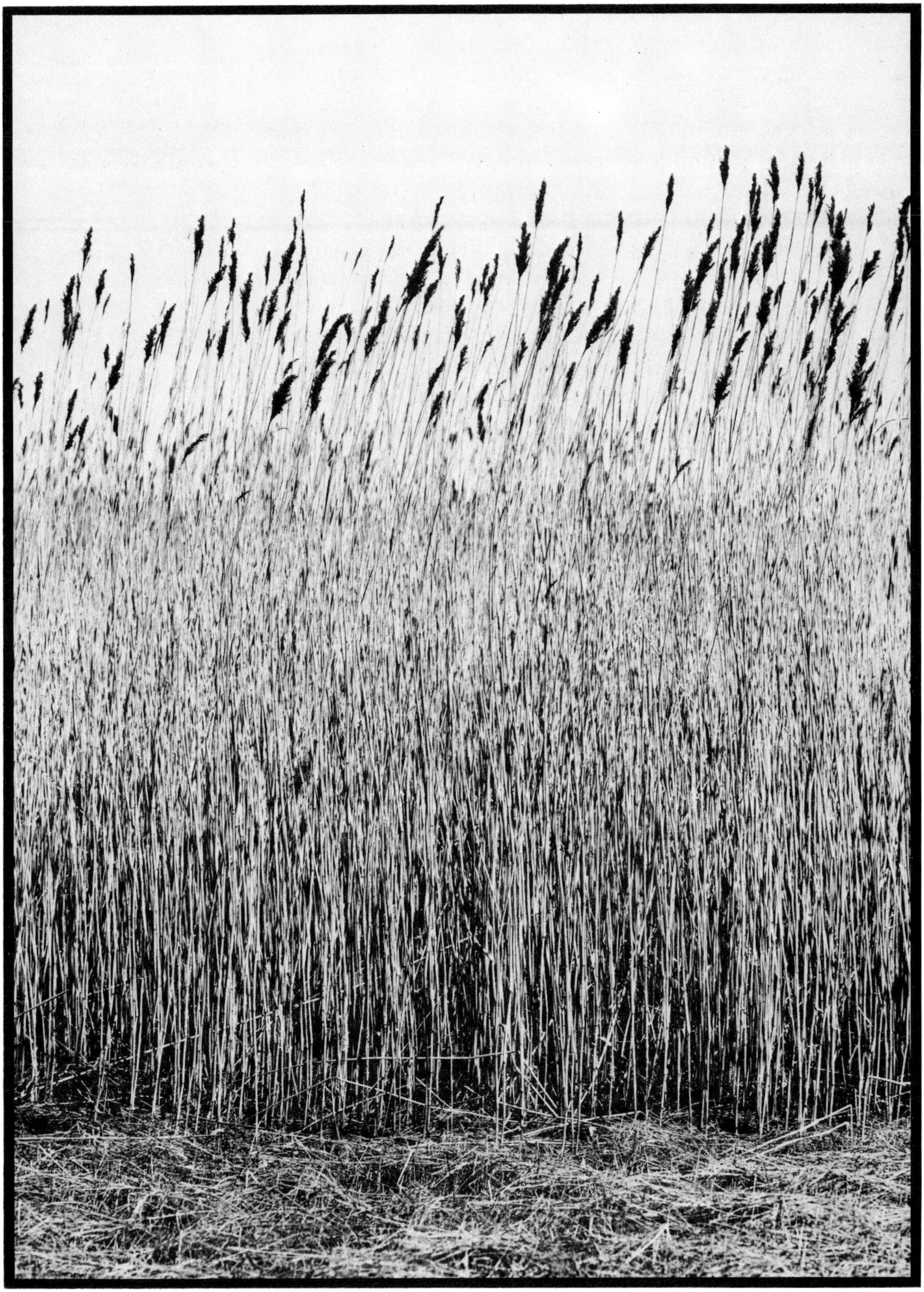

1

The meaning of a photograph

This brings us to the second aspect of the definition quoted at the beginning of this chapter 'Composition is a well thought-out arrangement'. So far we have only considered the 'arrangement', now we have to deal with the 'well thought-out' part. We have already discussed the photographer's role in choosing to arrange the elements of his picture. Indeed, the word 'arrangement' implies that there is no question of chance as far as the distribution or disposal of the pictorial elements is concerned. When taking a picture the photographer has definite intentions, ideas, feelings or whatever you want to call them, which he wants to form into an image. (This does not necessarily imply conscious cerebral activity, it might be a process which is partly or even completely governed by the subconscious.) In order to do so he must make use of the properties of his subject matter on the one hand and of the possibilities offered by the photographic process on the other.

So the first thing is the photographer's personality and his vision (generally speaking and as far as the actual picture is concerned). There are two aspects to his ability to create an image: first the subject matter and its properties and second his photographic equipment and technique and the possibilities which these offer. Composition is the means of bringing these two aspects together and to form an image according to the vision of the photographer. This is extremely important and you should think carefully about it, because it shows that composition is not mechanical and so concerned only with the tasteful distribution of pictorial elements on paper. On the contrary, composition is mainly a question of the *meaning* of pictures. If the photographer uses composition as a means to express his vision (whatever that may be), the composition provides the means by which the viewer may perceive the mood and/or meaning of the picture.

It could perhaps be explained this way: photographs are an 'optical' language. The properties of the subject matter and the scope of the photographic techniques employed constitute the vocabulary of this language. This leaves us with composition as the 'grammar' of this language, whose structure provides us with ways and means to make significant statements in the language of photography.

This description, which after all is nothing but an elaborate version of the definition of composition as a well thought-out arrangement, dictates the approach used in this book. The first and relatively easy part is to take stock of the structures of composition. The second and more complicated part is to find

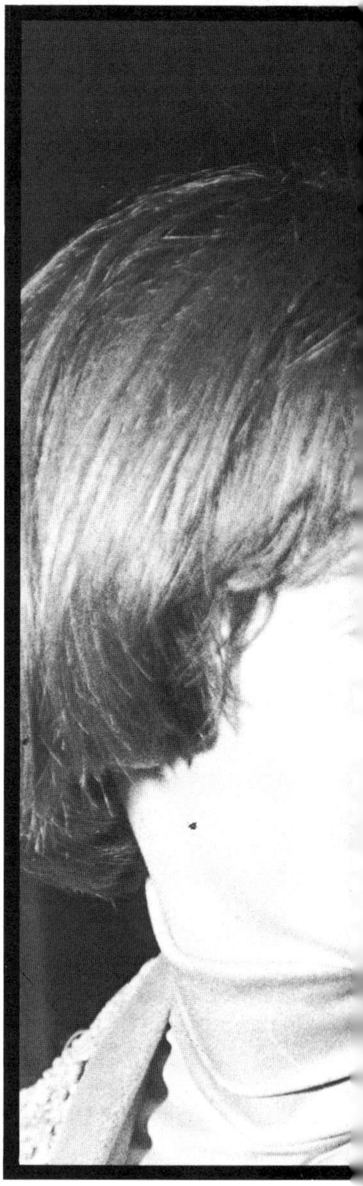

When photographing couples one of the strongest elements of composition is the direction of their gaze. This is true even if its physical representation is very weak, as in this picture, where you cannot even see their eyes. There are two reasons for

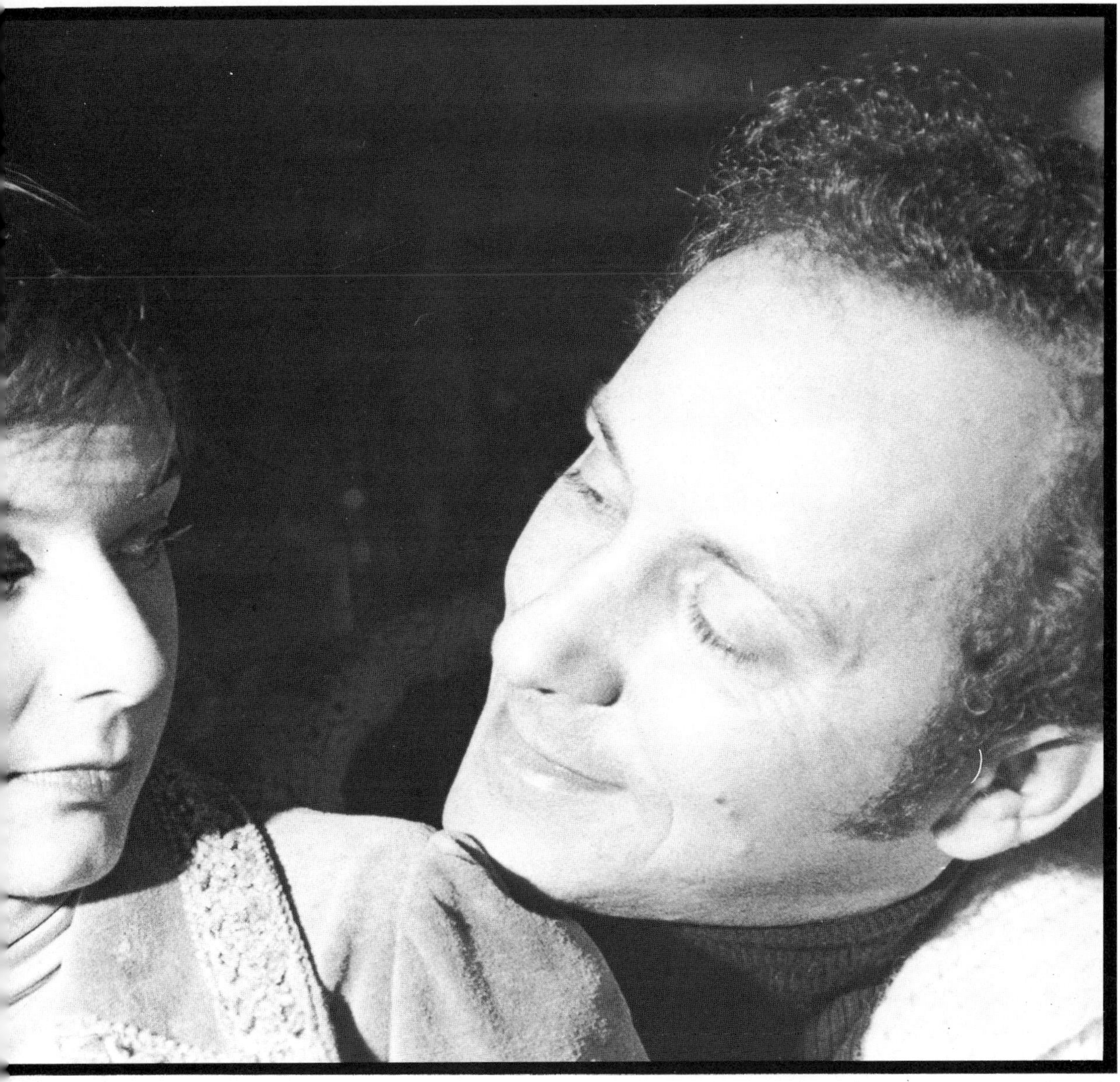

2

this: first, the way people look at each other and their surroundings can be psychologically very revealing. Second, this leads the viewer to a strong (albeit subconscious) reaction to this element of the composition. So always take great care with it.

out how these structures can be employed to impart mood and/or meaning to photographs. But, because this is a book and not a lecture or personal talk, I can demonstrate the points only with photographs which I have chosen for this purpose. They are nothing but examples. If you want to learn more about composition you will have to apply the statements and examples given to your own photography – doing it your own way and adapting them to your own ideas and intentions.

2 Some Rules of Composition

Everyone who is interested in art and/or photography seems to know some rules of compositon or at least seems to know of their existence. Unfortunately most people seem to have a wrong impression of the nature and the value of these rules. That is why I will first give you quite a simple example of a rule of composition so that we can find out what it means to the viewer of a picture, what kind of role it plays in the interpretation and description of the picture and how you, as a photographer, can profit by knowing about it.

Diagonal lines and composition

You have probably heard or read that it is preferable or advantageous to arrange pictorial elements along diagonal lines. The reasons given for this advice vary, but they generally boil down to this: a diagonal line from the upper left to the lower right corner of the picture plane is easily recognised and serves to give a semblance of order to the whole picture. On the other hand a diagonal line from the lower left to the upper right corner is dynamic, giving power and movement to a picture (*3*).

This may be true, as far as it goes, but it does not answer the question: Why does it work this way? Or: When or how should we make use of this so-called rule? In order to find out about this we will have to take a closer look at the perception of pictures. If someone looks at a rectangular plane he always perceives it in a certain way, generally without being conscious of the fact that he does so. He starts in the upper left corner (*4*) of the rectangle and his gaze travels over it as if he were reading the pages of a book. (This is to a very great extent dependent on our cultural habits and is, or was, different in other cultures and/or times. But we will overlook these complications for the time being.)

This reaction of the viewer to an 'empty' rectangle provides us with the most basic law of composition: The 'standard pattern of eye-movement' is changed by everything placed in the rectangle, thus providing the viewer with a set of responses which are triggered by the distribution of elements on the picture plane. For example if I draw some lines on a rectangular

3 4 5

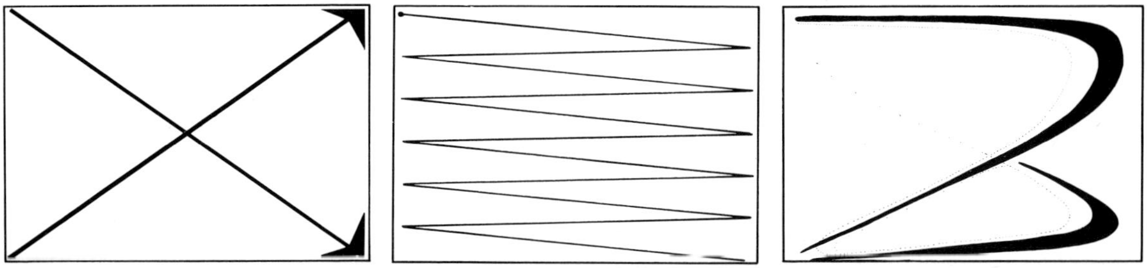

Patterns of eye movement.

piece of paper like those shown in the diagram (5) the pattern of eye-movement will not be like the standard movement shown in 4. Instead it will follow something like the course indicated by the dotted line in 5.

This is not a purely academic distinction. It has very practical consequences for the composition of pictures, because with the direction and sequence of eye-movement the quality of perception also changes. Elements which are arranged according to the standard pattern of eye-movement are easy to perceive because the gaze of the viewer meets with no resistance, but deviations from this routine introduce new elements, which evoke new reactions in the viewer. That is why a diagonal line running from the upper left to the lower right corner of a rectangle is generally associated with order but not with any dynamic impact, because the deviation between the pictorial element and the eye-movement is minimal. On the other hand a diagonal line from the lower left to the upper right corner follows the general direction of the eye-movement pattern (from left to right), but not the sequence of movements which run from bottom to top instead of from top to bottom. This deviation adds a very general dynamic feeling to a certain sense of movement.

I would like to illustrate these remarks with a set of three photographs. Illustration 6 gives a general view of the subject with which we are going to deal. It shows the ruined gable-end of a house, and a small path leading to it which is bordered by ferns and hemmed in by outcrops of rock on both sides. In my opinion this photograph is quite nice in that it gives a good feeling of the materials depicted. But as far as composition is concerned it must be classified as a failure. The path divides the picture into two sections, while the overall composition does not offer the viewer the possibility of seeing the picture-plane as a complete and integrated unit. This gives a disturbing quality to the photograph which seems quite wrong, because it does not fit in with its other elements.

In contrast, illustration 7 is entirely different although I did

6

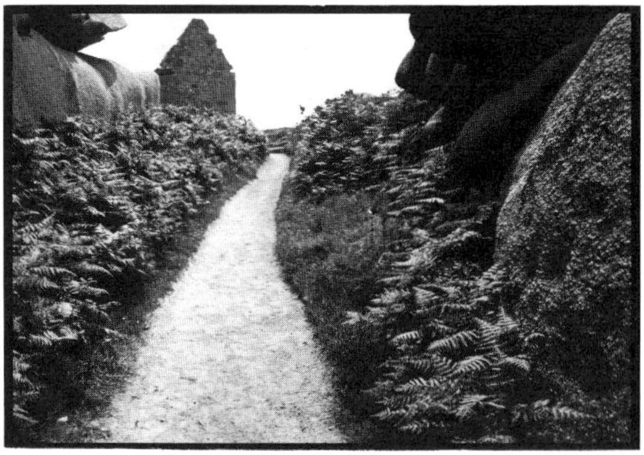

Right and below
A comparison of these three photographs and their accompanying diagrams shows the importance of the placing of the various parts of a composition.

7

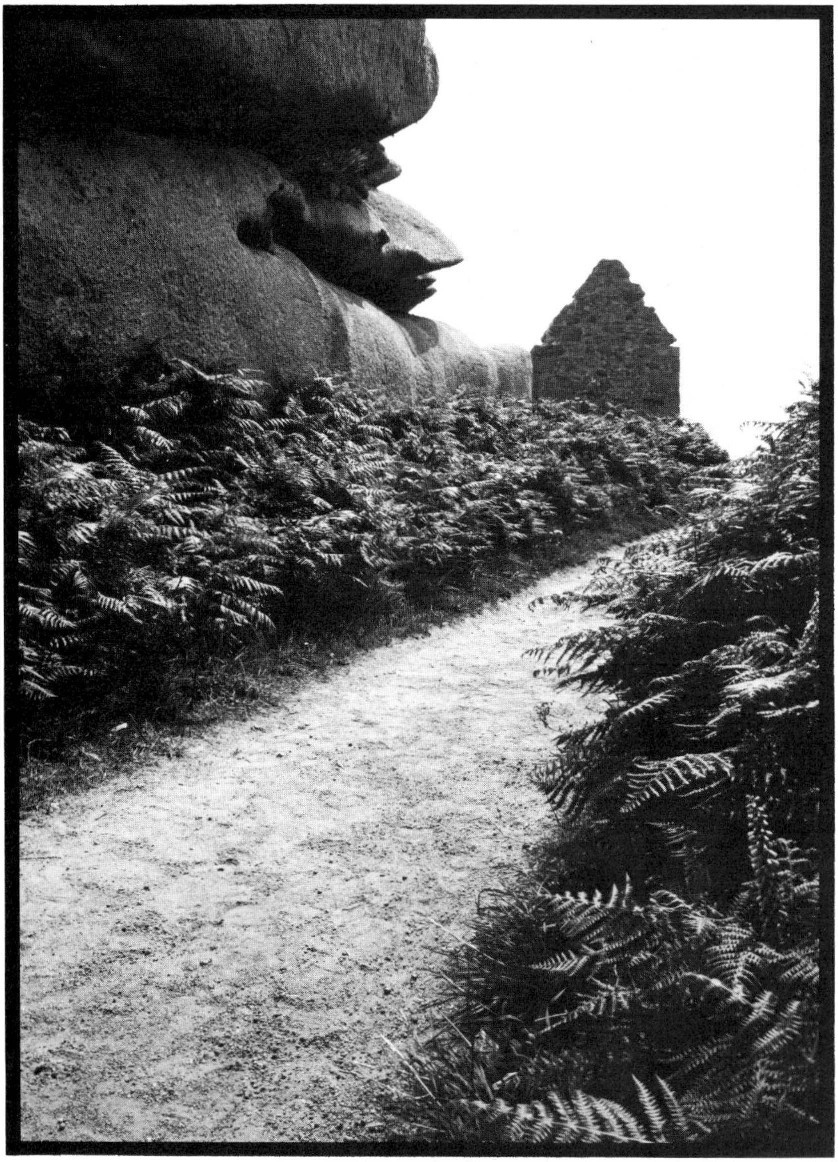

7a

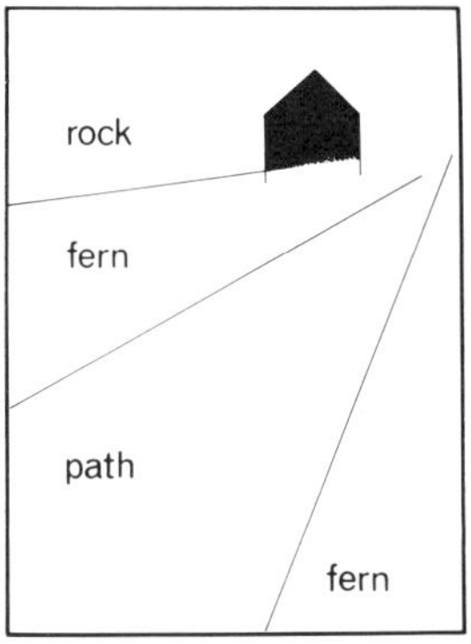

8

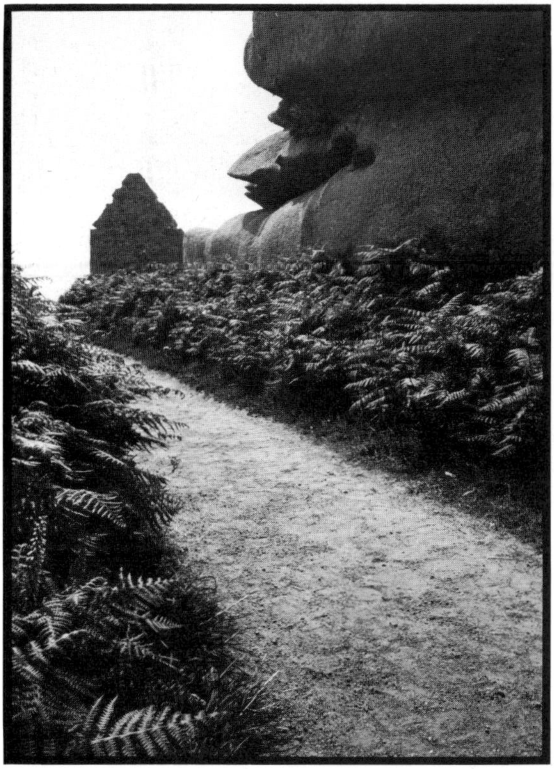

Illustration 8 has been reversed here so that you can easily see the difference between the impact of a diagonal line running from left to right and one running in the opposite direction.

nothing but change it from a horizontal to a vertical format and alter the viewpoint slightly. The path now runs along a diagonal line moving upwards, and divides the picture plane in a series of similar segments which are closely interconnected as shown in 7a. Because of the direction of these segments the gable-end of the house is stressed as the main element of the composition. At the same time the light-grey path is no longer a foreign element in the composition, because due to the similarity of outline of the different segments (*as diagram 7a shows*) it fits into the overall appearance of the photograph, at the same time serving as a counterweight for the otherwise overpowering mass of rocks in the upper left-hand corner. But we are still mainly concerned with the diagonal aspect of the composition which is provided by the path. That this is really what is responsible for the dynamic and forceful overall impression of the composition can easily be proved by a simple experiment: illustration 8 shows exactly the same photograph as illustration 7, apart from the fact that the negative had been reversed when I made the enlargement.

If you do not believe that the composition works equally well both ways, you might care to try the following experiment: show both illustrations to different people (of course without any comment) and ask them which of the two photographs they prefer. If you do this you will probably find that each photograph is chosen by an approximately equal number of people, the decision obviously depending on the state of mind of the viewer when looking at the pictures.

This leads to the conclusion that it is not the overall quality of the photograph which is different in the two illustrations. What *is* different is the mood which the composition conveys to the viewer and which makes him prefer one or the other picture. If you agree to this it now remains to pin down this difference and see whether we can attribute it to any specific property of the composition.

We have already seen that the composition of the first example (*7*) conveys an impression of forcefulness, monumentality and dynamics, the last being due to the diagonal line from the lower left-hand corner formed by the path. In the second photograph (*8*) the impression of monumentality remains, but without any suggestion of dynamism. On the contrary, the overall appearance of the photograph now stresses the qualities of tranquility and even melancholy.

It should be clear by now that these differences are caused by the different position of the diagonal line in the composition. (Please note that in comparing these two photographs we are not dealing with radically different concepts. We are concerned with nuances and you will have to look closely – both at the photographs and at your reactions to them – in order to appreciate them.) All this answers the first question which we asked at the beginning of this chapter: Why does it work this way? We now can give the answer: there is an interplay between basic forms of visual perception and the compositional arrangement of pictorial elements which induces certain reactions in the viewer.

This immediately leads to a conclusion which is of some importance to our photographic work. It would be nonsense to understand 'compositional rules' as a purely formal description concerning graphic elements of pictures. Composition is not a thing in itself. It exists in the relationship between the image and the viewer. That is why I cannot provide you with a set of rules to apply to your subject matter. If you did just that you might, at best, achieve results which are aesthetically pleasing. But if you disregard the meaning which is introduced into your photographs by the use of compositional elements you have actually achieved nothing at all. As I explained in Chapter 1, a photograph might be termed an optical message – and a message without meaning is not worth talking about.

It can be difficult to arrive at a compositionally convincing combination of people and their surroundings, but it is always a safe bet to work either on contrasts of forms or lines, or on similarities. Which approach you choose depends on what you want to express. In this photograph I chose to stress the similarities in a network of horizontal and vertical lines in order to arrive at a serene and tranquil overall impression, which enhances the slightly melancholy look on the girl's face.

9

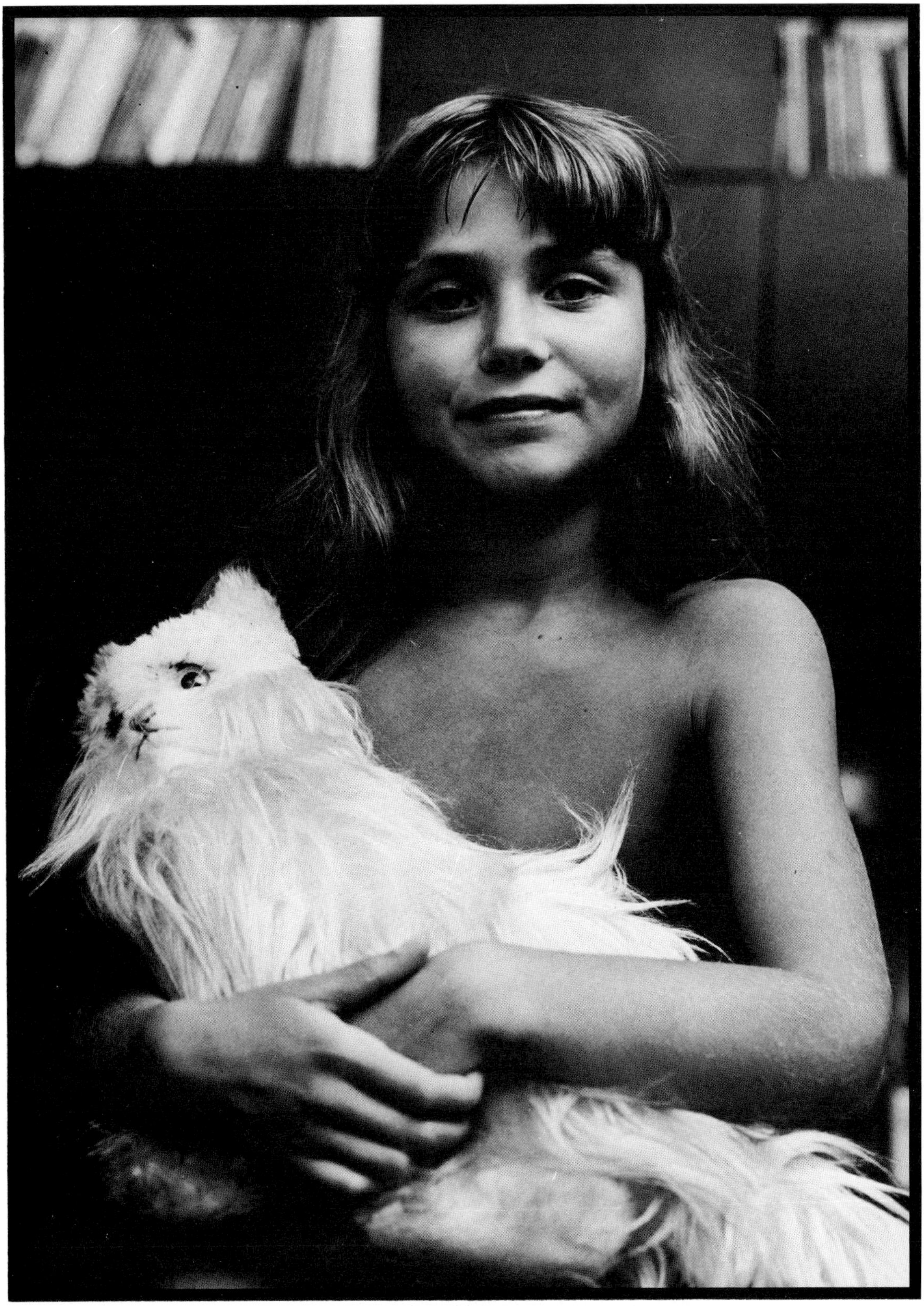

How to use rules of composition

This in turn answers the second question posed at the beginning of this chapter: When and how should we make use of this rule? The answer is this: Rules in the common sense of the word do not exist in composition. We can study the use of compositional elements and their impact on the viewer. This provides us with material for our decision-making when taking pictures, not in the way of set rules but more as points of reference which we can use for our orientation. That is why we always have to deal with three problems at once when we deal with composition. First, we are concerned with our intentions as

10

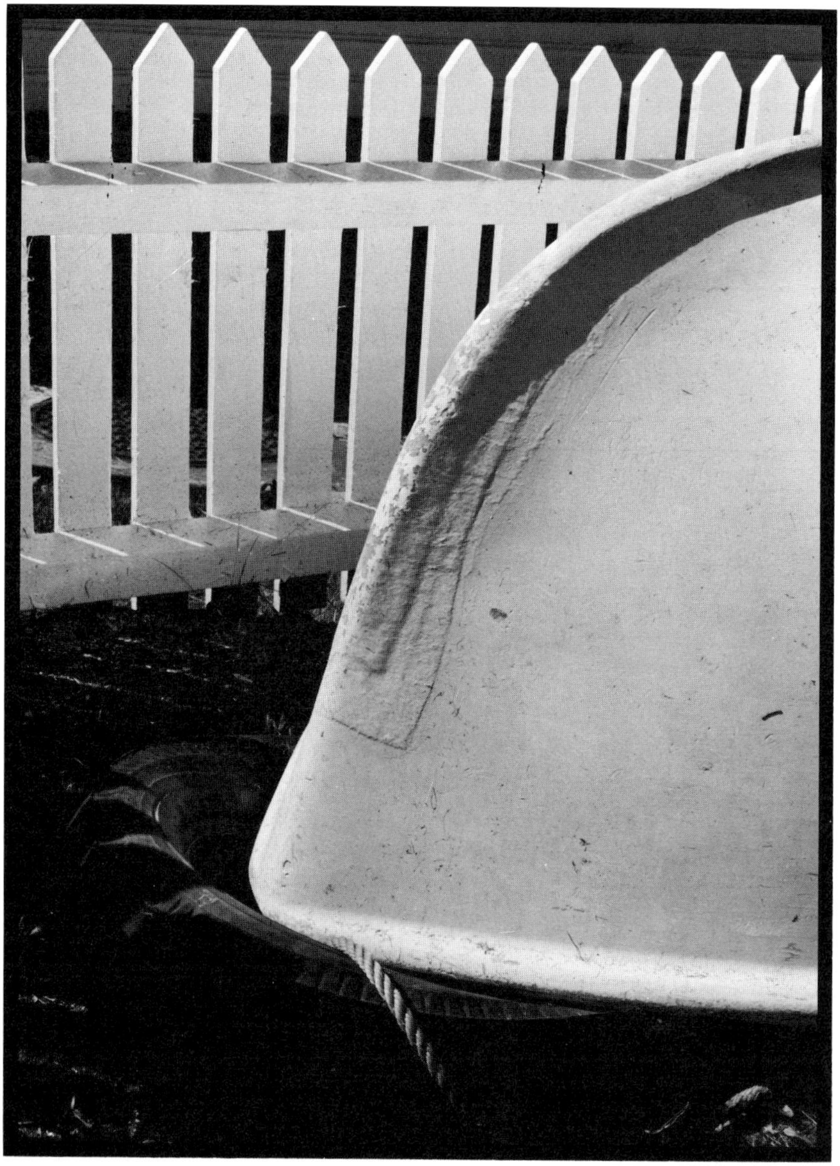

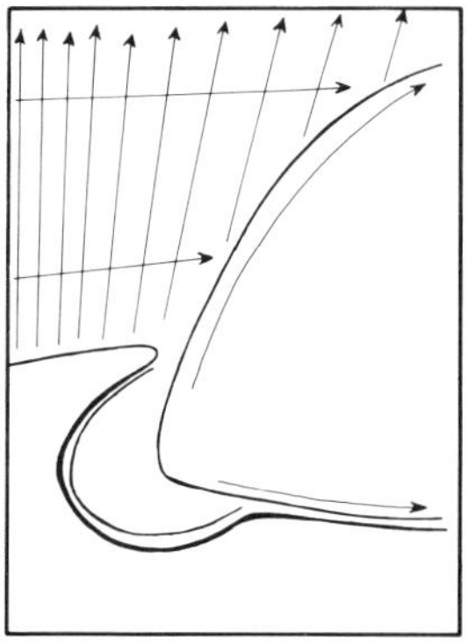

10a

This upturned boat which I found in southern Norway has been arranged in a composition which is both static and at the same time dynamic. The diagram shows how much compositional movement it contains, but the interlocking of the different lines is responsible for the static overall effect.

photographers; second, we have to deal with the response of the viewer to the photograph, and third we have to look into the ways and means by which this reaction has been produced.

This is why judging the qualities of a composition is so difficult. The photographer can judge whether he reacts to his own photographs in the way he intended to do. This is one basis for judgement. On the other hand, he might watch the reactions of viewers of his photographs and make a judgement according to the agreement between the actual reactions of the viewers and those he intended to create. Third, the viewer knows only the photographs themselves and his reactions to them. That must form the basis for his judgements. The fourth way has been employed throughout this book. The photographer (in this case myself) explains some of his intentions, shows how he tried to realise them and describes his own reactions to the photographs and those of other people who have looked at them. Thus you will gain some insights into the working of composition, although you might easily disagree with some (or all) of the conclusions reached, because your basis of judgement might be (and probably will be) different from that used here. (More about this in Chapter 13.)

Interaction of compositional elements

Returning to the function of the diagonal line in composition, we have already seen some of the ways of using diagonal lines in the preceding examples. By now it should be obvious that the impression a photograph conveys to the viewer does not depend on a single element which can be isolated from the rest. The reaction of the viewer is determined by all the elements of the composition working together, so that certain properties attributed to any one element can be enhanced or diminished by its combination with others.

An interesting example of this is provided by illustration 10. It shows part of an upturned boat in front of a fence, both painted in the same shade of off-white. The main factor of the composition is again a diagonal line, in this example formed by the boat's bow. But this diagonal line is bound into a network of other lines which I have indicated in the diagram (*10a*). All these lines lead out of the picture on the upper or right-hand side. This effect is further enhanced by the dark and round form of the tyre on which the bow of the boat rests. Together with the peculiar form of the dark lower left corner of the picture plane it serves to enhance the movement of the other lines. This gives a subject which might otherwise be associated with absolutely static and tranquil impressions a strangely disturbing quality. For me, looking at this photograph is as if I had caught an immovable object suddenly off balance – and this seeming contradiction is what makes the photograph interesting and sustains the interest of the viewer. It is quite obvious that you cannot isolate any one element of this photograph and study its impact on the viewer, it is the interplay of the different elements which is the most important factor and not any single property.

Compositional movement

Before we look any further at compositional elements, we should perhaps take stock of the situation and formally

11

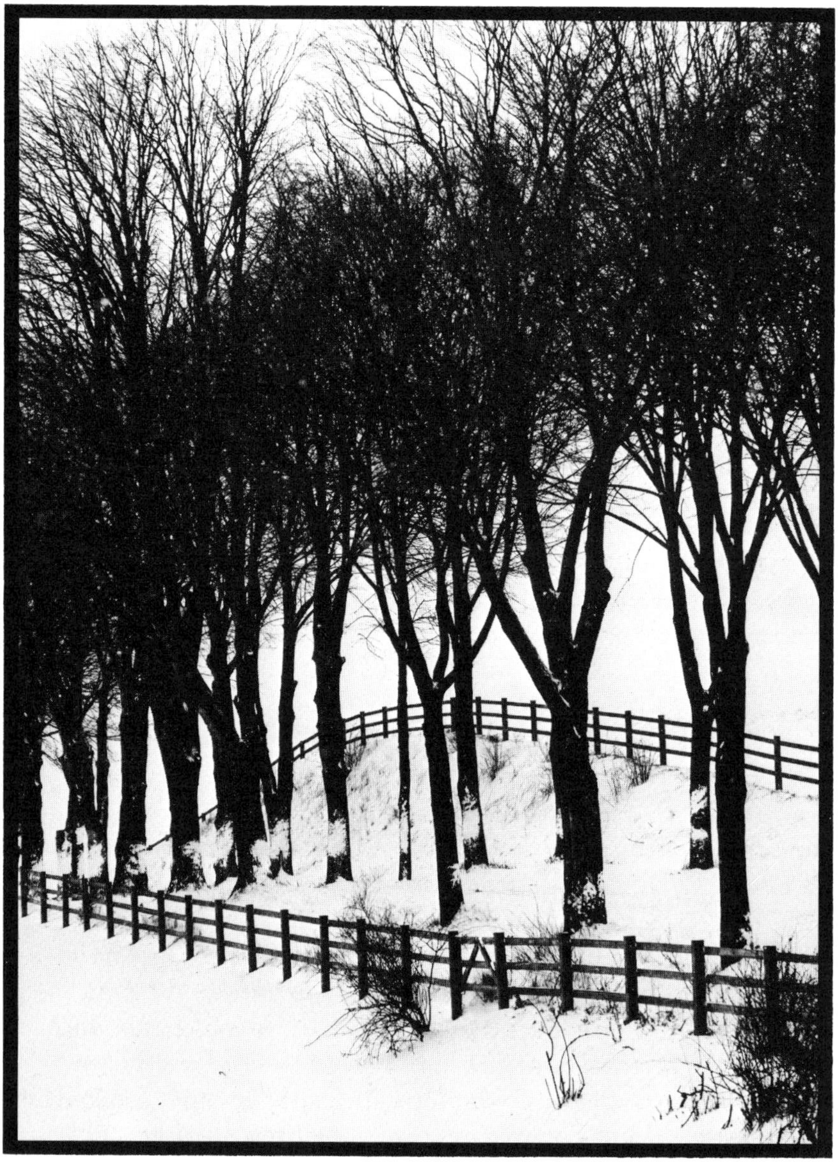

11a

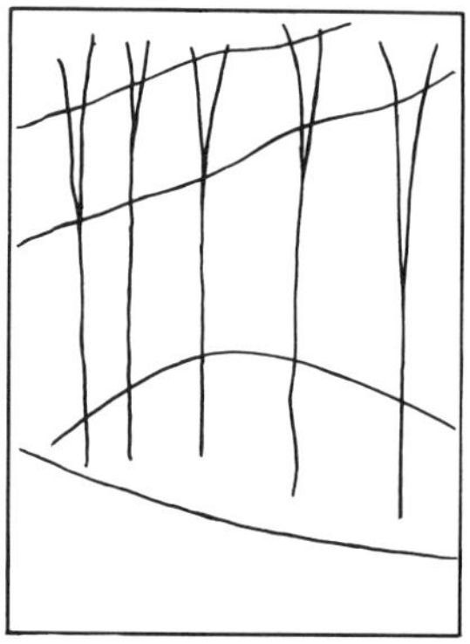

The Danish island of Mør provided another example of a composition of interlocked lines. When a picture consists of so many different lines running in different directions, the composition must be very carefully balanced if it is to succeed. Here, the strong black and white contrasts add to the impression of simplicity, although the composition is actually relatively complicated.

introduce a term which I have already used in the preceding descriptions of photographs. We started with the fact that there is a basic pattern of eye-movement which is subconsciously used by the viewer to perceive a rectangular plane. Then we found that this eye-movement can be changed and re-directed by the introduction of elements into the rectangular plane. This provides us with the concept of 'compositional movement'. The term 'compositional movement' means that we accord the quality of movement to the elements of composition although, of course, the actual movement is made by the eyes of the viewer. Examples illustrated demonstrate that we can arrange this compositional movement and so evoke certain responses in the viewer.

The first compositional movement which we dealt with was that of the diagonal line. There are of course other kinds of line which are important in the composition of photographs. Some people, for example, insist on reserving the term 'diagonal line' for those lines which really run from one edge of the picture plane to another. Consequently they do not call lines which deviate from this 'diagonal', but 'free lines'. In my opinion this differentiation is allowable only if you keep in mind that the difference is a gradual and not a principal one.

The next illustration (*11*) is an example of a photograph which does not contain any pure diagonal lines. Instead it lives on a variety of lines which more or less deviate from the diagonal. As you can see from the diagram (*11a*) the overall pattern of the composition resembles that of the fences depicted. It consists of vertical lines which are crossed by three zones which form various angles between the horizontal and diagonal lines: the lower fence, running downwards, the middle one, first angling upwards and then down again and the border formed by the crown of the trees, which comes closest to a diagonal line leading upwards.

Usually such a diversity of movement in one composition would make it hard to follow and confusing. But here the different elements are so balanced that the overall impression is one of integrity and order. This effect, of course, is enhanced by the strong black-and-white contrasts which help to distribute the importance attached to single elements of the composition evenly over the whole picture plane. That is why the photograph proves the point which I wanted to make. As you can see, the forcefulness of the lines and their importance for the composition depend, among other factors, on their angle to the diagonal and horizontal lines, but the differences are only gradual and not in any way of a principal kind.

12

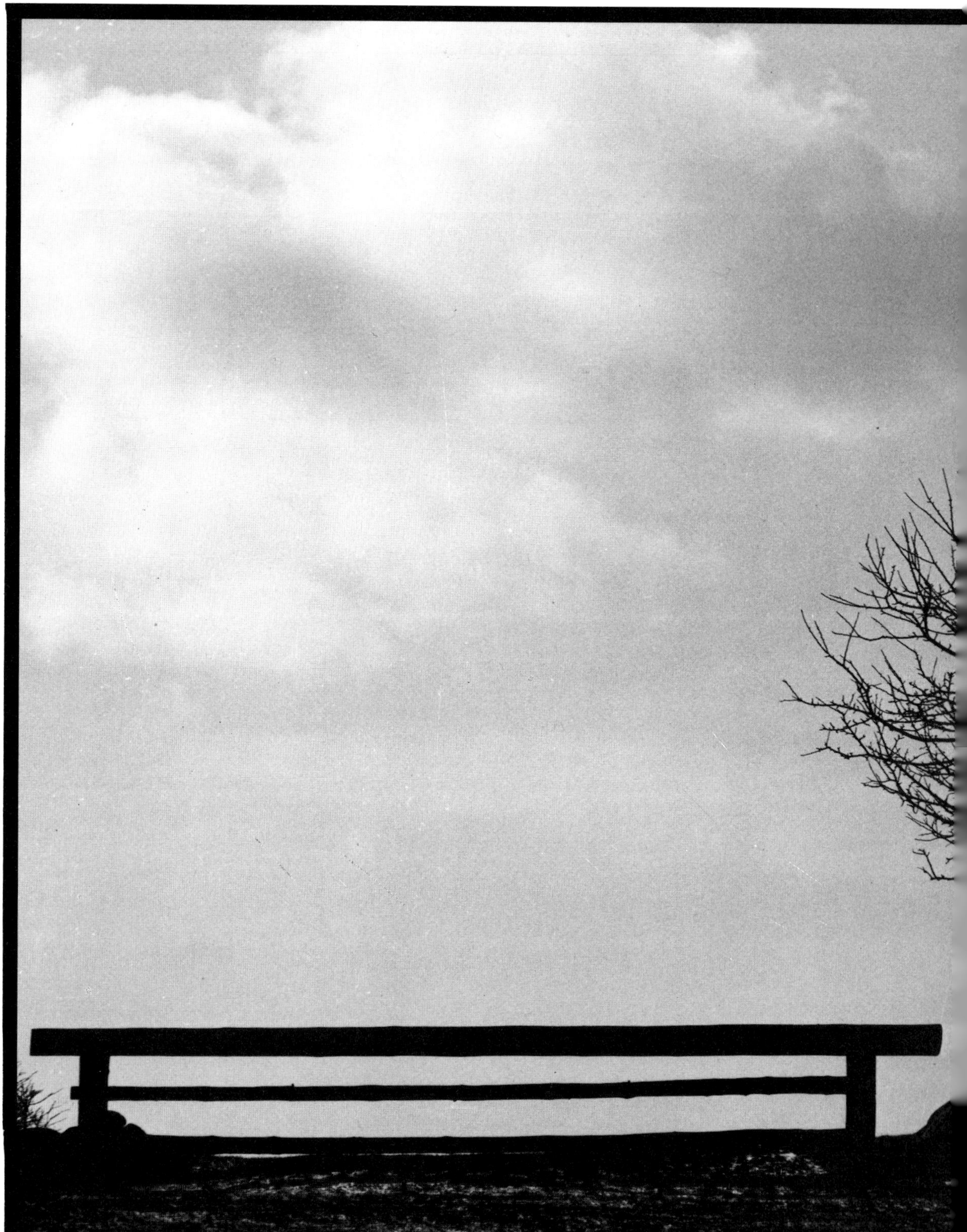

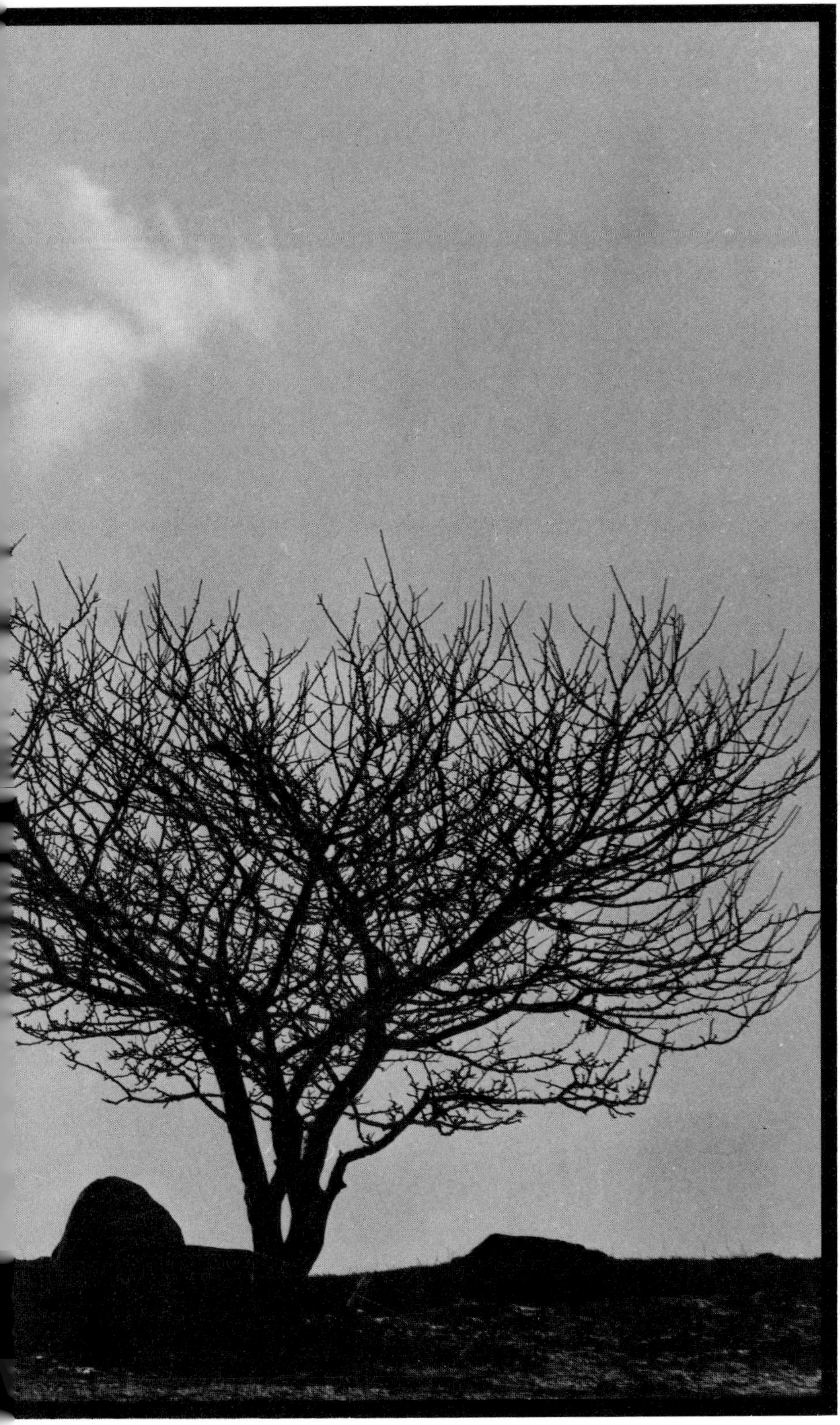

This illustration introduces a new compositional element: optical lines. These are the optical connections between the main elements of the composition – the tree, the cloud and the railing. Although these lines are not actually depicted, they are very important in understanding the composition.

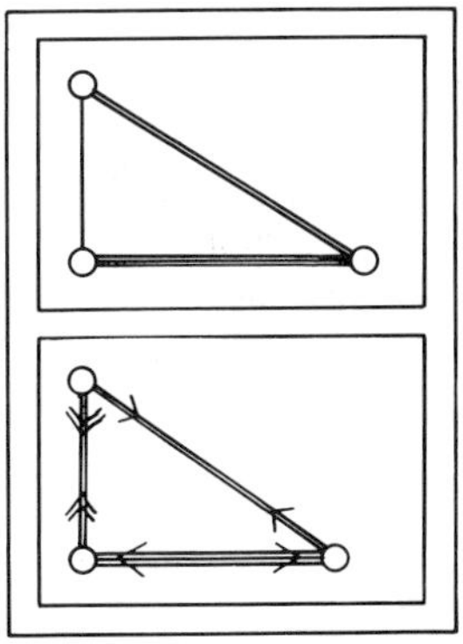

12a

This is entirely different when strictly horizontal lines are concerned. A horizontal line does not convey an impression of movement. It is not dynamic but inert, and thus different in principle from diagonal and free lines. In the next illustration (*12*) you will see three horizontal lines at once, but not one of them adds to the compositional movement by itself. What movement there is stems from the interrelation of the three main elements of the composition: the cloud, the tree and the railing.

This picture is worth analysing carefully because it demonstrates some new things as far as the working of composition is concerned. Apart from the three horizontal lines already mentioned there are no real lines in this photograph. However, the three main elements of the composition form a triangle (*diagram 12a, top*) whose sides work as 'optical lines'.

Optical lines

This term is easily explained. Optical lines are lines which are not actually depicted, but which come into being as the lines of eye-movement connecting different elements of a composition. In the preceding photographs we were concerned only with real lines, in this picture there are both: the horizon and the vertical bars of the railing form real lines, while the connections between the tree and the cloud and the railing and the cloud are optical lines only. Of these lines the strongest is the horizontal one, because here a real and an optical line come together. The second in importance is the diagonal line between tree and cloud because it coincides with the diagonal line of the picture plane and thus gains strength. The weakest line is that between the cloud and the railing. Taken at their face-value these connections would form an imbalanced composition, but so far we have not taken into account the relation between the elements themselves. In doing this now, I will confine the discussion to their two main properties for the sake of simplicity and clarity. I will classify them according to their form and their placement on the grey scale.

There are two kinds of form in the picture:

1. a 'free' form with undetermined border-lines (tree, cloud)
2. a geometric form with well-defined border-lines (railing)

And there are two placements on the grey scale:

1. black (tree, railing)
2. 'white' or light grey (cloud)

This means that all the elements of the composition contrast with each other. But they do so in different degrees as the list shows:

Overleaf
This photograph is almost a double portrait. The very close relationship (compositionally speaking) between the girl and her doll causes the viewer to look for relations between them, so that the 'personality' of the one seems to reflect and influence that of the other. Note how the vertical and horizontal lines of the background are echoed and taken up by each 'person', thus strengthening the withdrawn atmosphere of the photograph.

a) contrast between: cloud – tree
equal values: form
different values: grey scale
b) contrast between: railing – tree
equal values: grey scale
different values: form
c) contrast between: railing – cloud
different values: form
different values: grey scale

Thus the strongest and optically most effective contrast exists between the cloud and the railing, while the other two are of about equal optical importance. If we now add this to our assessment of the real and optical lines, we will get an adequate review of the composition. The elements of the composition are grouped in a triangle which has a very strong and dominant base, while its two other sides are balanced and of equal importance (*diagram 12a bottom*). We have seen that four compositional elements were necessary to achieve this effect. They were:

likeness (of form and grey values)
contrast (of form and grey values)
real lines (compositional movement)
optical lines (compositional movement)

We have already discussed the importance of lines in the composition and seen how their values (or position) in a picture could be described and explained in terms of compositional movement. Now we can add some new terms to the repertory. The abstract concept of likeness or contrast between compositional elements defines their relationship and with that the optical connections (optical lines) between them. Thus likeness and contrast determine compositional movements as much as do the optical and real lines. At the same time these terms are concerned with the shape and general appearance of compositional elements. Just as lines create associations and impressions in the viewer – as we saw when discussing the first photographs in this chapter – so do the shapes and other determining factors of compositional elements. But the latter directly influence the mind of the viewer and thus work on a different level.

I have already stated that in a very general frame of reference, for example within the limitations of the middle European cultures of the second half of this century, the 'standard patterns of eye-movement' are quite similar in most people, so that reactions to this level of composition might be anticipated with a great degree of accuracy. On the other hand,

13

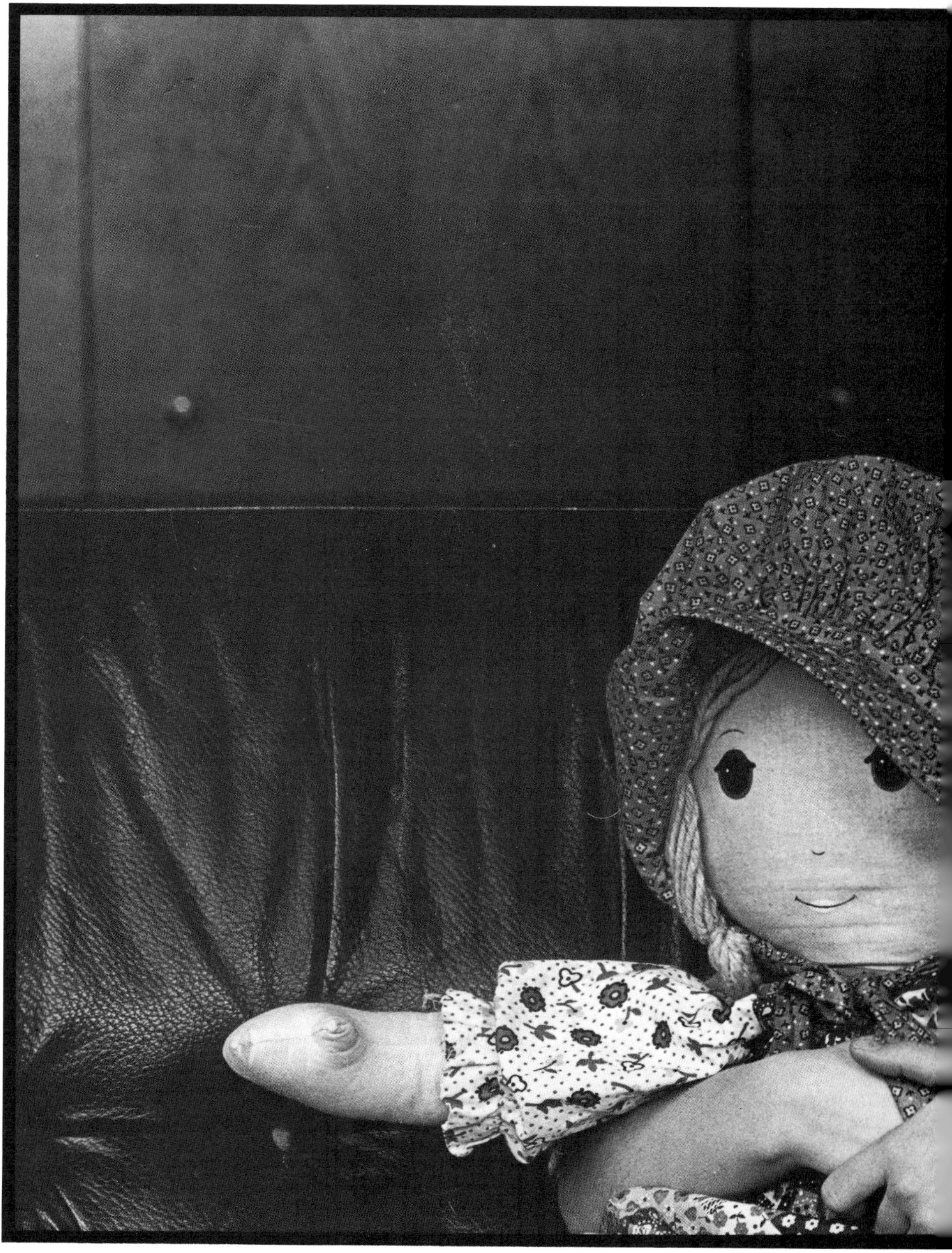

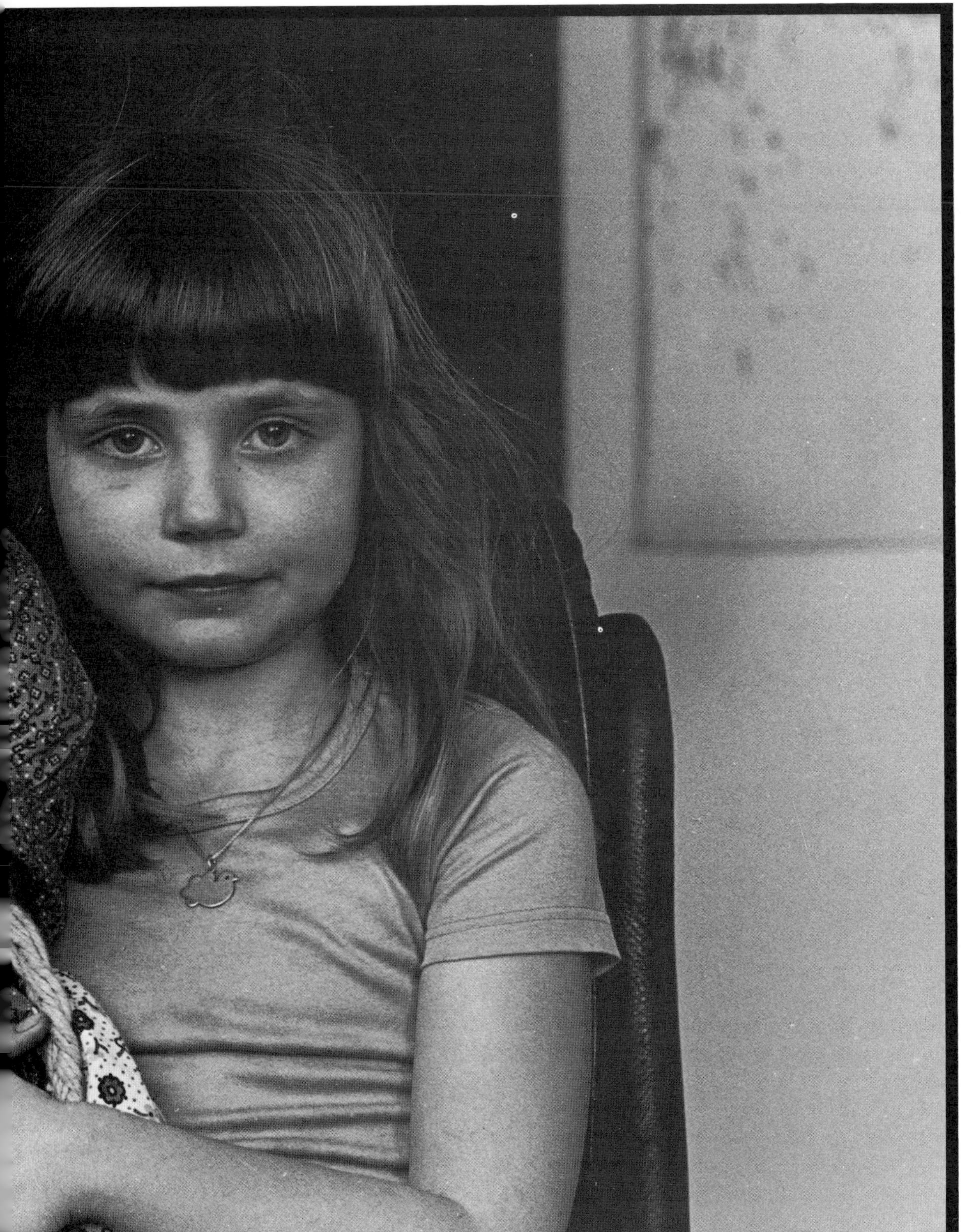

the direct influence of shapes and related properties of compositional elements works on a very personal background, which is strongly influenced by changing moods and the other imponderables of a viewer's mind, so that there we are reduced to mere guesswork.

The personal element

The reason for this purely theoretical discourse is that it allows us to introduce a highly important, and very practical, distinction between two categories of photographs. A photograph whose impact relies mainly on the configuration of its elements (that is, a network of real and optical lines) cannot only be described with a fair degree of accuracy, its impact (or lack of impact) on the viewer can be predicted reasonably well. Thus it will be appreciated by a majority of people – or not, as the case may be. On the other hand, a photograph which relies on the shape and related qualities of its elements is highly personal and its acceptance or rejection by others is uncertain.

14

This is no reflection on the quality of the photographs belonging to one or other of the two categories, but it is important to understand this distinction if you are concerned with pictures in any way and it might help you to assess other people's reactions to your own photographs. Illustration 14 is an example of this. It shows a photograph which I like very much. But the chances are that you will not see anything in it at all (judging by the responses which I have had from other people). The reason for this lies in the fact that it belongs to the second category described above. In contrast to picture 7, for example (or most other photographs in this book), it does not work along generally accepted lines, but its perception requires a frame of mind which cannot be taken for granted – and that is why I am not even going to try to explain it.

This leads us to the conclusion that not all levels of composition are open to verifiable descriptions and interpretations of the kind with which we are dealing in this book, and it shows why I have limited the examples illustrated and discussed to those on which a general agreement should in my opinion be possible.

But on the other hand you should not draw a wrong conclusion from all this. If you thought that it would be safe to limit your work exclusively to the kind of compositional treatment described in this chapter, you would be quite wrong. If a photograph (or any other picture) completely conforms to any given set of rules, it will be both boring and meaningless – a statement which we will examine in the next chapter.

The extreme simplicity of this picture and the reduction of its composition to a few elements is not agreeable to many people, while others are attracted to its austerity. This shows that the quality of a composition and its appeal to a viewer cannot ever be predicted and judged at all objectively.

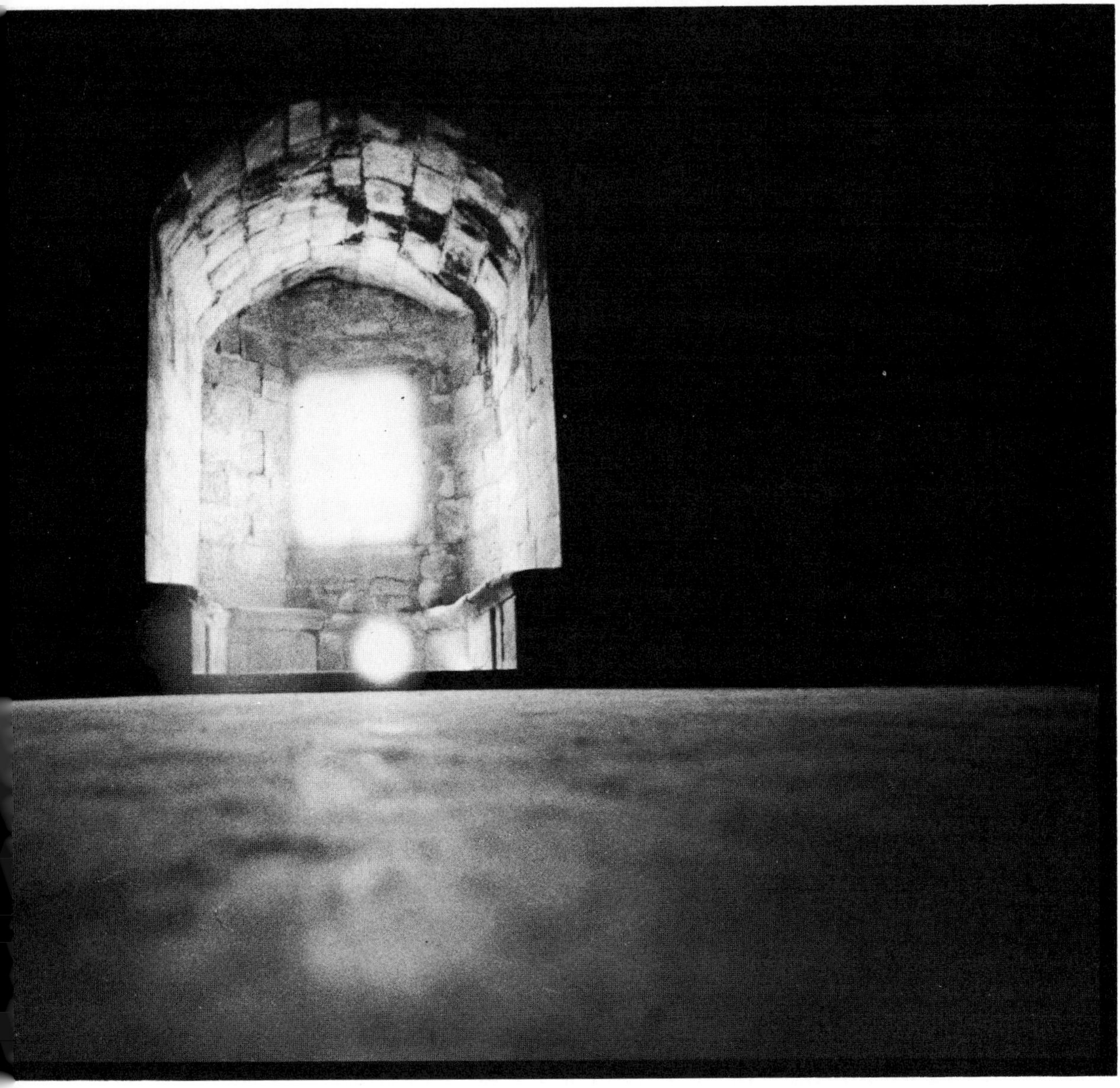

15

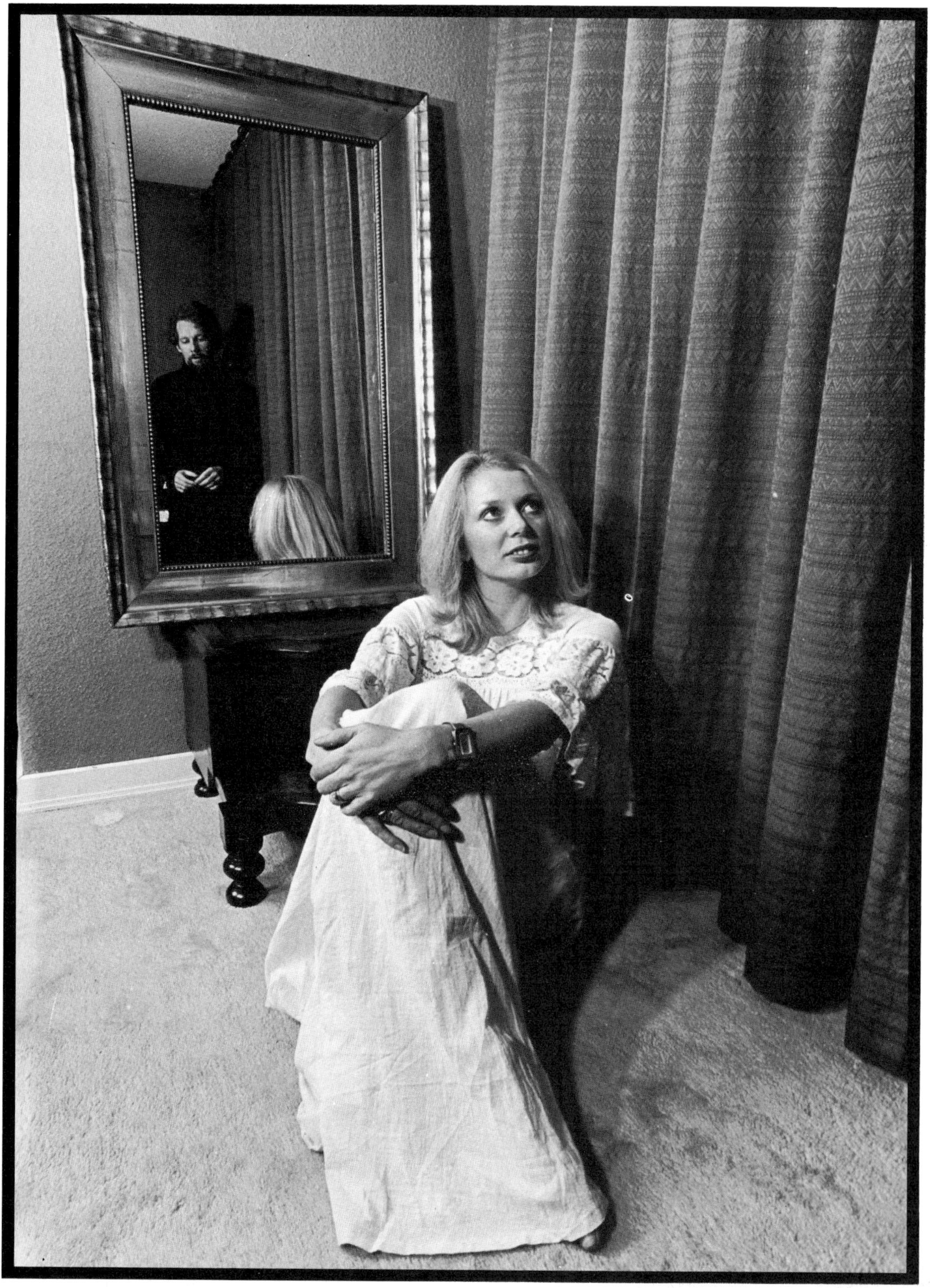

3 The Importance of Originality

I am not going to launch into a philosophical discussion of composition and reality because it would be out of place here. Nevertheless, there are some more comments which I wish to make upon these very general and basic concepts because they influence your work and its reception by others whether you like it or not.

Let us start with the question of the originality of a photograph by looking at illustration 15. This is a portrait of a couple taken in their bedroom. It is nothing out-of-the-way, neither in its subject matter or in its composition. But in my opinion it is nevertheless quite original. First of all it has been taken with an extreme wide-angle lens (17mm on a 35mm-camera). Considering that one is generally advised to use long focal length lenses for portrait-photography, this can be called unusual. At the same time it is original because it is not just a trick, but the basis of the effectiveness of the photograph as a portrait. On the one hand, this lens provides the strange spatial distortion which is especially visible in the shape of the mirror and the proportions of the seated woman, thus making a comment on the relationship of the people depicted. This lens also enabled me to show two people in conversation in a very unusual way, for although you know that the two persons are really looking at each other, in the photograph both confront the viewer, the man looking to the left and down, the woman looking to the right and up. At the same time the heavy frame of the mirror gives the effect of a 'picture within a picture'. The subject of the photograph seems to be the woman, while the relationship between her and her husband seems to be to that of a picture in the background.

To use a 17 mm lens for a portrait is unusual. To do something unusual (and therefore original) is not an end in itself, but this illustration shows that unusual means can be used to convey unusual meanings, feelings and impressions – and it is these which make an original photograph.

Although the concept of originality is very personal (what is absolutely new and fascinating for me might be old hat for you), it seems safe to say that this photograph is original. It shows a 'standard' subject realised in an unusual way, thus containing both elements of the concept of originality. First of all it contains a lot of elements which you as the viewer know, but secondly it is realised in a way which is, I hope, new to you. In order to succeed a photograph needs both elements. If you have something new (and therefore original) to say you must do so in terms which are at least partially known to the person looking at your photograph, so that he can learn to understand it. But it is equally obvious that a photograph must contain something new so as not to be meaningless and boring.

Let me give you an extreme example of this. If you have something to say which is sensationally new and entirely original you could, of course, invent a new language with a new vocabulary in order to express yourself. But the result would be that nobody could understand you.

In terms of composition this means:

a) If you regard photography exclusively as a means of self-expression (which of course is a perfectly legitimate thing to do), then questions of composition and meaning do not arise at all. b) If you regard photography as a means of expressing something (or yourself) *to others* (i.e. between yourself and the viewer of your photographs), composition is the tool which you use to convey your meaning (mood, feelings or whatever you want to call it). Then the whole concept of originality boils down to this: what you have to say should be original, it should be your very own (if not it would not be worth saying). If this is so, your photographs will necessarily be original. You will, however, have to realise them by means which are at least partly or potentially known to the intended viewers of your work. But, at the same time, if you stick completely to what is safe and well-known you will say nothing and your pictures will mean nothing.

The unimportance of 'rules'

This leads to the main point of the argument. You are probably aware of the very popular 'rules of composition' which you will generally find in the simpler works on photography. There, for example, you are advised to look for a foreground for your pictures. If there is none, you are told to place your wife (or husband, or child) there – in the case of colour photography preferably in a red dress. You are advised to 'frame' your subject (with trees or whatever else you might find). Then you are told that your subject should fill the whole frame, that the horizon should not divide the picture in half, that you should have nice clouds in the sky (where else?), that your picture should contain a complete grey scale, including black and white, etc., ad infinitum.

I would like to be very rude, but will just state that this is utter nonsense (I will deal with these ideas in later chapters.) If you stick to these so-called rules your pictures – with some luck

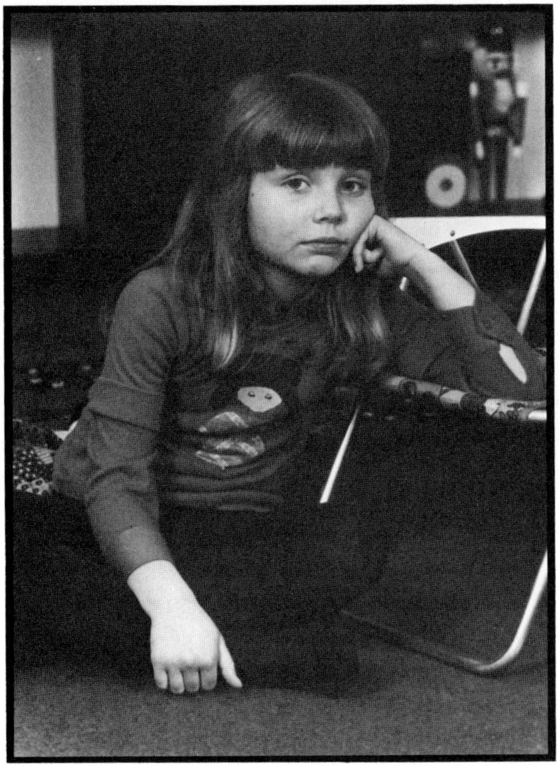

16

To pose someone and then to take a photograph is the easiest way to keep the composition of a picture under control, but more often than not the results look stiff and unnatural. It takes much longer (and uses up more film) if you wait and allow people to arrange themselves naturally and unselfconsciously. That photographs taken this way can be compositionally as convincing as posed ones is shown by this illustration. (The same applies to all the photographs of people in this book, because the same technique was used in them all.)

– will look aesthetically pleasing, but they will be utterly meaningless and can have no appeal to a viewer because they contain nothing which could arouse his interest. They would be nothing more than repetitions of pictures which we have already seen a million times. It would be much better and easier to buy postcards or books of photographs than go to all the trouble to do it yourself if you just do what others did before you – and perhaps did even better.

You are you, you are unique as a personality and your photographs should reflect this fact by being as original and unique as you are. To do so, you must know the possibilities of composition: that is, you do not have to know any rules of the kind described above, you just have to find out what can be done with all the different photographic means available and how this will influence or change the appearance of your photographs.

An example of this would be the use of interchangeable lenses. These are, in fact, among the most versatile of ways with which to compose a picture, so they are dealt with at some length in the next two chapters.

4 Different Lenses – Different Effects

Everybody knows that you can use telephoto-lenses to photograph distant objects, animals or people. Without these lenses we would have been spared sneak-shots of celebrities in the nude, but we would not have pictures of dangerous or shy animals. On the other hand it is well known that wide-angle lenses can be used to take pictures in restricted spatial circumstances. Travel agencies, for example, need them to show mere holes of hotel-rooms as palatial apartments.

These practical considerations, however, do not come into creative photography at all. The reason for this is that each lens of a given focal length gives a rendering of the spatial relationships between the objects depicted which is quite specific to it and different from the effects provided by lenses of other focal lengths. This is what makes them so valuable for composition and is the reason why we should understand completely the influence of interchangeable lenses on the appearance of our photographs.

The camera and the eye

Most people start their photographic life with what is generally called a 'standard' lens with a 'normal' focal length. This lens will be the starting point and point of reference for our discussion. This lens is not called 'standard' or 'normal' because most cameras are equipped with it, but because it produces an image which comes closer to what we see with our eyes, than the image produced by any other lens.

Although this statement seems to be quite true and is a well-known platitude of photographic literature, it is more wrong than right because it is based on the assumption that the camera and the eye are very similar. Mechanically or physically speaking this may be true: both have a lens, a diaphragm (iris) and a plane on which the image is projected. But here the similarities end and I must strongly warn against giving any importance to this comparison because composition (and indeed the whole of photography) draws its impact from the dissimilarities between camera and eye.

That statement probably needs some explaining. A camera

produces photographic images, if necessary automatically and without human influence. The eye cannot 'see' by itself – *we* see, using our eyes. This means that seeing is a process which involves not only our eyes but also our cerebral system and has nothing whatever to do with the production of photographic images. I have tried to sum up some of the most important differences below. You will see that these differences each indicate one of the compositional possibilities of photography:

1. The photographic process produces a two-dimensional image. We 'see' (experience) the world in the spatial perception. (The transformation of space into planes gives a first means for composing a picture.)

2. The spatial effect of photographic images can be changed (for example by the use of lenses of different focal lengths). The perception of space depends on seeing with two eyes and on eye- and body-movement. The perspective effect of the perception of space is unchangeable. (That is why changes of this kind work especially strongly in composition.)

3. The photographic image has a clearly defined distribution of sharpness and unsharpness. (This can be influenced by the choice of lenses and other factors, thus giving us an additional means of composition.) In seeing, the field of perception is scanned in steps with changing sharpness, partly unconscious, partly controlled by our interest and the situation.

4. The photographic image is 'total' or 'complete' in that everything which can be shown with the given technical means will be contained in the final image. In contrast to this, human perception works 'selectively'. It is subjective and we do not necessarily 'perceive' everything that we 'see'. (Which, by the way, was pointed out by Sherlock Holmes to Dr. Watson during one of his cases.)

Although this comparison could be continued, this should be enough to show that the photographic process (and its results) are entirely different from human perception. The photographic image never shows us 'a true image of reality' or anything of the kind, at best it contains our interpretation of it, 'filtered' and changed by the composition.

Before discussing the nature of these changes and how to use interchangeable lenses to effect them, it is important to know what is actually changed by the use of these lenses. Although it is quite true that the geometric perspective of pictures of a given subject is always the same, irrespective of the focal length of lens used (except fish-eye lenses), the appearance of that perspective changes with the use of lenses of different focal lengths.

Perspective and the lens

This merits a closer look. First, I want to demonstrate that the geometric perspective really does not change in photographs taken with lenses of different focal lengths, provided that the distance between subject and camera is not changed. Illustration 17 shows a subject photographed with a standard lens. The next illustration (*18*) shows the same subject, photographed from the same viewpoint, but using a telephoto lens. The diagram (*19*) shows the relations between the two pictures. Illustration 20 shows an enlargement of part of the negative which was used for illustration 17. If you now compare the

17

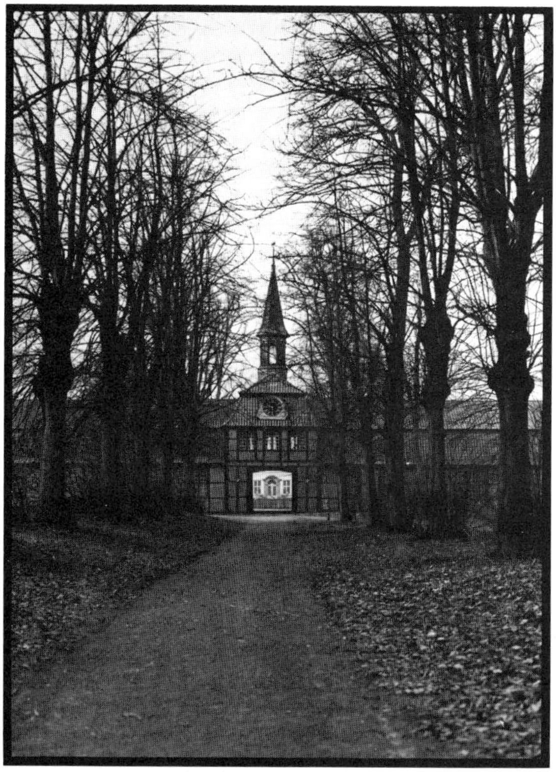

18

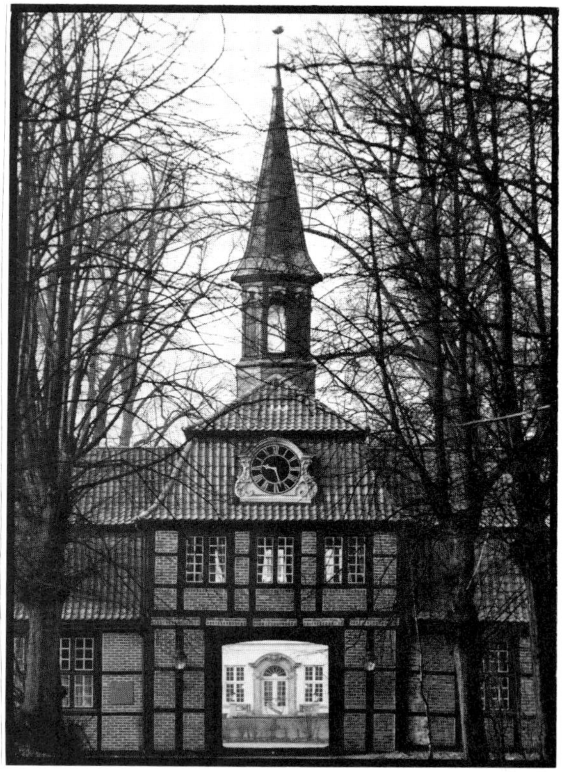

19

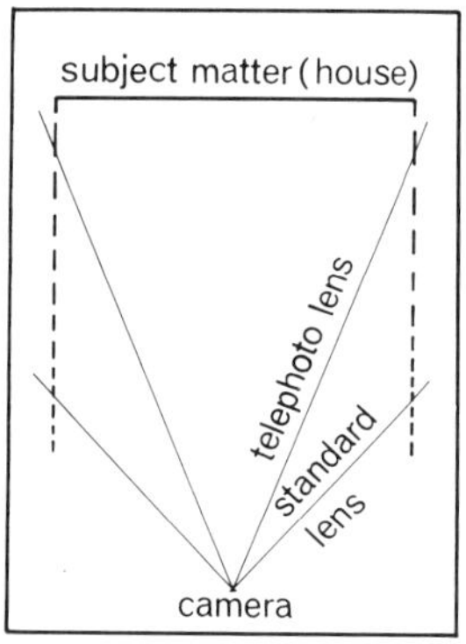

Above and opposite
This set of photographs and the diagram prove that the geometric perspective of a photograph does not change with the focal length of the lens used (provided that you do not change the viewpoint!).

The first picture (17) was taken with a standard lens, the second (18) with a telephoto lens. The third illustration (20) is an enlargement of part of the negative of 17 and it coincides exactly with the one taken with the telephoto lens.

picture taken with the telephoto lens (*18*) with the appropriate section of the standard picture blown up to the same size (*20*), you will find that they are exactly alike. This conclusively proves that the geometric perspective of both pictures is the same, although they were taken with lenses of different focal lengths.

This is a basic fact which does not help us much in itself if and when we want to influence the composition of a photograph. But it is nevertheless quite important to know, because it immediately leads to other different effects, for example if you change not only the lens but the distance between camera and subject at the same time. What happens

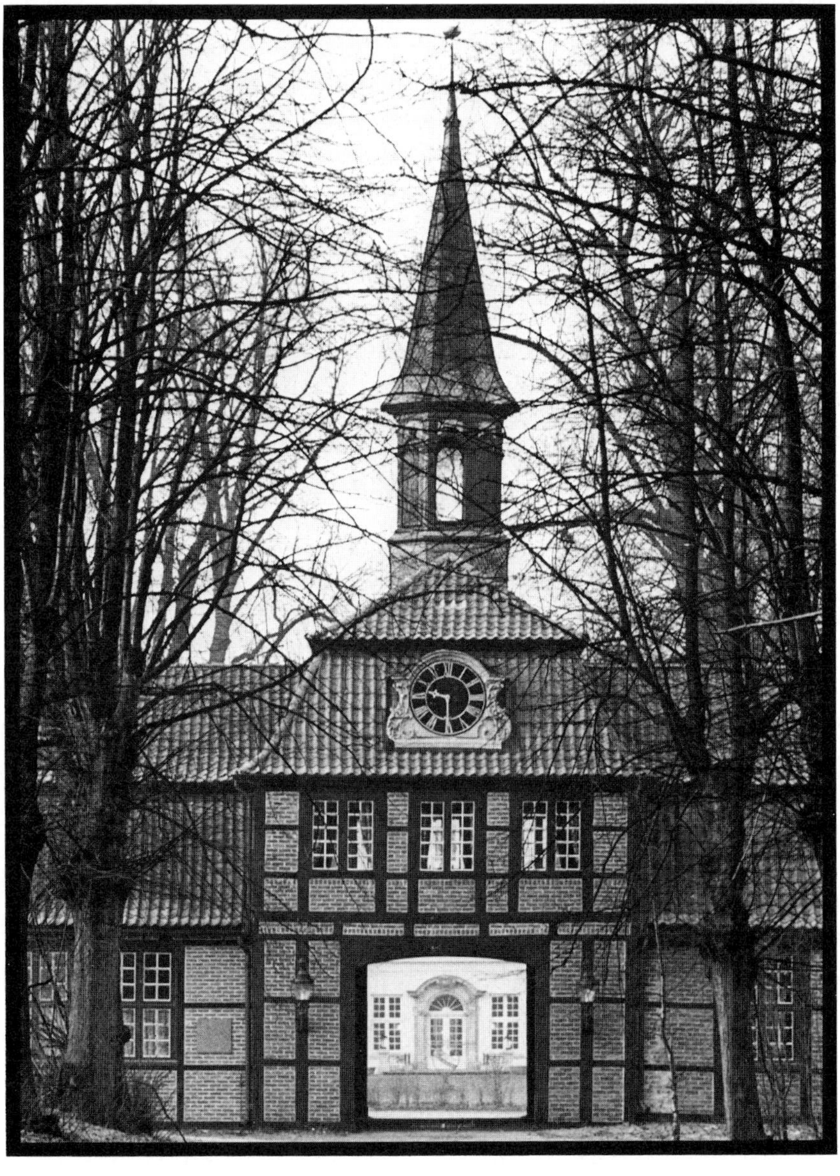

20

21

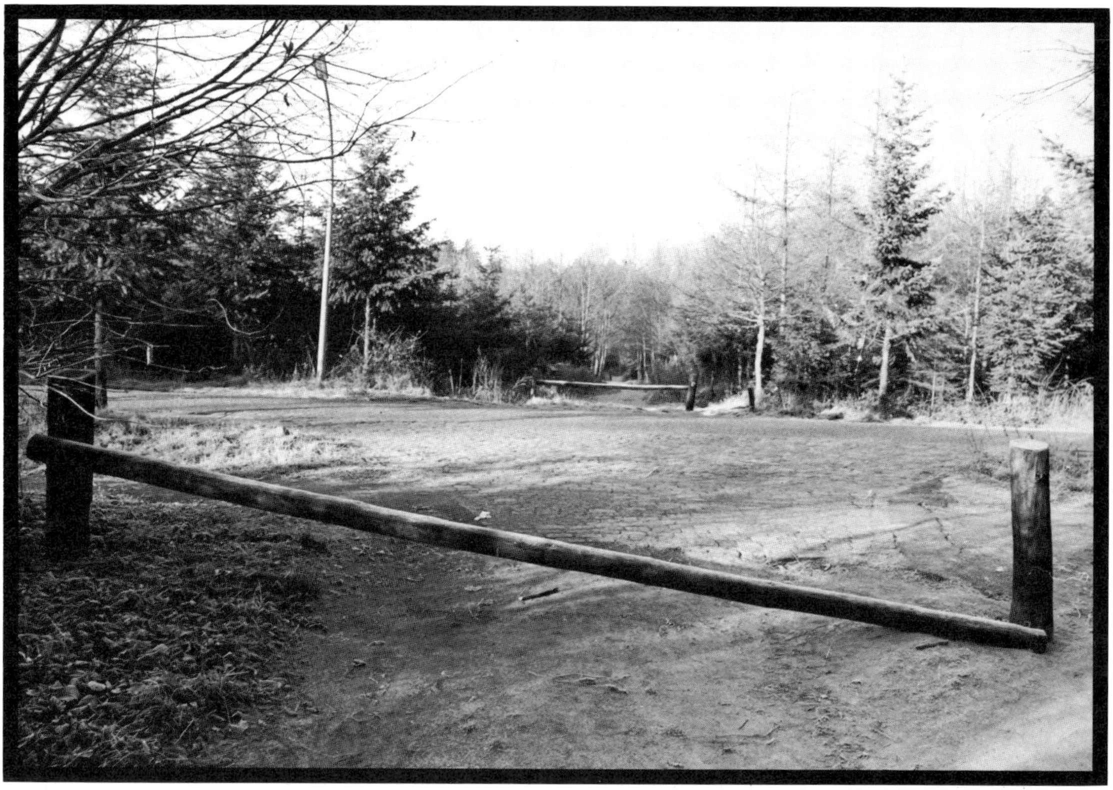

22

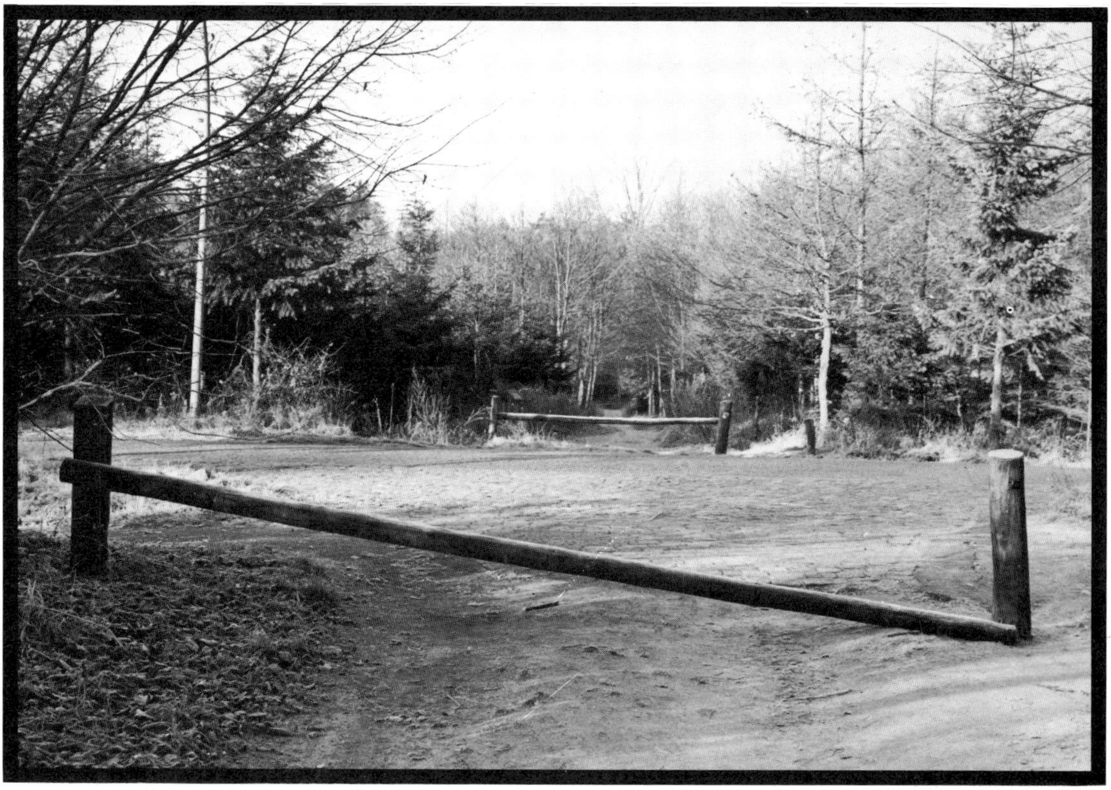

23

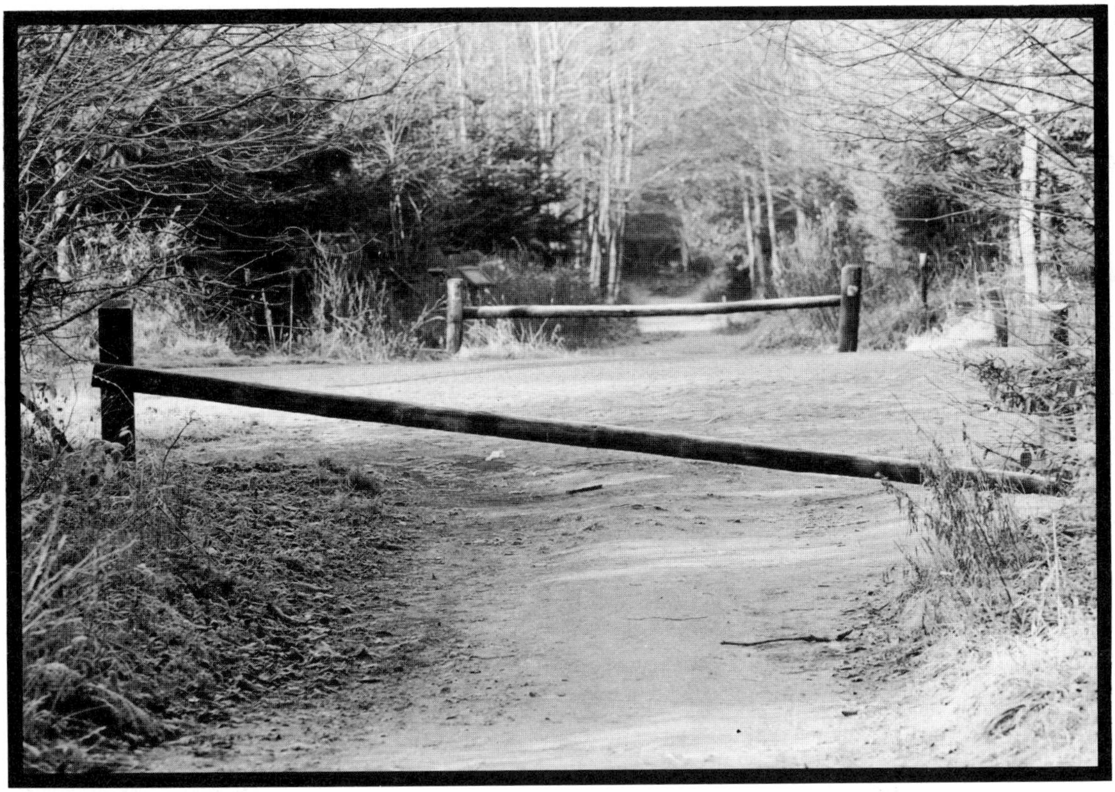

24

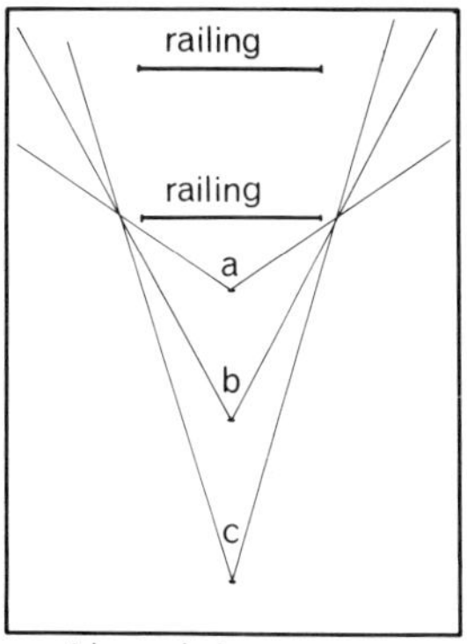

a wide angle lens
b standard lens
c telephoto lens

Above and opposite
These three pictures show that the spatial effect of a photograph can be changed with the use of different lenses, if the viewpoint is changed as well. The diagram (24) gives a key to the combinations of focal length and viewpoint which led to the three photographs.

then is demonstrated in the next set of illustrations.

The first of these illustrations (*21*) was taken with a wide-angle lens, the second one (*22*) with a standard lens and the third one (*23*) with a telephoto lens. In each case the distance between the camera and the subject was chosen so that the railing in the foreground of the picture always appeared the same size on the negative. (Compare with diagram 24.) You can see now that the relations of size between foreground and background change drastically with each lens used. (In reality the two railings in each picture were both of about the same size!)

That shows clearly that we can change the spatial effect of a subject according to our compositional ideas or aims by changing the focal length of the lens used and/or the distance between camera and subject.

I would like to compress these possibilities of changing the spatial effect of photographs into two 'rules':

1. If you want to keep the effect of depth in a picture, but want to change the framing of the subject at the same time, you will have to use the same lens but change the distance between camera and subject.
2. If you want to change the effect of depth in your picture but

retain the framing, you must change focal length and photographing distance in the same proportion (ie if you double the focal length, you will need twice the distance).

It should go without saying that all kinds of combinations between these two basic factors are possible and will yield appropriate results. This means that it is absolutely not irrelevant for the effect of your photograph whether you get closer to your subject or change the lens instead – each of these measures will change the composition of your photograph in a different way! If you wanted to classify these effects under the headings 'wide-angle lenses' and 'telephoto lenses', you would arrive at something like the following:

1. Proportions: *Wide-angle lenses*: The proportions of things depicted are changed according to their distance from the camera. Things close to the camera look much bigger than ones far way. *Telephoto lenses*: The proportions of parts of the subject are not changed to any great extent. Especially when using long focal length lenses, things are shown close to their natural relations to each other with regard to size.

2. Extension of space: *Wide-angle lenses*: The distances between parts of the subject look bigger, especially if they are close to the camera. *Telephoto lenses*: With extreme telephoto lenses there is almost no recognisable extension of space, in other cases it appears to be much shortened.

3. Depth of field: *Wide-angle lenses*: With large distances the depth of field is extremely great, using small *f* stops and very short focal lengths it might range from close to the camera to infinity. *Telephoto lenses*: With long focal lengths the depth of field is very small, it might diminish to a few centimetres.

Because these things change with each lens, the decision as to what focal length to use for a given subject is one of the most important compositional decisions which you will have to make. This is the reason why the practical considerations, which in 'applied' photography are usually the deciding factors on what lens to use, should not play any part at all in 'creative' photography. You are (or should be) concerned with the question of how to compose your photograph, and not thinking about the kind of lens which you will need. If, for example, you decide on an extreme wide-angle lens to impart the desired 'mood' or 'feeling' to your intended photograph and then discover that you cannot get close enough for that kind of lens,

25

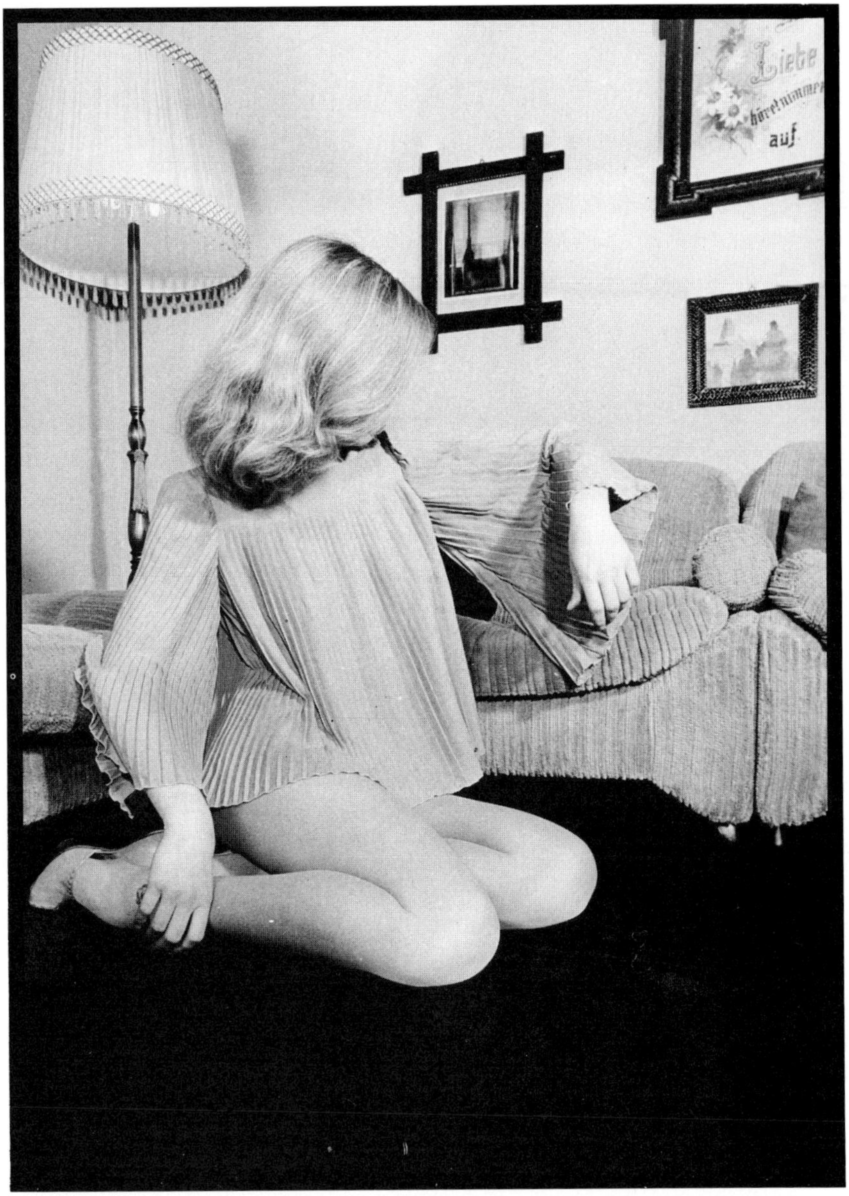

An unusual viewpoint or lens should not be chosen just for its own sake. But sometimes they serve to enhance, or even to create, exactly the kind of atmosphere you want. Here, the 17 mm lens and the viewpoint, which was very close to the floor, drastically change the composition from the conventional to one with an unusual distribution of masses and to an almost confusing change in proportions. The atmosphere thus created has an unreal feeling, which is further enhanced by the very dark floor, on which the model seems to float.

it will not do to substitute a longer lens, the effect of your photograph would change and it would not represent what you had in mind. That is why you should then try for an entirely different realisation – or for none at all.

These things are of course nothing but the basis of composition with interchangeable lenses. Again there is no substitute for your own work and the experience which you will gain from it. But when you consciously start to employ your interchangeable lenses for compositional purposes, you will very soon find out that you can do much more with them than you might at first have suspected. We will discuss another aspect of this in the following chapter.

5 Interchangeable Lenses and the Rendering of Space

Perspective

Let us assume that you want to photograph the turret of a castle. If it is to fill the greater part of your negative there are several ways in which this can be done. You could, for example, use a telephoto lens (let us say a 150 mm lens) and take the picture from a relatively great distance. On the other hand you could use a wide-angle lens (for example a 21 mm lens) and choose a viewpoint very close to your subject.

The question now is: What kind of differences between the two photographs are you going to get? If you look at them, you will probably notice the different rendering of perspective first. In the photograph taken with the telephoto lens the turret will look quite 'normal', that is without what is usually termed perspective distortion (*see diagram 26*), while the wide-angle rendering of the same subject contains several converging lines (*see diagram 27*).

Although this kind of perspective rendering is no property of the lens used, this so-called perspective distortion usually goes with wide-angle lenses, while telephoto lenses are generally associated with a 'correct' rendering of perspective in this context. The reason for this is quite simple. If you use a wide-angle lens you must get relatively close to your subject in order to fill your frame with it. In consequence you have to tilt the camera upwards in order to get all the subject on the negative. On the other hand you will need a greater distance with a

Different perspectives commonly associated with different lenses. 26: distant viewpoint gives parallel verticals because the camera is more or less level with the subject. A long focal length lens is used to give a large enough image. 27: close viewpoint with wide-angle lens tilted upwards to include the whole subject, giving converging verticals. 28: relative camera positions.

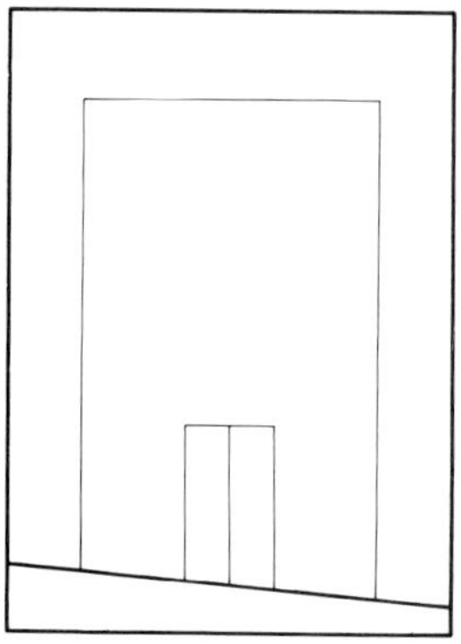

26

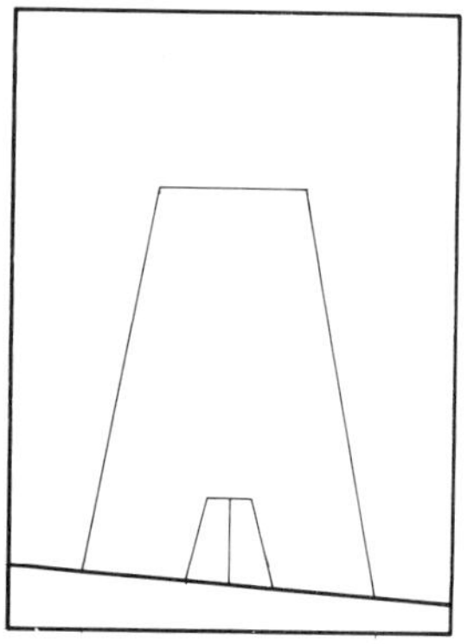

27

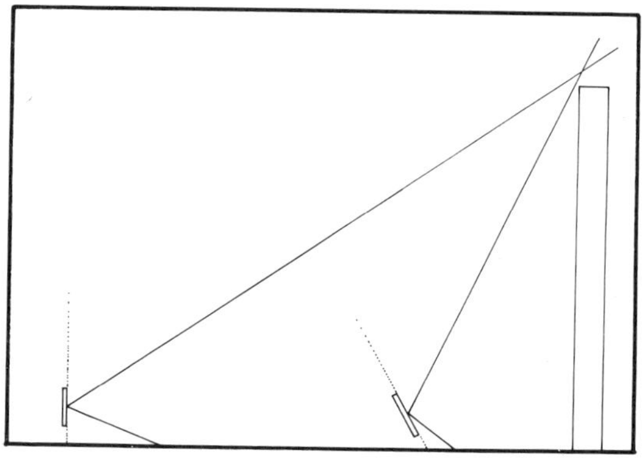

28

telephoto lens, which allows you to hold the camera parallel to the subject, which results in no distortion at all (*diagram 28*). In some cases, however, it does result in an apparent foreshortening of the distance between objects and a flattening of the field. There is also less apparent difference in the relative sizes of objects in a scene when viewed from a greater range.

So the conclusion is this: perspective distortion is no function of lenses (apart, of course, from fish-eye lenses). The distortion depends solely on the tilt of the camera. In practice, you will get more distortion with wide-angle lenses because when you need them it is more often necessary to tilt the camera than with longer lenses. That is the first reason why the choice of a certain lens influences the composition of a photograph. Depending on the angle at which the camera is tilted, the lines in the photograph will run differently, thus giving a different impact to it.

Incidentally, if you are the fortunate owner of a view camera you have much more freedom in the composition of your pictures than with any other camera. You can change the degree of distortion by using the movements of your camera without changing the lens or your viewpoint. Thus you are able to combine the other characteristics of lenses (for example in the rendering of the extension of space) with or without distortion or no no-distortion, just as you please. Owners of other cameras are not so lucky and must look for the best possible compromise.

Having clarified this, I would like to stress one point: what is usually called 'distortion' in the rendering of perspective actually is – geometrically speaking – quite correct. In 'seeing' (as discussed in Chapter 4) we unconsciously correct converging lines, they appear 'natural' to us. In a photograph the situation for our perception is entirely different. The photograph is usually rectangular, thus giving points (or better, lines) of reference for the lines which are contained in the photograph. In addition, the angle of view and other conditions under which we perceive the photograph are different from those used in the picture itself, thus creating a contrast which leads to the (optical) conclusion that the rendering of perspective is distorted, although it really is quite correct. Obviously this contrast, which leads to a kind of optically induced tension in the viewer, can be used for compositional purposes. Strengthening or diminishing it by changing the angle at which your camera is tilted means changing the emotional impact of your photograph.

We should, however, keep in mind that converging lines

work both ways. The usual procedure is to tilt the camera backwards, which results in lines which converge in the upper part of the picture (*compare 29 and diagram 29a*). It should go without saying that the reverse is equally possible: if you point your camera downwards, the result will be lines which converge in the lower part of the picture (*compare 30 and diagram 30a*).

The role of the viewpoint

A look at the two photographs, which were taken from almost exactly the same viewpoint, will convince you that the composition is quite different in each case and – with that – the

29

29a

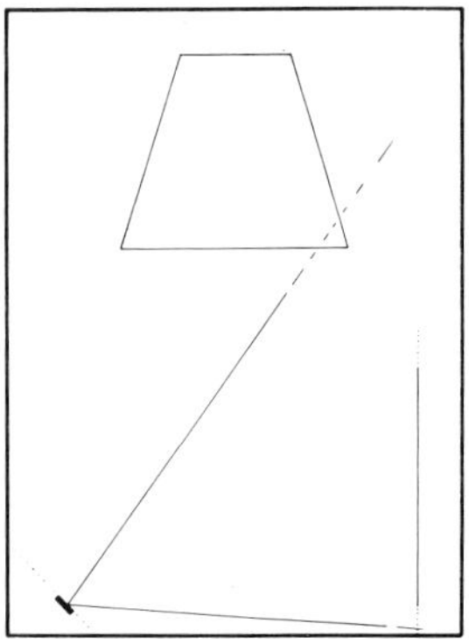

Left and opposite
The Château de Suscinio in Brittany lent itself to this demonstration of diverging and converging lines. If the camera is pointed downwards, vertical lines are shown as diverging, while they will converge if the camera is pointed upwards. This is not distortion but a geometrically correct rendering of perspective.

emotional impact on the viewer. The first photograph is mainly concerned with the castle itself, while the second one stresses the relationship between it and its viewer. This immediately indicates the second thing which usually changes with the lens used and which is, apart from that, always important in the composition of photographs. The viewpoint is not only enormously important in the rendering of perspective (as I have already explained in the preceding paragraphs), it also adds to the impact of a photograph in its own right.

A lens with a long focal length usually leaves you no freedom as far as the height of your viewpoint is concerned.

30a

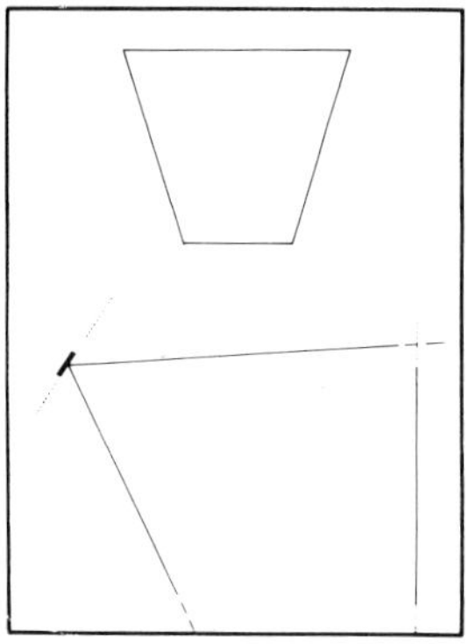

As a comparison of the two pictures show, these effects can be used to change the impact of a photograph at will.

30

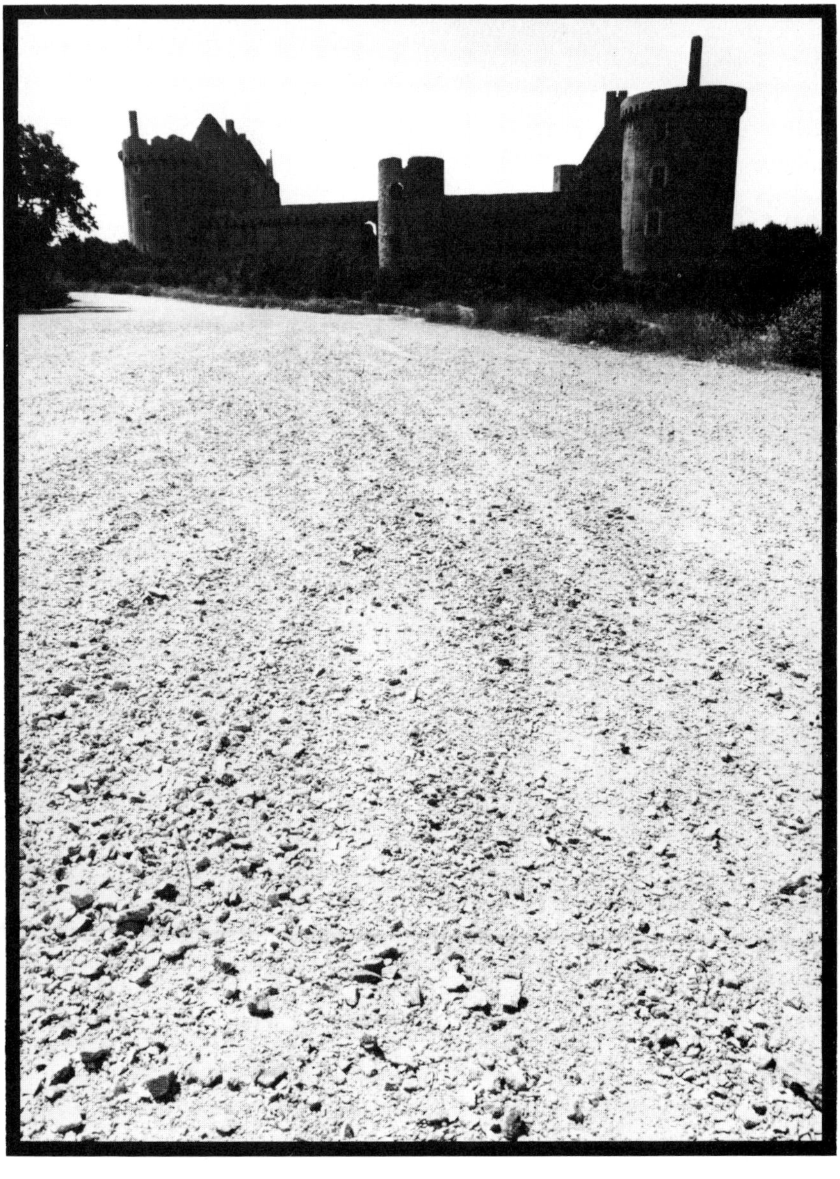

31

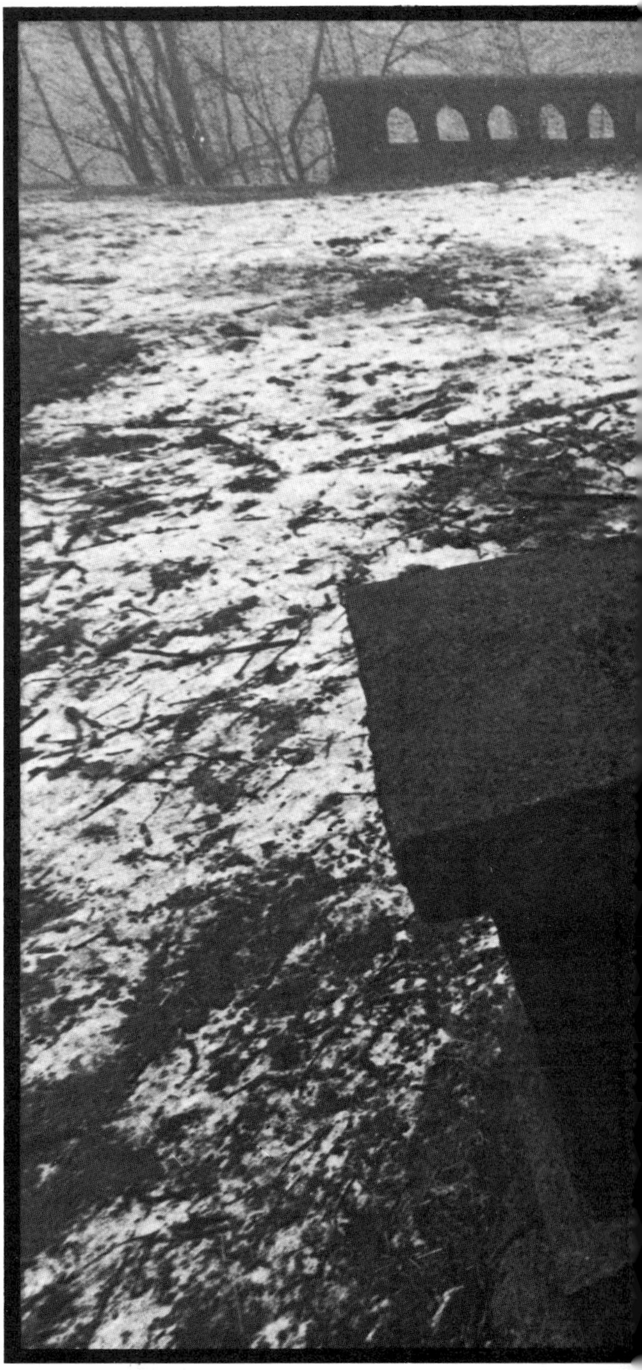

Extreme wide-angle lenses (in this case a 17 mm lens on a 35 mm camera) allow you to use diverging or converging lines to the greatest possible extent because you have the most freedom in the choice of viewpoint and in the tilt of the camera. With a 17 mm lens even a small deviation from the strictly vertical position of the camera will lead to considerable 'distortion'.

Even if you change it considerably (for example by climbing a tree or using a ladder), the appearance of your picture will not change at all (with extremely long lenses) or only very slightly. On the other hand, when you use wide-angle lenses small changes in the height of the viewpoint can radically change the composition and impact of your photographs. The height of the

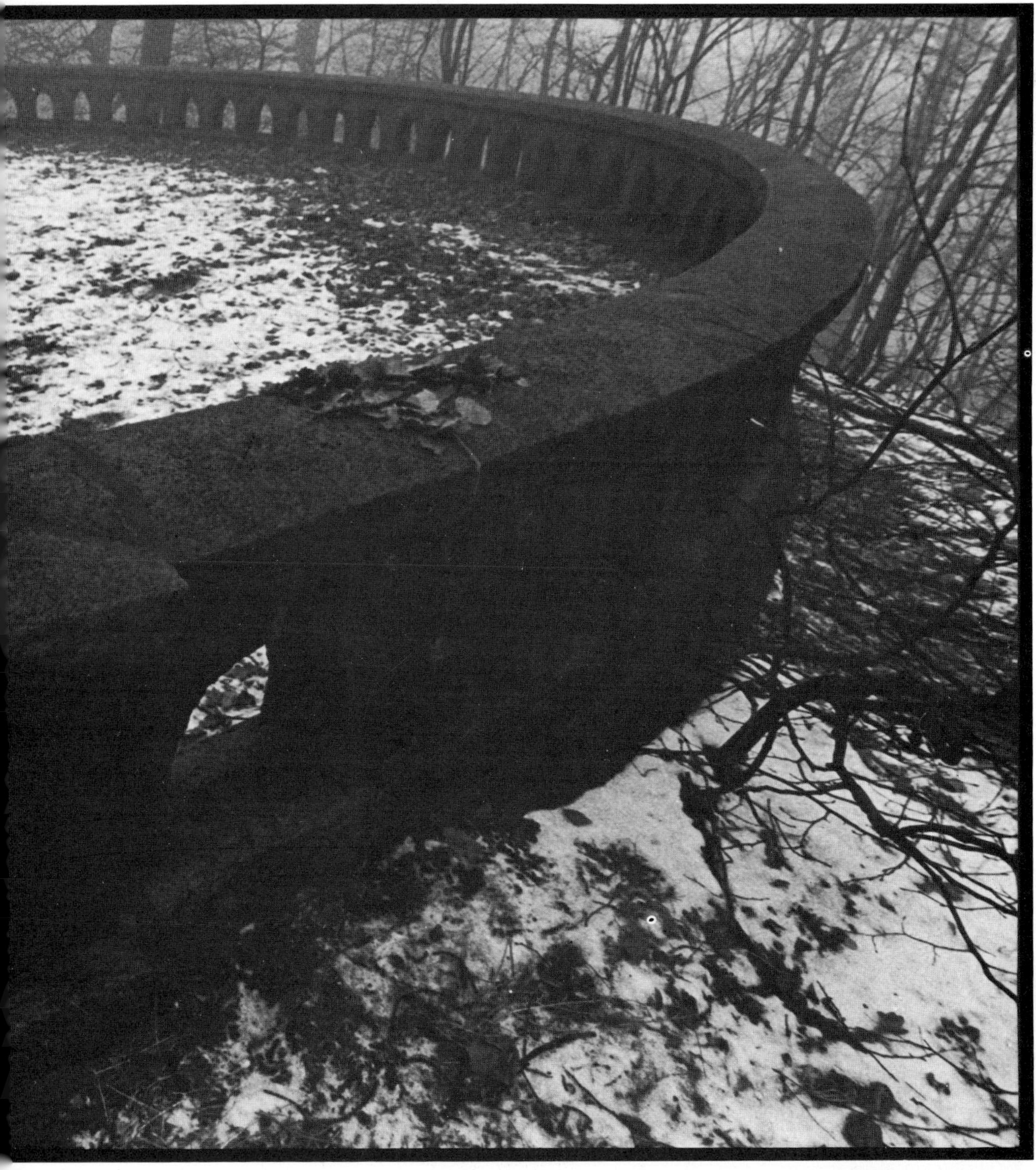

viewpoint in photographs 29 and 30 differed by about only 1.7 m. The first one was taken from eye-level standing upright, the second one from ground-level.

This difference between telephoto and wide-angle lenses is one of the reasons why the latter usually stress the extension of space in a photograph, while telephoto lenses seem to compress

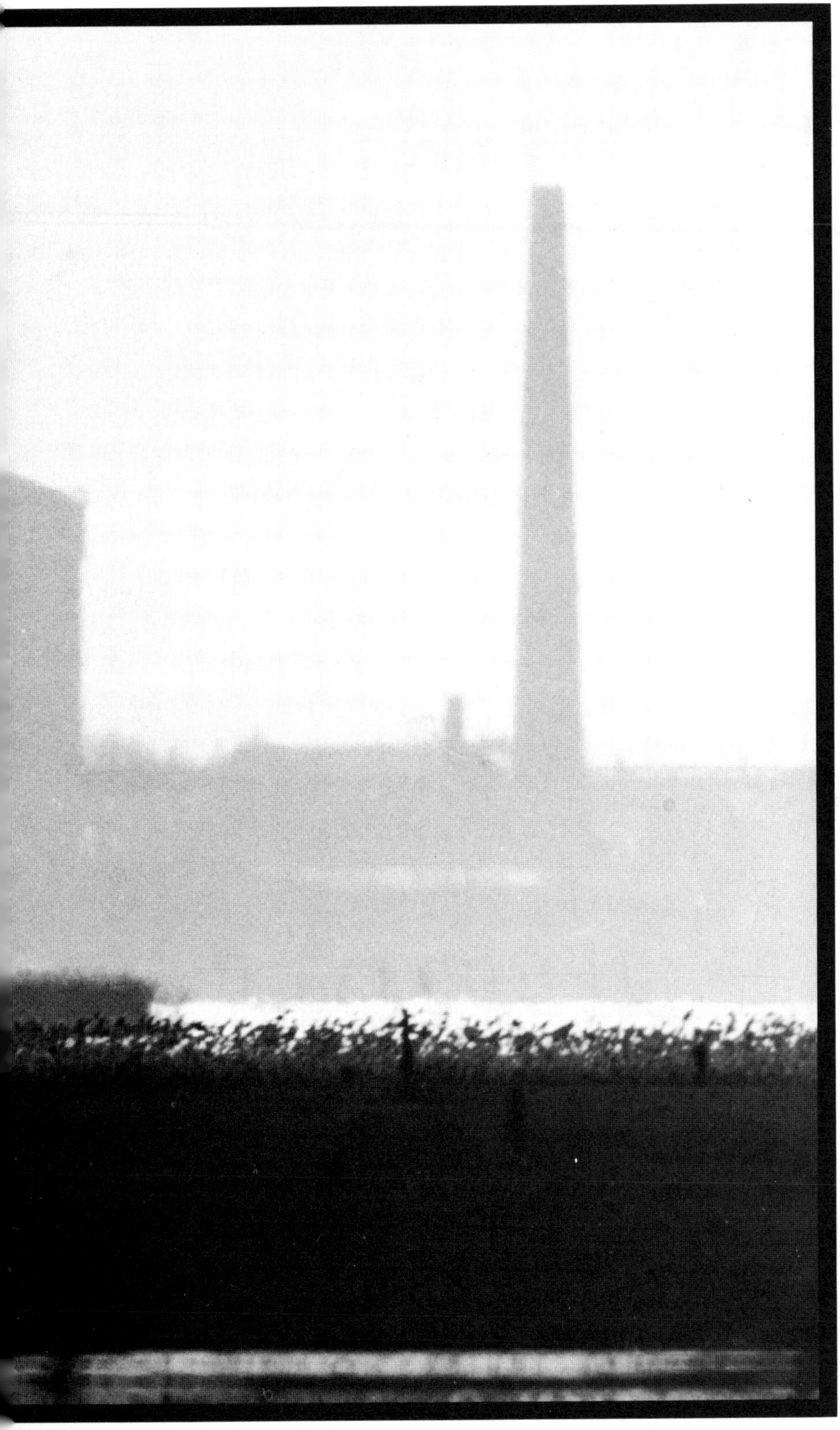

Extreme telephoto lenses (here a 1600 mm lens was used with a 35 mm camera) have very small fields of view. Therefore you do not have much of a choice as far as the viewpoint and the tilt of the camera is concerned. It is practically impossible to have diverging or converging lines in a photograph taken with a lens of this focal length.

it. With telephoto lenses you generally 'look' straight at things; with wide-angle lenses you can show the ground between things (and with that the extension of space). This is illustrated by the next two photographs. The first one (*31*) was taken with a 17 mm lens (on a 35 mm camera). Due to the very close range which is possible with this extremely short focal length lens, the camera was pointed almost straight down on the closer part of the stone structure, thus showing the ground between it and the distant 'wing' of the balustrade. The impression of the extension of space is further strengthened by the rendering of the proportions of the things depicted.

As I explained in Chapter 4, the difference of size is stressed with the use of wide-angle lenses. In reality both ends of the balustrade are of the same height, but they look entirely different in this photograph – much more so than they would look if you really saw them. This disagreement between what you subconsciously expect due to your perceptual habits and what you actually see in the photograph strengthens the impression of a wide space. (In this picture it is further enhanced by the haze or fog, which partly obscures the depth of the subject matter.)

As far as the rendering of space is concerned, the next photograph (*32*) shows the greatest possible contrast. It was taken with a 1600 mm lens (on a 35 mm camera) and in order to gain an idea what this means in practical terms, you should realise that the factory shown in the background of the picture was about ten kilometres distant, as I found out when I later looked at a map. The only indication of depth in this photograph is the distribution of the two grey zones, the distance being symbolised by the haze which in turn is responsible for the lighter grey of the background. This backdrop-like appearance is the typical way to show the extension of space with telephoto lenses. It is not depicted directly as is the case with wide-angle lenses, but indirectly, by implication.

This difference in the rendering of space is not only important in itself, it gives us freedom to arrange the elements of our photographs according to our intentions.

The next photograph (*33*) was taken with a 21 mm lens (on a 35 mm camera) not only to show the still elegant form of the wrecked ship, but also because this lens gave me the possibility of stressing the low viewpoint, which in turn emphasises the mass and size of the ship and allows the orientation of the mast, crossbeam and the hull, which makes for the strong as well as static composition. At the same time the background is

The use of a wide-angle lens (a 21 mm lens was used for this illustration) usually leads to drastic changes in the proportions of the things depicted because its use is generally combined with a change in viewpoint. If you use a wide-angle lens and get closer to your subject at the same time, the background will become smaller and more insignificant, which often strengthens the impact of the main subject and allows you to clarify the composition.

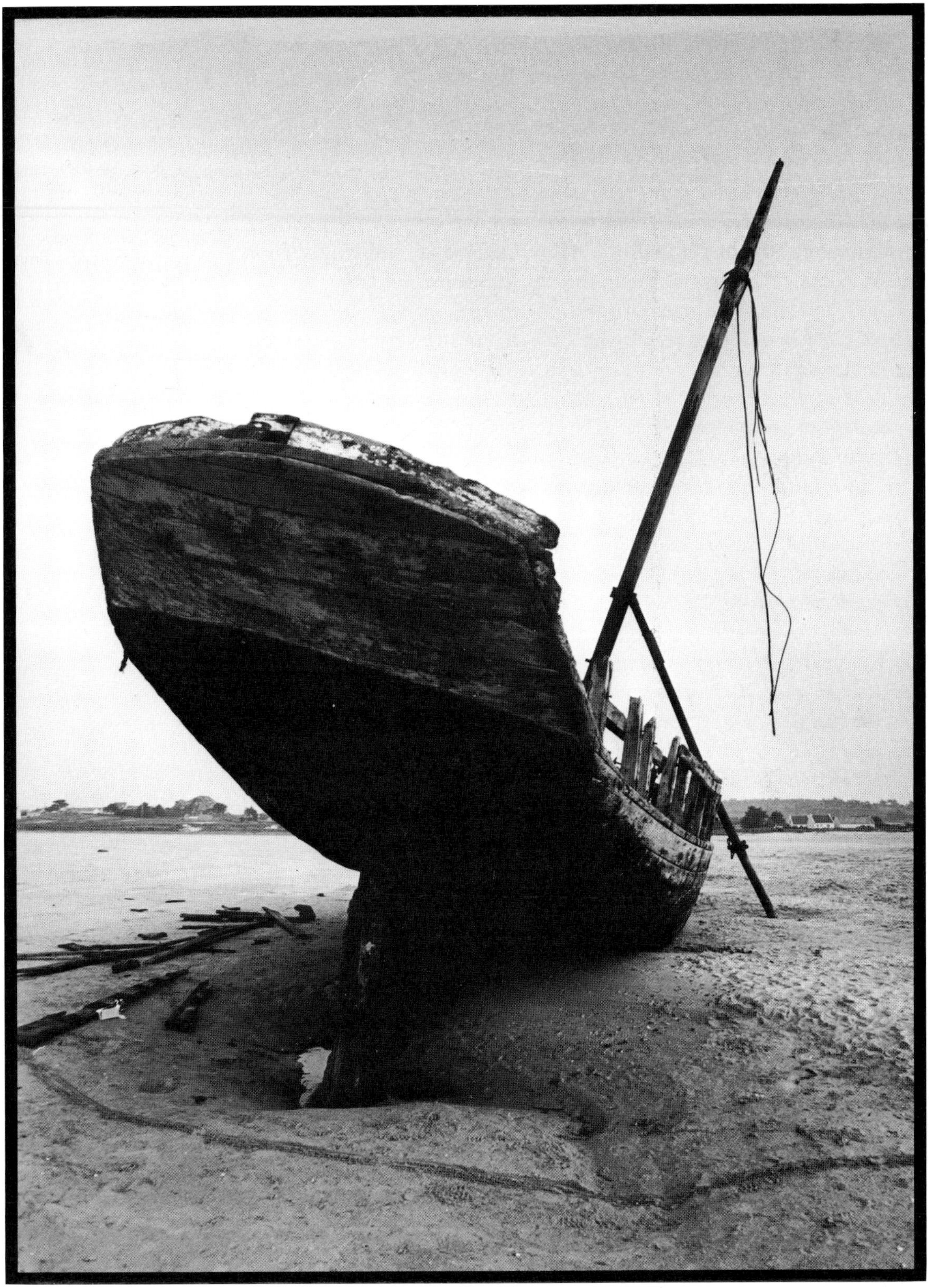

suppressed, which was the main reason why I used a wide-angle lens. Emotionally speaking, the background does not seem to belong to the subject and formally it did not fit in either, because it was very chaotic. So although the wide-angle lens was first used to keep the background as small as possible, all its effects come together to form this composition.

It is quite obvious that the use of a telephoto lens gives the reverse effect: background and foreground (the latter usually containing the main subject) are drawn close together, thus stressing the relations and/or contrast between them.

You now have an idea of the importance of the representation of perspective and the effects of the viewpoint on the composition of your photographs. The third (and last) of the factors which we have to look at is depth of field.

Depth of field

How to employ depth of field in the composition of photographs is actually the best known of the factors described in this chapter, that is why I can be very brief about it.

As you well know, depth of field decreases with the use of lenses of longer focal lengths and increases with smaller *f* stops. That leaves you with a wide field for experiment. You can start by changing the *f* stop in order to arrive at the effect desired, and if that does not work you can change the lens. But, as I have already explained, a change of lens gives a completely different image – not only another depth of field! That is why you will have to find a compromise which combines all the elements of composition as far as they are influenced by your choice of lens, in order to arrive at the closest possible approach to your ideas. But whatever you do, you should never consider a change of *f* stops as a means of getting a practicable exposure time. Depth of field is much too important a factor in composition to be sacrificed to these purely practical considerations. If you run into difficulties, you should first think about the use of faster films or of a tripod. If neither of these measures help, then you can start to compromise by giving up on your *f* stops.

This warning implies something else. Working with a modern SLR-camera you will generally not be able to see the depth of field in the viewfinder without some kind of manipulation. I have noticed that this results in many people not bothering at all. Do not follow the bad example of others, but always check on the depth of field! This very small additional delay will not only help you to make better pictures, it might even get you thinking about what you are doing and thus lead to even better realisations of your ideas.

Although much more could be said about the use of interchangeable lenses, these two chapters should give you quite a good idea of what to look for when you are working along these lines. But reading about it is, of course, not enough. You should get out and try all your lenses on some subject – not just haphazardly shooting away with whatever happens to be at hand, but really thinking about the effects which each lens will have on your photographs. In order to help you I have summarised the things which I have discussed (and some more, which you might want to explore yourself) in a table below.

Changes in the effect of space

The effect of space becomes smaller	The effect of space is caused by:	The effect of space becomes greater
long focal length	perspective rendering	short focal length
viewpoint at eye-level	level of viewpoint	lower, higher
parallel lines	tilt of camera	converging lines
smaller	depth of field	greater
distant	shooting range	close

effects of long focal lengths	effects of short focal lengths
smaller depth of field	greater depth of field
greater photographing range	shorter photographing distances
smaller tilt	greater tilt
smaller variations in level of viewpoint	greater variations in level of viewpoint
stronger aerial-perspective	less aerial perspective
stronger colour-perspective	less colour perspective
in all: impression of the extension of space is weaker	in all: impression of the extension of space is stronger

34

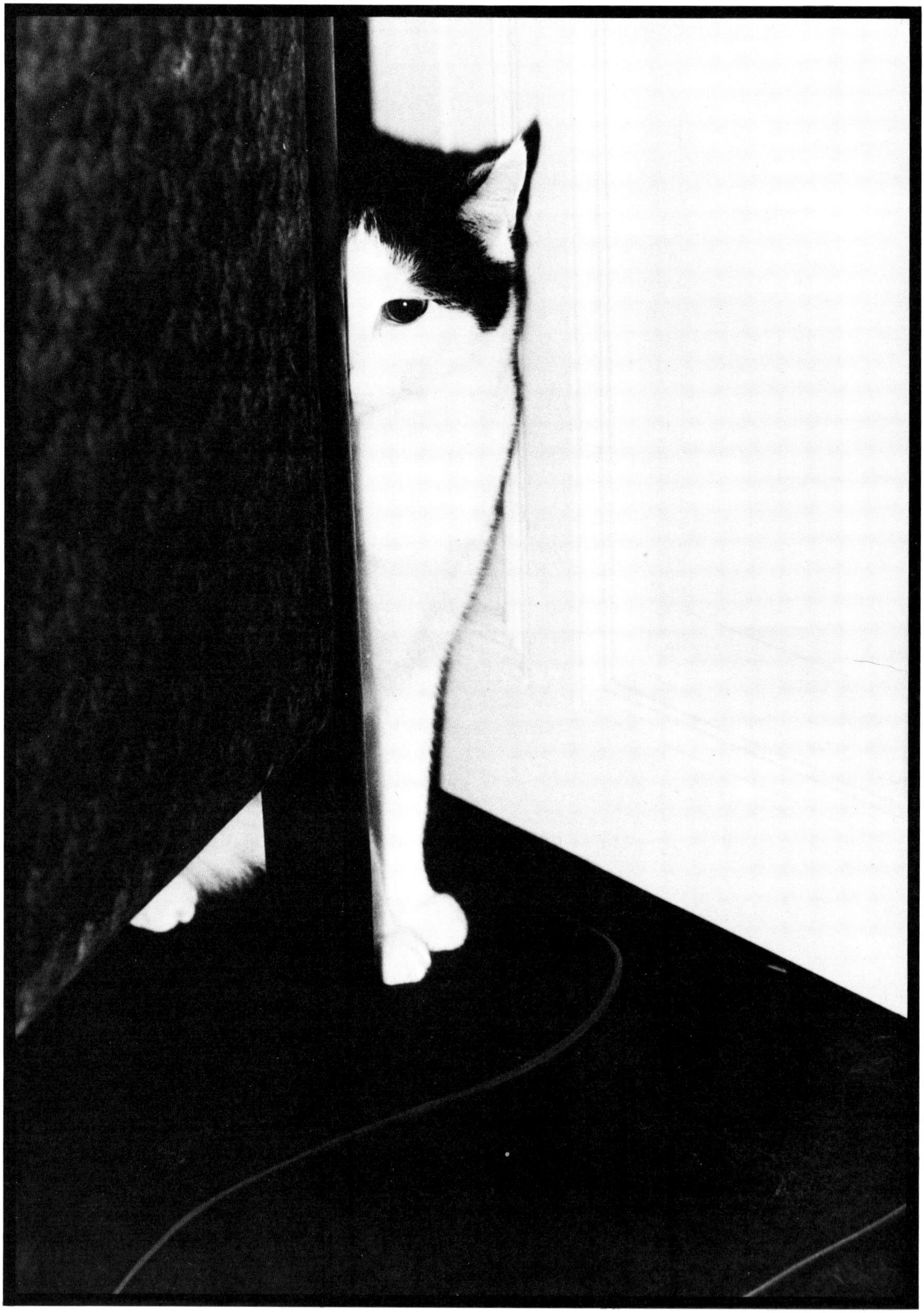

6 Colour or Black-and-White?

So far we have discussed two things which are basically different. On the one hand we looked at some elements of composition in the conventional sense of the word (ie compositional movement, lines, etc.). On the other hand we looked at some ways of influencing those elements according to our ideas (interchangeable lenses, viewpoints, etc.). I have tried to show that there are no safe rules which tell you how best to arrange the elements of composition. You have seen that the formal arrangement of pictorial elements depends solely on what you want to express with your photographs. This implies that photographs which are constructed according to some purely formal 'rule' do not succeed. Although at first they may be aesthetically pleasing, they cannot (and do not) have real

Opposite
Animals and people have at least one thing in common: they move at the worst possible moment. That is why it took me two rolls of film to produce this shot, where everything fits together exactly as it was meant to do. This composition lives by the strong contrast between the rigidly composed angles and planes of the furniture and the rounded and fuzzy contours of the cat. The very thin border of black shadow (determined by juggling around with the flash light) was very important because it set off the white of the cat against that of the door and the curved line of the extension cord in the foreground, which creates a connection between the different elements of the composition.

Right
Colours do not have to be garish in order to appeal to the viewer. Indeed, pictures which are almost monochrome, with only very subtle hues and changes in colour have quite an impact in the world of clashing and 'loud' colours, which is our usual daily environment.

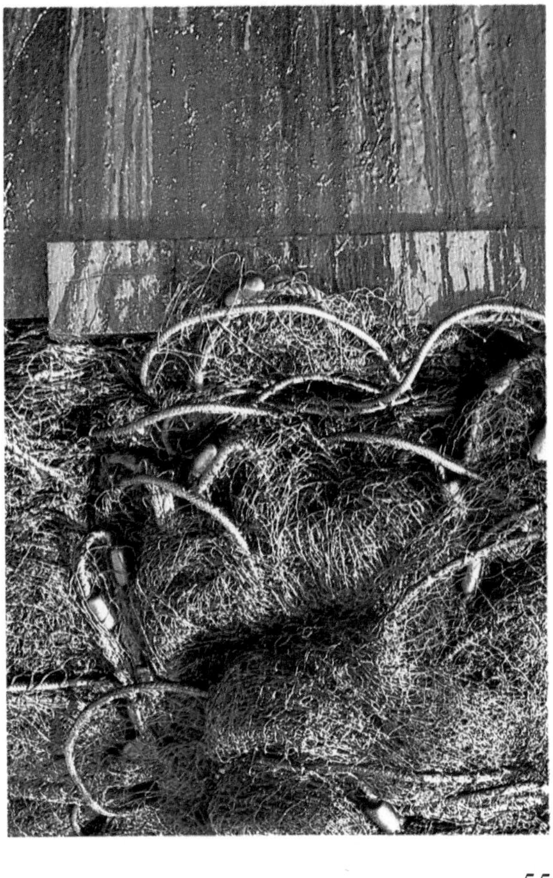

35

impact on the viewer, because they carry no message, mood, feeling, meaning or whatever you want to call it – they are 'empty'. Nevertheless, it is important to know as much as possible about the working of compositional elements, because you will thus gain insight into the possibilities of transposing your meaning (in the broadest sense of the word) into photographs which can be appreciated and understood by others.

This represented one side of the discussion. The other side was represented by some examples of how to influence the composition of pictures by photographic means. Here we are on safer ground, because we deal with facts and 'rules' when discussing it. If, for example, I say that this or that will happen if you use a lens of a certain kind, this is true and can be tested objectively – assuming, of course, that I worked things out correctly!

This means that you will have to do two things if you want to learn about composition. First, you must get some idea about the relationship between photographs and their viewers, that is, you will have to find out how to adapt the formal elements of a composition so that they will carry your message. This, as I have shown, is a subjective matter and I can give you nothing but pointers, you must do your own walking.

Second, you must learn about the influence of photographic means on the appearance of your pictures in order to be able to handle the 'language of photography' properly and successfully.

Then, of course, there is another utterly vital aspect of composition which is entirely and exclusively personal: you must have something to say.

There are, however, some things which are not specific to any one of these three categories, but which touch all of them at once. One such is the question of whether to use colour or black-and-white for your photographs. For some people this is almost a religious or moral question and accordingly real wars sometimes rage between the believers in colour and the protagonists of black-and-white. On the other hand some people do not think at all: they do this or that because it is the done thing. Another argument that you sometimes hear is that colour-photography is much easier than black-and-white photography (or vice versa).

You will probably have guessed that I do not think much of any of these views. In my opinion black-and-white and colour photography represent two entirely different and distinct means of expression and of realising pictures. Choosing one or the other is not a decision for 'better' or 'worse', but an option to

Overleaf
These three pictures show three different ways of handling colour. The saturated and strangely contrasting colours of 36 impart an air to the subject which might be described as friendly, lively and appealing. It looks somehow very southern, although it was taken in Denmark. The same subject has an entirely different impact in the almost completely monochrome rendering of 37. Here it looks withdrawn, severe and very cold and northerly indeed. Between these two extremes is 38. The composition relies on very simple forms in an equally simple arrangement, which is further enhanced by the subtle changes in colour.

use a specific means to realise an idea. This decision should not be one of principle. It should be reached after careful consideration of what kind of realisation you want for each photograph. This is, I must admit, not always an easy decision. I prefer black-and-white-photography, and sometimes I do not take a photograph at all, because I know that it should be done in colour. But you know the saying: Don't do as I do, do as I say!

How to decide between colour and black-and-white
Joking apart, the question remains: when should you use black-and-white and when would colour do the job? As should now be obvious the answer to this question is not subject to hard and fast rules. We will look at some examples and try to find out why they were done in colour and whether we can draw any conclusions or generalisations from this.

The second picture (*35*) seen here is an example of a subject which, in my opinion, would not work in black-and-white at all. It shows a tarred fishing-net lying on a concrete surface and except for some very small and slight blue reflexes it consists entirely of black and grey tones – and that is exactly why it had to be photographed in colour. Apart from the formal configurations of the different parts of the net and the contrast between its undulating forms and the rectangular black concrete-block, the appeal of this subject consists of the fact that it is grey and black. If the subject had been photographed in black-and-white the viewer could not even guess at the colours of the things depicted and this would take away most of the impact of the still-life. The contrast between the net and the concrete-block is integrated and suspended by the unifying overall colour, thus providing the calm and withdrawn mood of the picture.

Another example of this kind of reasoning for using colour photography is shown in illustration 37. But before we talk about the use of colour here, I would like to remind you of our discussion in Chapter 5 of converging lines and camera-tilt. A 17 mm wide-angle lens was used here in order to allow a great amount of camera-tilt and, with that, converging lines. The result is that the building looks squat and powerful, this effect being further enhanced by the pronounced foreshortening, which goes with this kind of perspective rendering.

The importance of colour in composition
The subject of this picture appealed to me because it gave an exceedingly strong impression of the dreariness, monotony and

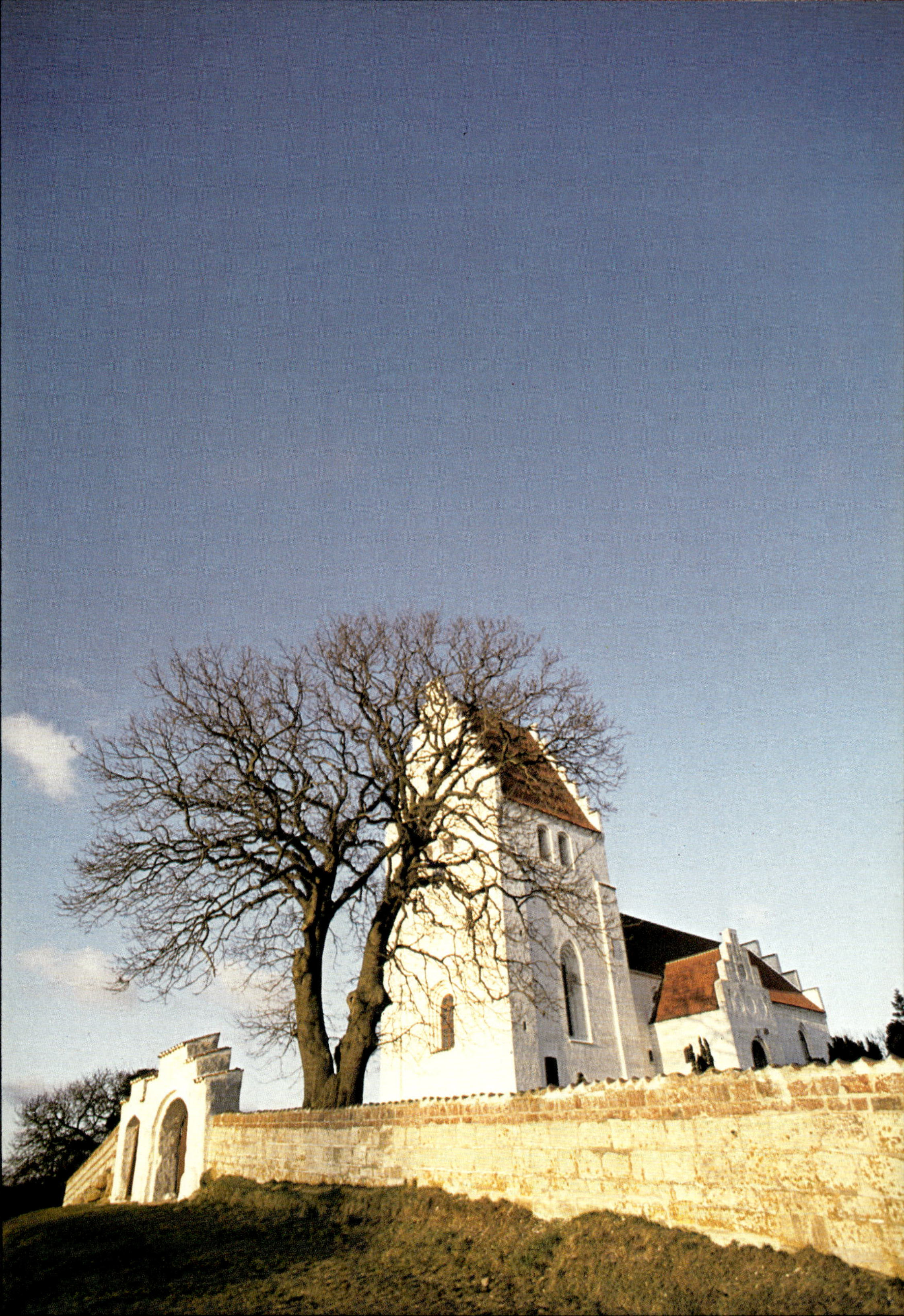

37

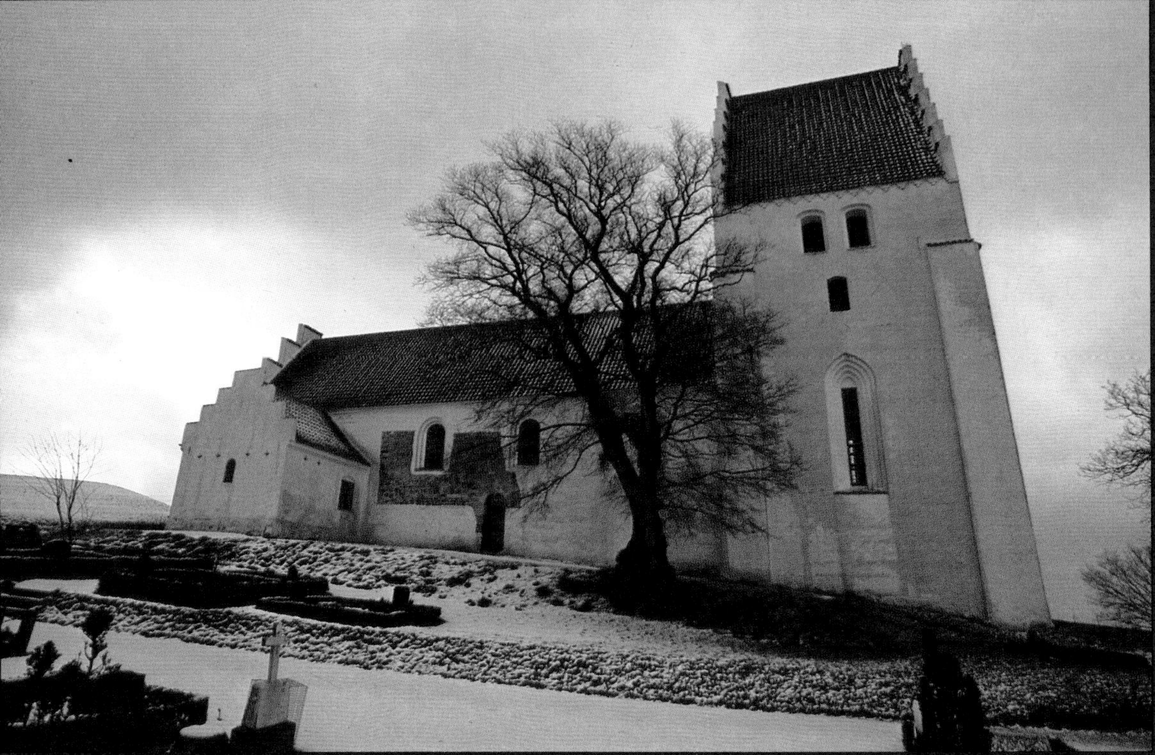

38

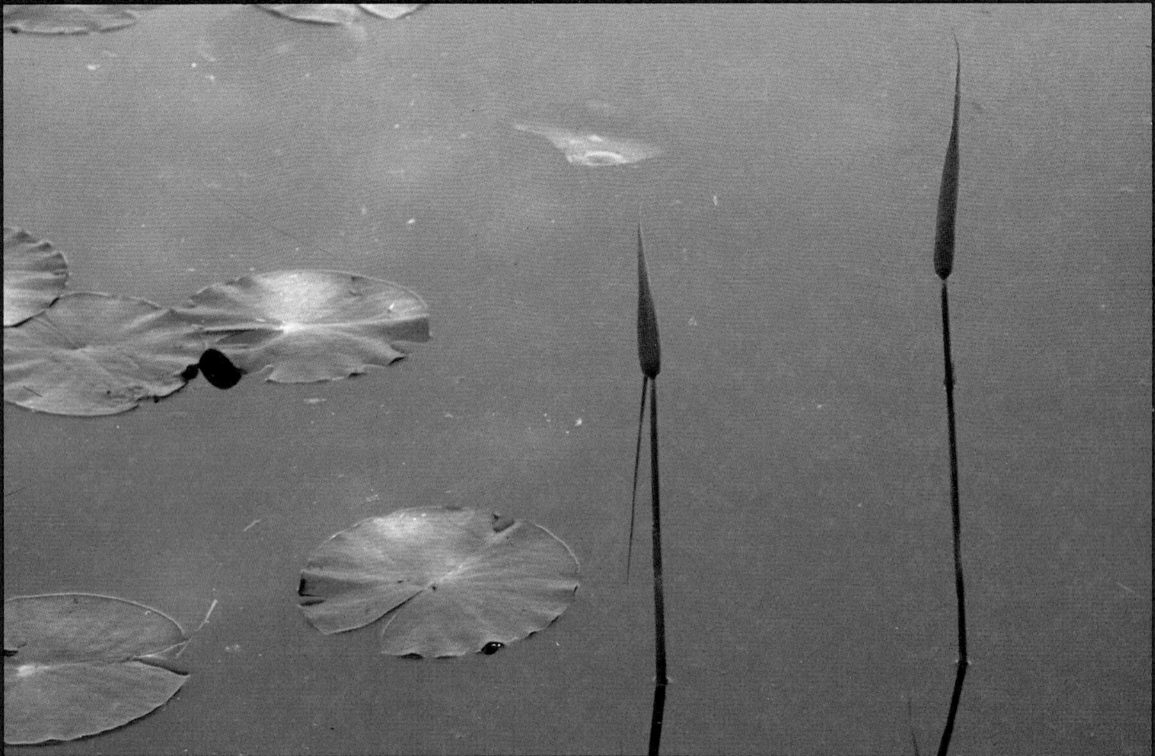

solitude of a winter morning. As in the previous photograph these qualities are mainly expressed through the dominating blue-grey and green-grey colours and, accordingly, by the almost complete absence of other colours. Again it is quite obvious that this is best expressed in colour, black and white would not have been at all effective.

In order to show you what a change of colour can do to the impact of a photograph, I have included another shot of the same subject (*36*). This picture was taken on the same day, but some hours later. The snow and fog had gone and the sun shone. I find the change in colour (note, for example, the roof of the church) really quite amazing. The impact of the photograph is now entirely changed and it looks almost as if it had been taken in some southern country. This goes to show that the mood of the scenery, as I saw it at the time and as I tried to relate it in my photographs, depended on the colours of the subject, which accordingly had to be recorded on colour-film.

This leads us to a first conclusion: colour photography should be used when the colour, whether in its intensity, its type, its distribution or for any other reason, really is an essential part of the subject and is consequently important for the photograph. Although this sounds like a platitude it is not as easy to realise as you might think. People like colour, whether it is something special or not. That is why they tend to include it in their photographs without thinking about whether it is superfluous or really adds something to the pictorial quality.

It is, however, also important to understand that a subject which does not work in colour does not automatically make a good black-and-white photograph. A black-and-white-photograph is not just a picture without colour! Both kinds of picture require an entirely different quality and degree of abstraction, they are different from their very starting point, which is in the mind of the photographer. That is why the decision to use one or the other is so subjective and personal, and it is also why I can only point out that the problem exists and show some solutions to it, solutions which may or may not work equally well for you.

We will assume that you have made your basic decision to use colour. Let us now have a look at what happens next. First we meet again some of those so-called 'rules of composition' which are as nonsensical as those already described in connection with black-and-white-photographs. There is, for example, the famous 'red spot', this time not on Jupiter, but

said to enliven your photographs. A red spot, be it a flower or the dress of a person placed in a landscape or whatever else, can actually work in two ways. Either it is not noticed at all if the picture consists of a multitude of different colours which are more or less randomly distributed over the picture-plane. Or it might destroy the composition if it is placed in a monochrome or strongly contrasting surrounding. It is just not true that a colour photograph needs some colour-contrast or other in order to be interesting. Again, it all depends on your intentions. Illustration 38 shows an example of this kind of thing: The photograph consists of blue, green and violet tones which are so blended as to appear almost monotone. The interest of the viewer is centred on the monochromatic nature of the colour and the contrast between round and straight forms. Just imagine what the introduction of a 'red spot' or some such artificial 'compositional device' would do to this photograph!

The scorn which I pour on such 'rules' should not, of course, lead you to believe that they never work. As with everything else in composition sometimes they might meet your requirements exactly, and then you should use them without hesitation! The next illustration (*39*) shows a case in point. As far as the colours are concerned, the impact of this photograph indeed rests on the concentration of the 'warm' colours in one relatively small spot, which strongly contrasts with the dominating blue-green tones. I will not hide from you that I created this contrast artificially, by using in daylight a film intended for artificial lighting. This use of film is an interesting way to change the colour-composition of your photographs. All parts of a subject which are of an intensely 'warm' colour (for example bright red) appear relatively unaffected in the finished photograph, while all other colours are changed to a more or less intense blue.

But to get back to our main concern: what I described in some detail concerning the 'red spot' goes for any other of the 'rules' which you may have read or heard about. Take, for example, the 'balanced proportions' of colours. It is said that a picture which contains about one-third of warm to two-thirds of cold colours (or the other way around) is especially harmonious. This indeed is true, as far as it goes, but why should anybody want to make a rule of it and strive to apply it? If harmony is what you strive for in your photographs, it can be achieved in a lot of different ways, for example by the very uneven distribution of colours over the picture plane. Have a look at illustration 40 and decide for yourself whether the very small amount of green in this photograph which otherwise

Below
If the colour balance of a subject does not satisfy you completely, you should not hesitate to change it to match your intentions. Here I used in daylight a film intended for artificial lighting. The resulting shift to predominantly blue and green tones conveys more of my impression of this scenery than a natural rendition of the colours would have done.

Right
Photography at night (by artificial light) usually leads to shifts in the colour balance, if you use daylight-type films and long exposure times. For documentary purposes it might be necessary to correct this, but in most cases the 'wrong' colours of the photograph (as in both this illustration and 46) have a much greater impact on the viewer.

39

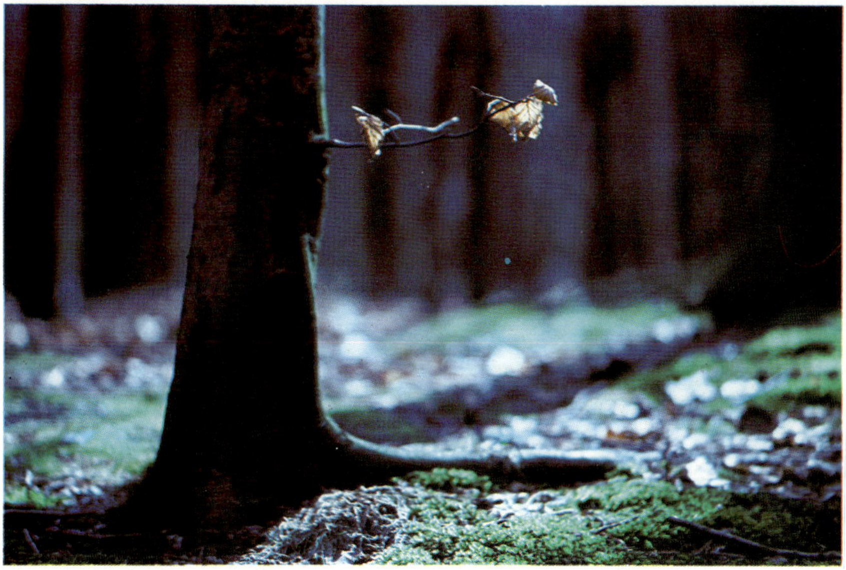

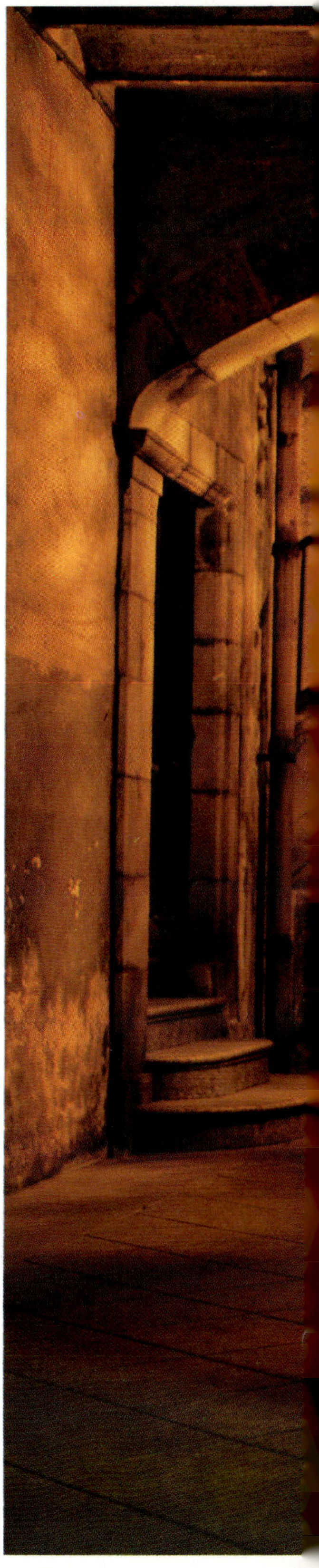

consists entirely of yellow-orange tones adds to or distracts from the overall effect of harmony and quietude.

Apart from that you should keep in mind that complete and perfect harmony (compositionally speaking) tends to be boring and meaningless. Pictures of this kind do not offer the least stimulus or resistance to the viewer – it is not even necessary to look at them a second time once you have seen them.

I will leave it at that, but if you do not believe me on the last point, I strongly advise you to have a really hard look at the photographs you are thinking of and to analyse them along the lines shown here – you might be surprised by the results!

Apart from the basic question of when to use colour and when not, my approach to colour photography has so far been of a rather negative kind, although I hope that you have profited by it, because knowing what not to do can be as important to know as the reverse. We are, however, going to have a closer look at some positive aspects, that is at some cases where we can confidently state that colour is used to special advantage in the composition of the photographs.

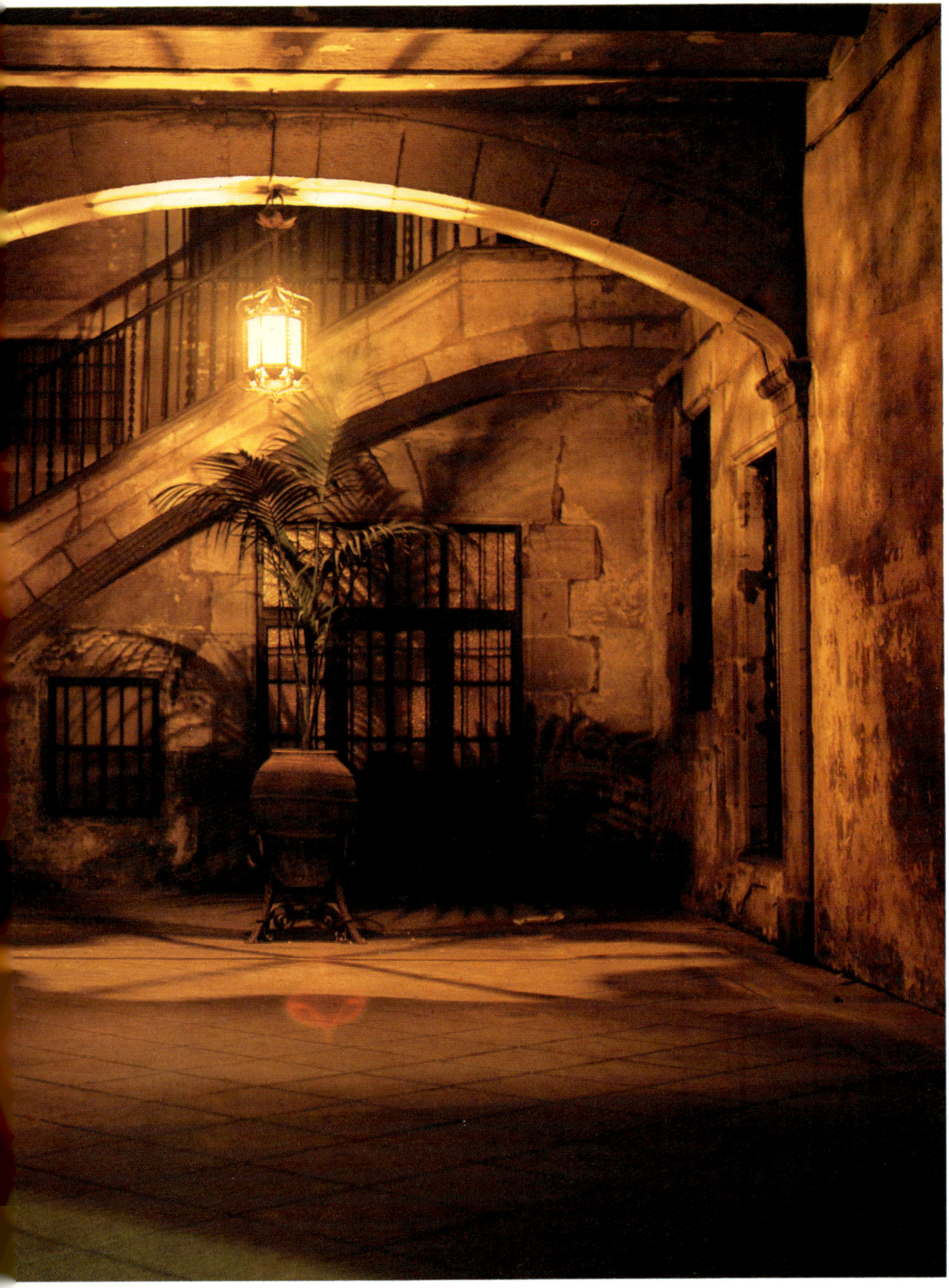

40

7 Colour and Meaning

The first two examples in this chapter are the most extreme cases for colour photography which I can dream up, because the colour itself is the subject of these pictures.

Colour and abstract compositions

The thing shown in picture 41 is actually the front of a metal wastebin which I once happened to see in a park. As far as the viewer is concerned, this picture shows an abstract configuration of colours. That is why I called it an extreme case of colour photography: the colours themselves are the subject and if you take them away nothing remains.

The strength of such a photograph rests exclusively on its composition. There is no other subject, or indeed any other aspect of the picture, which might draw the interest of the viewer if the composition is boring or contains any flaws. But this does not necessarily imply that the interest of a photograph of this kind begins and ends with its formal arrangement. This might be the case if you had been interested in some quality of the colour itself and took the photograph for this reason. On the other hand it is often the associative quality of a pattern or an arrangement of colours which arouses interest and which might accordingly be transmitted to the viewer. In this case the associative quality of a picture can be found in either of two things, or sometimes in both at the same time. First of all the arrangement of forms and colours could remind the viewer of something, that is, he might associate it with an entirely different subject because of some more or less superficial resemblance. Second, the composition could be constructed along the lines described previously (compare Chapter 2), that is, it might generate certain feelings or impressions by itself. (A diagonal line, for example, could evoke a dynamic impression.)

The second photograph (*42*) shows quite an interesting example of the associative power of abstractions, for in my experience viewers are invariably reminded of a wave, although the photograph depicts nothing of the kind. This association is easily explained by the dominating blue tones and the form, which indeed faintly resembles the well-known study of a wave

by Hokusai. In contrast to the first subject which just occurred naturally, this one was especially made to be photographed and was deliberately designed to provoke this association. Although this is not our real concern, you might be interested to know what the thing shown really is. The round form and the stripes at the bottom are pieces of clear adhesive tape (the former having been cut out with a punch), while the 'wave' consists of a piece of colourless plastic sandwich-wrapping. Everything was mounted between the glass of a 35-mm slide-frame and photographed in polarised light.

But regardless of whether you create your own abstractions or whether you find them in nature, you should always be sure of one thing: the colours and their forms carry the whole impact of the photograph and therefore must be strong enough to interest the viewer. Ideally, they should not just be pleasing or interesting in an undefined manner, they should carry a meaning (or should look as if they did!), which the viewer should feel he could find out if only he looked long enough! And do not be surprised if someone really seems to find a meaning in a photograph of this kind. It is not really there, it is created in the viewer's mind, the picture just serves to trigger the associations which lead to it.

This fact is important, and 'non-abstractions' contain this level as well, although most people are not conscious of it. Apart from the subject, the composition of each photograph (including its colours) works just as the 'abstractions' shown here. As the viewer responds to the subject matter, so he does to the composition, although this response is generally on a subconscious level. If both sets of associations work in the same direction, the impact of the photograph is strong. But if there is a difference or even a contrast between these two levels, the viewer will either react with confusion or not react at all. Then the photograph is a failure.

That, incidentally, is why a picture of – let us say – a cabbage leaf can be a much better photograph than a picture of a sensational occurrence or of a far-away place never photographed before. (I do not want to belittle the latter kind of picture with this statement, but we are here dealing with the aesthetic evaluation of photographs, and not with news-value and related categories.)

Before we go on to the next kind of picture, I would like to point out that the subject of an 'abstraction' need not necessarily be unrecognisable. In picture 43, for example, the subject can be clearly identified as a bench and an air-vent on the deck of a ship. But this identification is entirely irrelevant

41

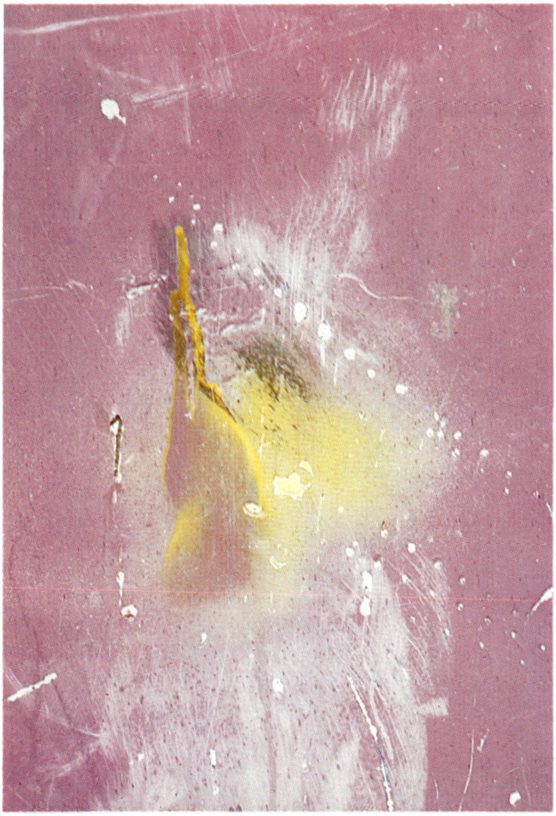

Left and below
Colour has a very strong appeal in itself. Evenly coloured walls and other surfaces can influence you psychologically. This is even more true for a combination of colours with abstract forms. In such cases it does not matter whether you find these abstract compositions in nature (41) or whether you make them deliberately (42). What counts is their impact on the viewer.

42

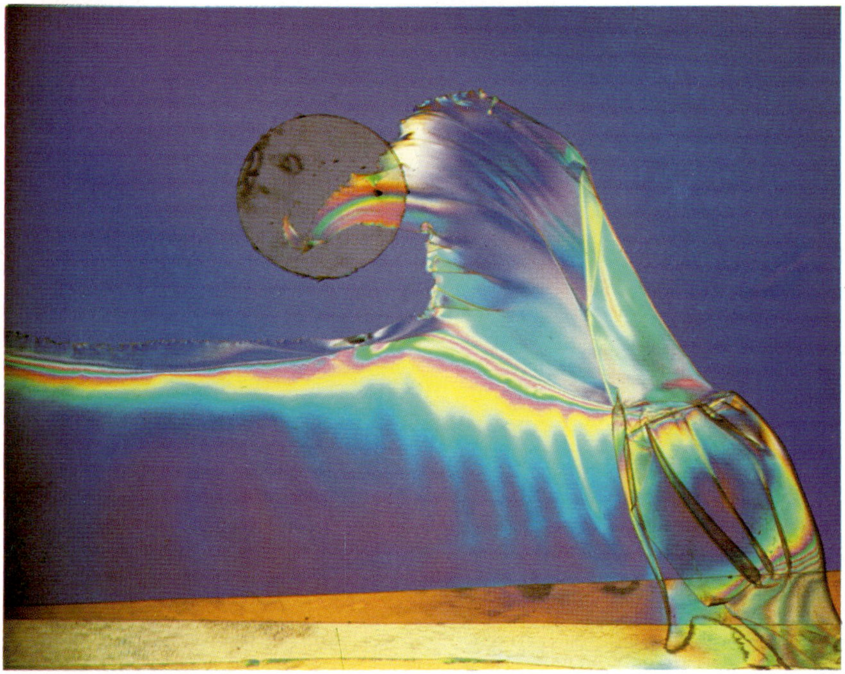

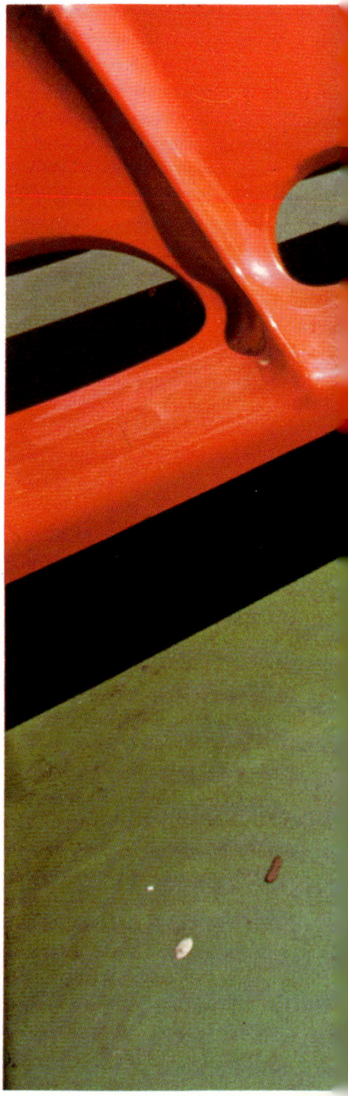

In some cases the impact of the colour of a subject and its arrangement can be so strong that it does not matter if you cannot recognise what the photograph shows. Here the distribution of light and dark areas and of the saturated colours is much more important than the picture's subject.

43

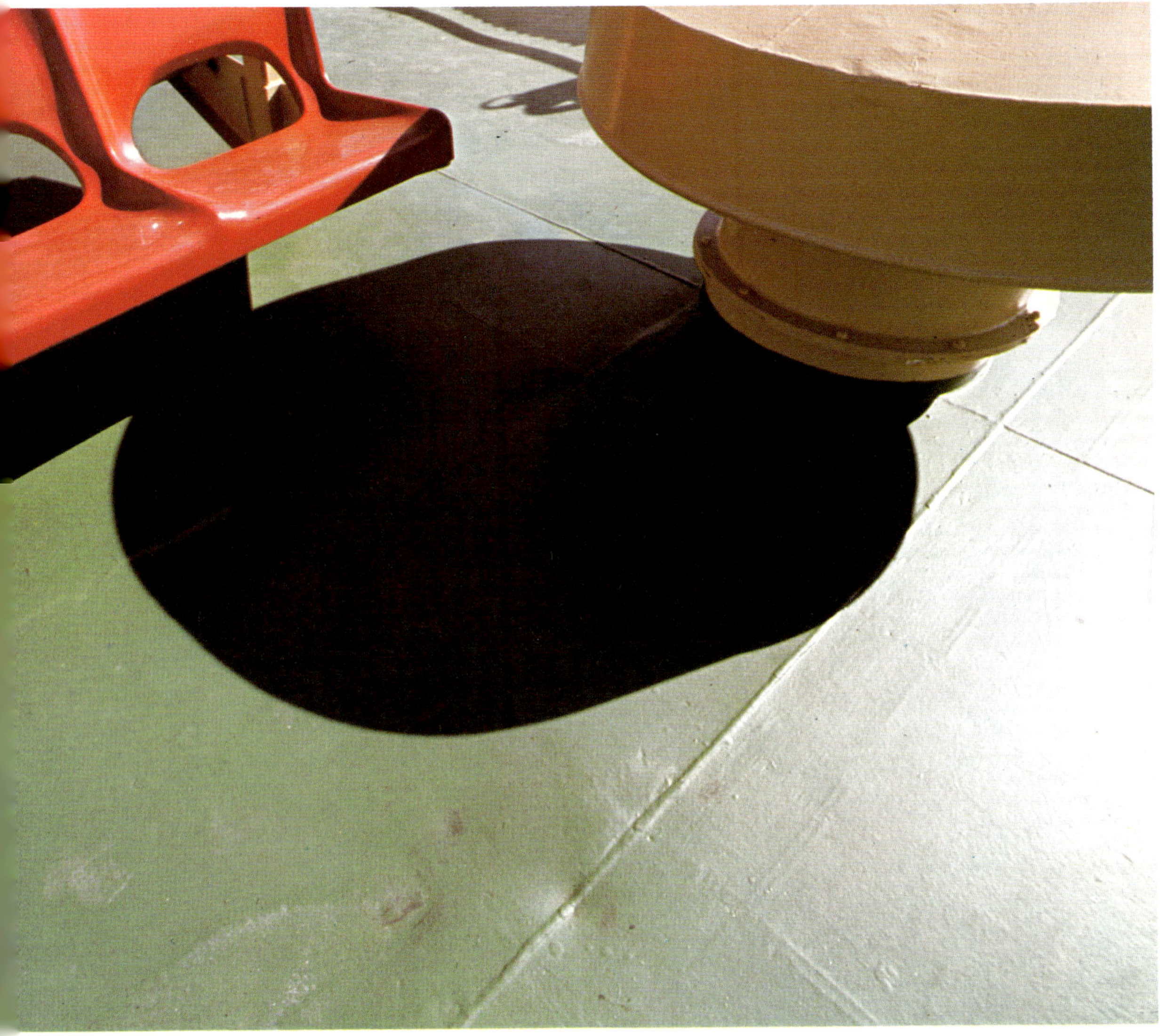

for the impact of the photograph which rests on its composition, that is, on the colours and their distribution on the picture-plane. A look at some photographic magazines will show you that this kind of 'abstract photography' was in vogue in Europe at the time of writing (1979), but this should not keep you from trying it yourself.

Turning from these examples, where colour is the only means of expression contained in a photograph, we will now deal with another set of pictures, where colours furnish additional information or give the possibility of achieving a satisfying composition.

Colour and subject matter

The next two photographs show quite a different application of colour. Everyone who is engaged in close-up photography knows from his own experience that one of the main problems to be dealt with is depth of field, which always seems to be much smaller than one would like it to be. This not only leads to difficulties in rendering the subject matter, it poses additional problems the moment you are concerned with the composition of close-ups. If photographed in black-and-white, the background of a picture is usually a more or less uniform grey, and the problem lies in arranging a meaningful or at least a pleasing surrounding for the subject. This problem can be reduced or even turned to an advantage if you use colour. Two reasons for this are demonstrated in the next illustrations. The first shows some kind of grass in front of mountainous scenery (*44*). The mountain, however, is only recognisable as such because it is shown in colour, which gives additional information as to its structure and the material of which it is composed. If this photograph had been taken in black-and-white, as indeed I tried, you would probably not have been able to identify the scenery at all.

In the second example (*45*) there are two compositional problems: the colour of the subject and the lack of contrast between subject and background. The subject is three fungi which are entirely black-and-white. Technically speaking, a rendering in black-and-white would work as well as one in colour. But we saw in the preceding chapter that both give quite a different impact to the photograph and so we have to decide what we want to express with our picture and choose the appropriate technique.

In this case the solution was easy because the second problem seemed to make the use of colour preferable. Although the subject itself is mostly light grey and the background would be rendered as mid grey, the contrast between them would not be great, and this photograph needed the greatest possible difference between subject and background. The use of colour, therefore, was almost a foregone conclusion.

Now look at some pictures where colour adds to the information contained in the picture or creates a greater impact on the viewer – not always the same thing! Logically, the next step should be to look at some examples where colour gives a different type of information or impact. What this means in practice is best explained with reference to the illustrations.

Illustration 46 shows a view of Barcelona taken at night (*compare 40*). Although the scene was artificially lighted, this light was exceedingly weak, so that the exposure took some minutes. The result is a photograph which shows some things and colours which I could not see at the time and others which I had not noticed. Generally speaking, light must have a minimum intensity in order to allow us to see colours. If it is weaker we can discern only grey tones – or nothing at all. That is why photography at night is one of the cases where we can show different information and thus add to the impact of our photographs. (You may have noticed that I carefully avoid a direct comparison with seeing when I talk about 'different' information. The reasons for this are explained in Chapter 4, where I described the basic difference between seeing and photography.)

All pictures where we change the so-called 'natural' colours of the subject by photographic means belong in this category. This change can be very small, indeed almost imperceptible, as in illustration 47. For this a telephoto lens (250 mm on a 6 × 7 cm format camera) was used to enhance the aerial-perspective of the scenery, which resulted in the overall blue-green tones and the slightly bleached appearance of the background.

In contrast to this a strong change in colour might be achieved by the use of coloured trick filters, infra-red films and related means. An example of this is given in the next illustration (*48*). This picture was taken using a prism in front of a standard lens. The result is a photograph which shows the spectral colours (or at least some of them) of the subject as

Below
Apart from its purely compositional value, colour often serves additional purposes. In pictures where large areas are rendered out-of-focus (which is usual with most close-ups), colour heightens the recognisability of the objects. If this photograph had been taken in black and white you would have been unable to identify the mountain in the background as such, it could just as well be a mound of earth.

Bottom
Very low contrasts tend to look 'muddy' and confusing in black and white photographs. In such cases it is generally advisable to use colour in order to clarify the composition of your picture.

Right
If the intensity of light drops below a certain level we cannot discern colour at all. That is why photography at night in very weak light can lead to interesting surprises. Although quite pleasing, the composition of this photograph has some flaws, simply because I could not see most of the things shown in the picture when I took it.

44

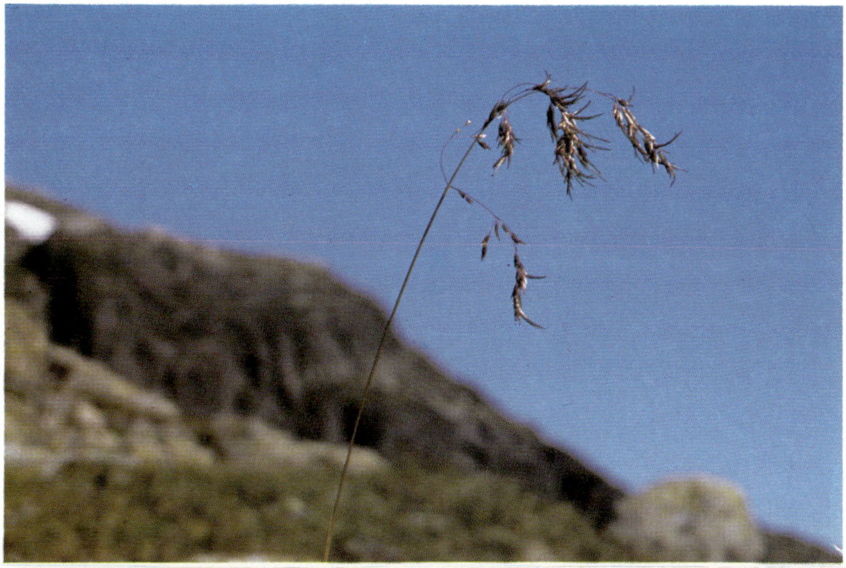

45

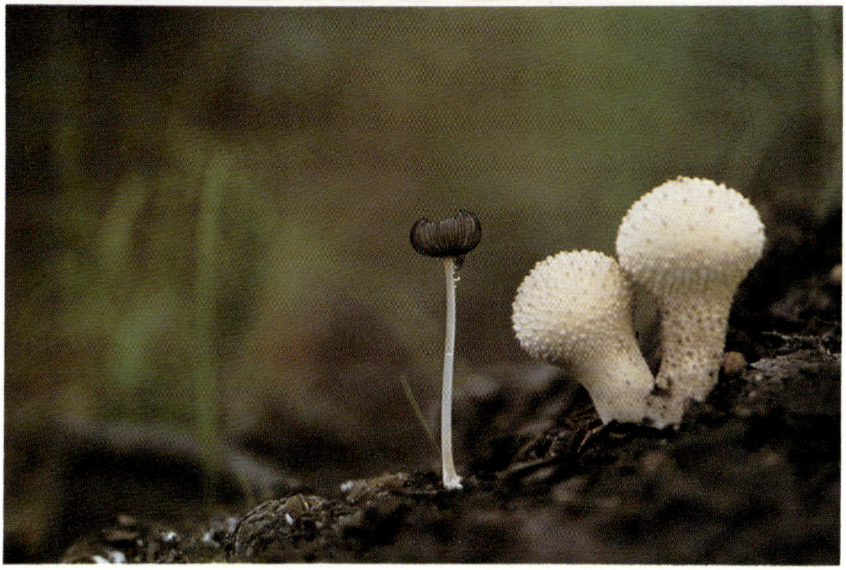

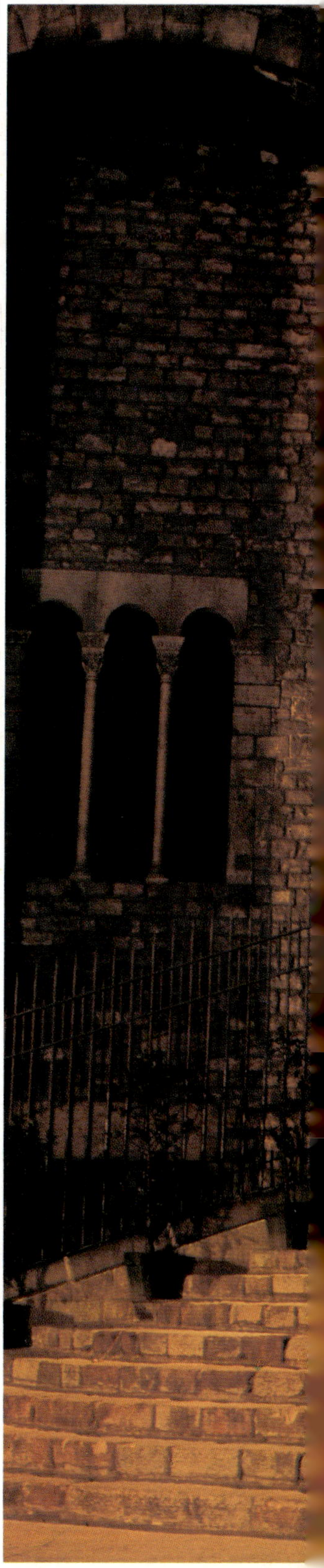

46

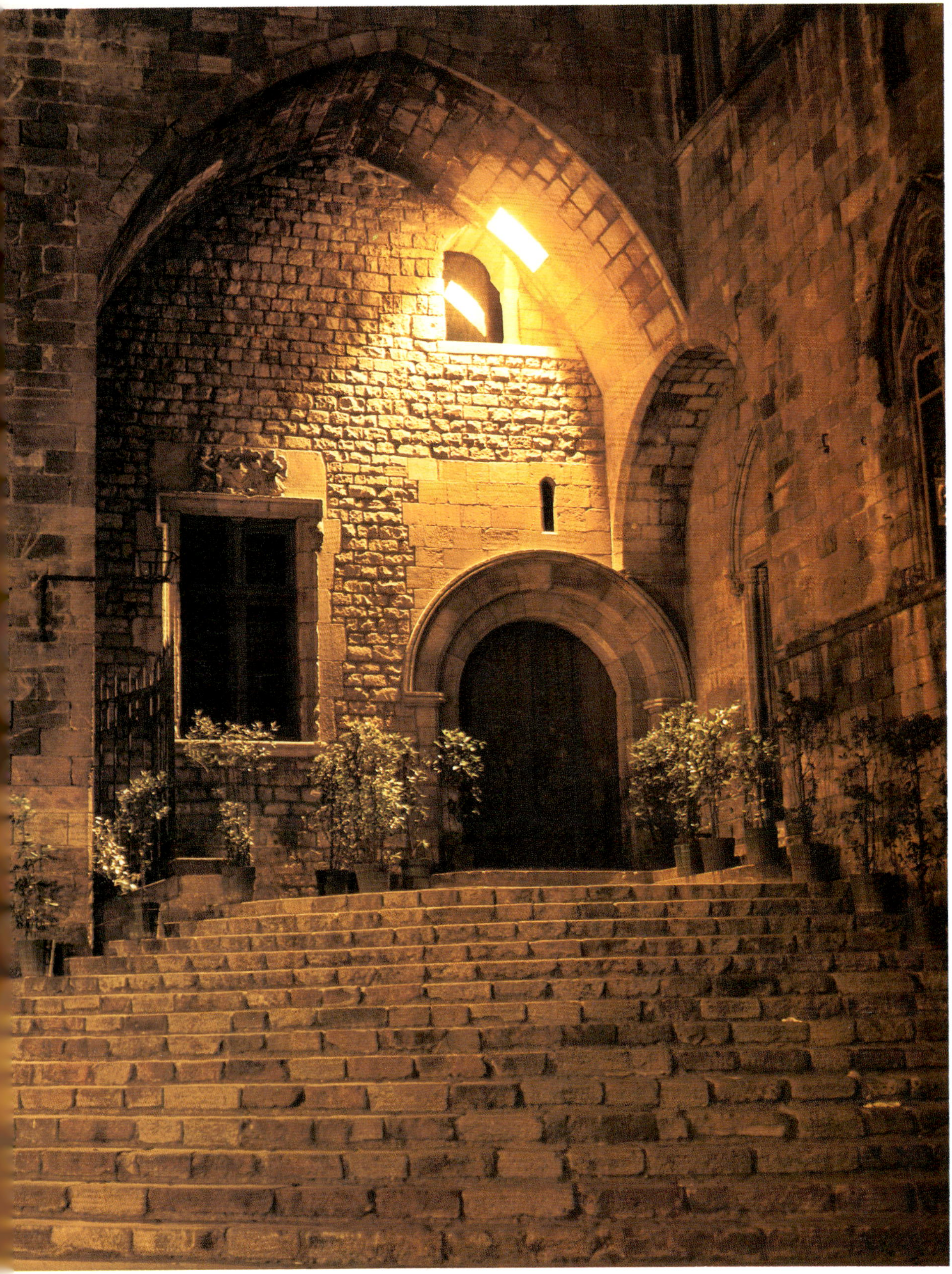

rainbow-coloured borders around the things depicted. The necessity for colour in this kind of realisation is self-evident, so that I need not elaborate on it.

Artificial colours

The last example for the use of colour is a bit more out-of-the-way than the others. Illustration 49 shows a black-and-white enlargement which has been toned and coloured. Although, strictly speaking, this might not belong in the realm of composition, I would like to point out some of the 'how's' and 'why's', because it could add to your repertory of expression and serve as an introduction to an entirely different field of colour-composition.

As you know, toning and colouring was first introduced in photography as the only known means of showing colour, no other technique existing at the time. This of course leads to the question: why should it be employed nowadays when we have easy-to-use and almost perfect colour-processes at our disposal. The answer to this lies in the fact that these colour-processes are relatively automatic. Their starting point is always the 'natural' colour, and changes to it invariably change the appearance and balance of all the colours in a photograph. Furthermore, all colour processes use dyes, which generally give the same overall appearance and texture. That is the reason why processes like toning and colouring are still used today, because if you know how to go about it you can use them to create colour-effects in your photographs which conform completely to your intentions.

As far as the technique is concerned, there is absolutely no limit to what you can do except your knowledge and manual dexterity. You will find explanations of toning-processes in dark-room-manuals. Everything else you must try for yourself. It is usual to start colouring with watercolours, but you can use crayons as well. Even oil-colours, especially those of the transparent variety, work very well on resin-coated (RC) paper. You can also remove part of a photograph by painting or spraying over it, or you can add something by painting or drawing it in. Of course, there really is no reason why you should do any of this, but equally there is nothing to keep you back if you think that it will help to achieve the effect you want. There is no rule which states that a photograph should look like this or that, and nobody can prevent you from tampering with a photograph in any way you can think of –

what counts are the results. But please note (again): a thing is not necessarily good because it is new or far-out. You must be your own judge when it comes to deciding whether you should or should not do something radical like this.

Colour or black-and-white – the photographer's choice

This more or less cryptic utterance gives me the opportunity to introduce the last point for consideration in this chapter. If you are to be your own judge on matters of this kind, why do I insist on discussing the question of whether or not to use colour in a photograph in all this length and detail?

The answer is that this is not only a question of composition, but one which is concerned with the psychology of the photographer as well. In my lectures and general dealings with photographers I have noticed that most people tend to accept colour-photography as *the* photography. Black-and-white photography is more often than not ignored completely, or else is regarded as an outdated technique with no right to exist in the modern world. In documentary and scientific photography this might be true because in colour photography you just have more material to work on when you are going to transpose reality into a photographic picture. But in creative photography, with which we are dealing here, when talking about composition this is entirely wrong. Black-and-white photography and colour-photography, as well as such intermediate forms as toning and colouring, are equally useful and interesting modes of expression.

As I have shown so far, there really is no reason at all to prefer one or the other on general grounds, because each of these techniques gives you an entirely different means of expression, and therefore different ways to realise your intentions. On the other hand, that does not mean that you should refrain from preferring one or the other. As I have stated earlier I generally prefer black-and-white photography and the reason for this is undoubtedly to be found in my psychological make-up, in exactly the same way that other people undoubtedly prefer colour photography.

But whichever you use, you should always be conscious of the fact that a preference of this kind imposes a limitation on the means of expression available to you. This does not matter at all, as long as you are aware of it and know what you are going to miss.

47

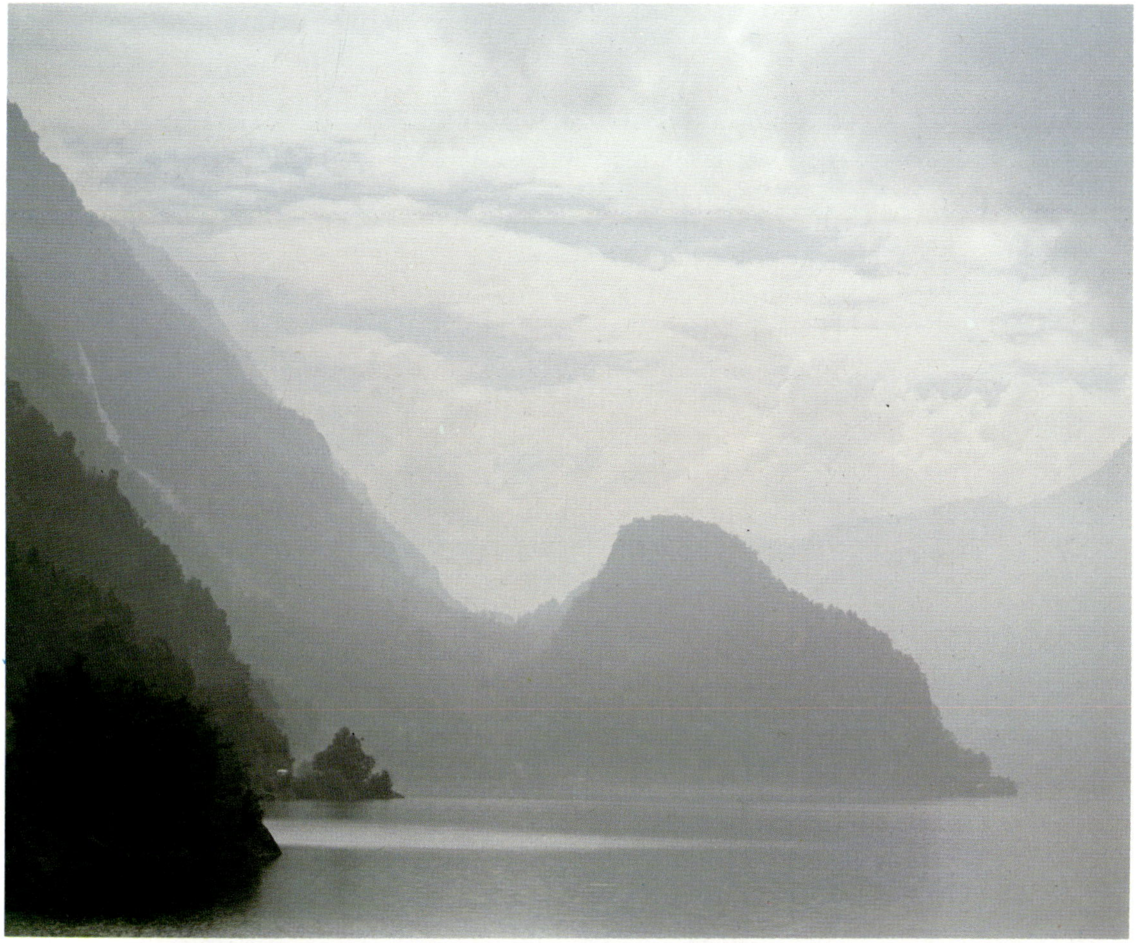

48

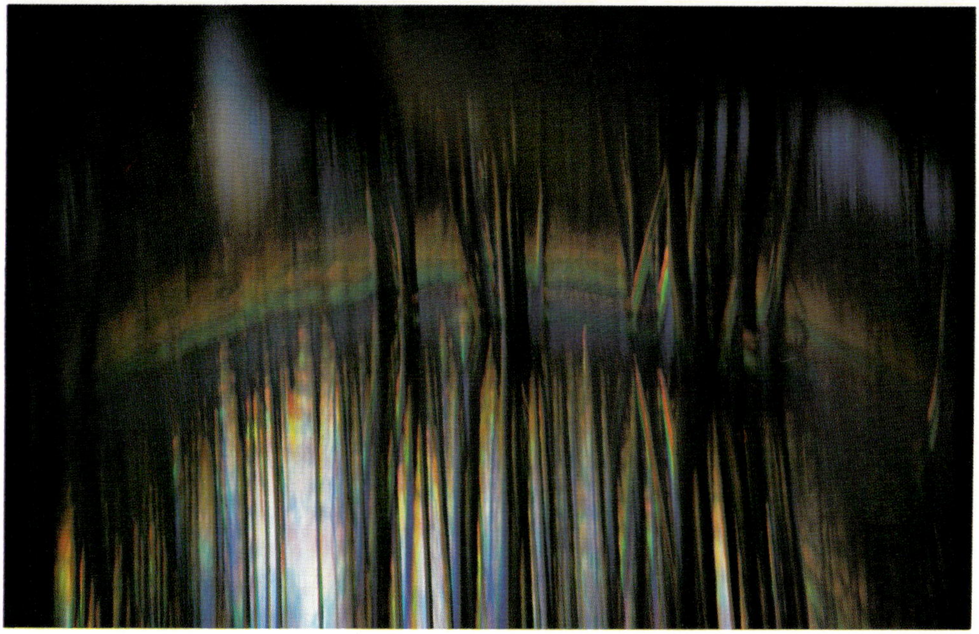

49

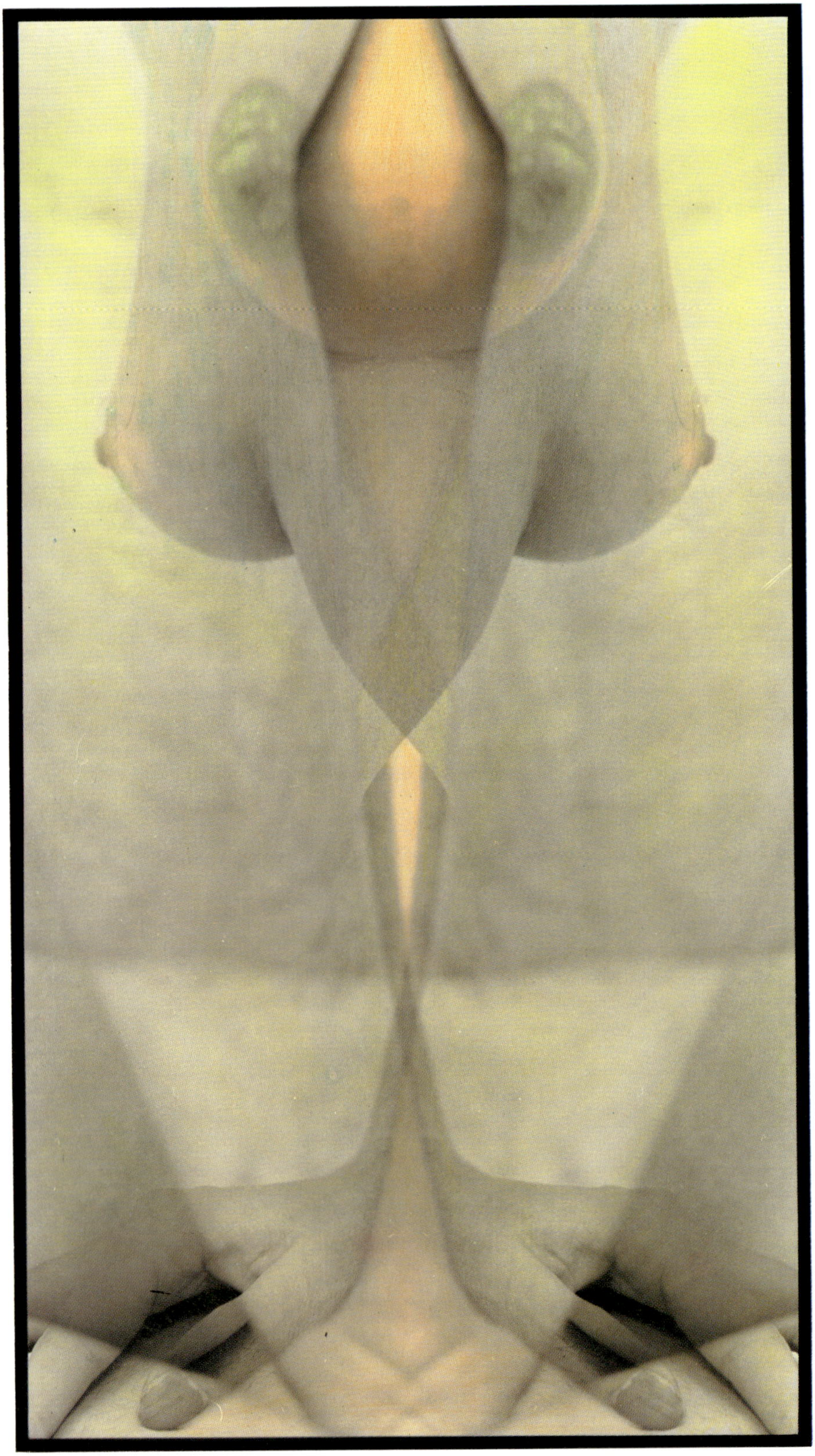

Opposite top
Haze leads to muted and usually bluish colours. This effect can easily be strengthened by using a telephoto lens (250 mm on a 6×7 cm camera) and by omitting the foreground. Views like this are almost invariably a bit romantic and melancholy.

Opposite below
Most effects which depend on coloured trick filters and related means must be shown in colour. In particular, the very subtle changes in colour, like the rainbow-coloured borders of this picture, would not work in black and white at all.

Left
Sometimes you may be dissatisfied with the 'natural' colours of your subject and with the changes which you can introduce by using various films and filters. You then have the possibility of taking a black and white shot and toning and colouring it precisely as you want. The enlargement was first toned brown (sulphur toner), then part of it was treated with gold toner (red) and then the whole was coloured with crayons and oil colours.

8 Expressing Your Ideas

In the preceding chapters I have dealt with composition mainly from the theoretical point of view. This served (or should have served) to lay the foundations for what we are going to do next. I will now demonstrate the basic approaches to a photographic theme by giving you examples of what I did. I will discuss some pictures and try to generalise the results in order to find out what can be learnt from them. It is not enough just to show some pictures and talk about them. I will have to explain why I took them, how I took them and why they look as they do. If I were to follow the usual routine, I would show you a picture of,

50

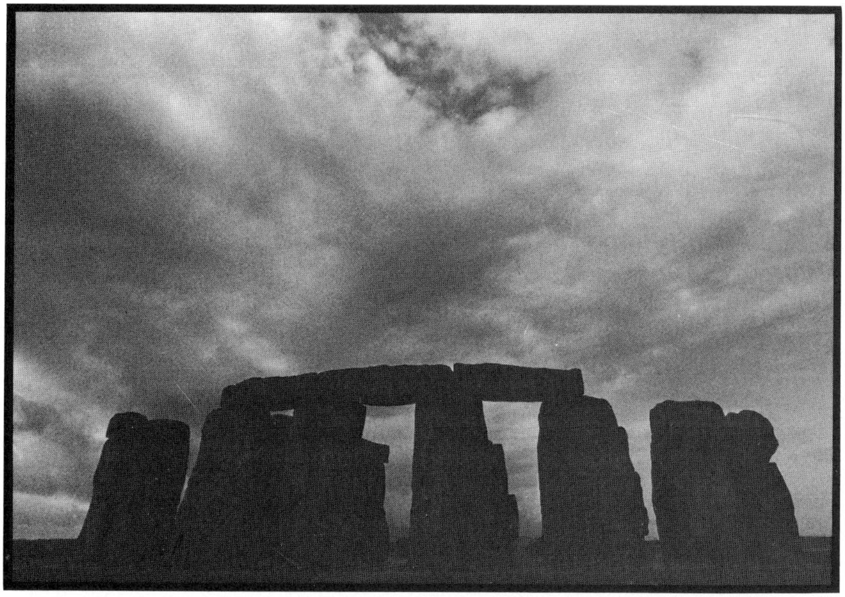

This overall view of Stonehenge shows a very simple and stark composition. The main points are the worm's eye view and the reduction of grey tones to almost completely black silhouettes and a few grey tones in the sky. The diagram shows the distribution of the compositional elements.

50a

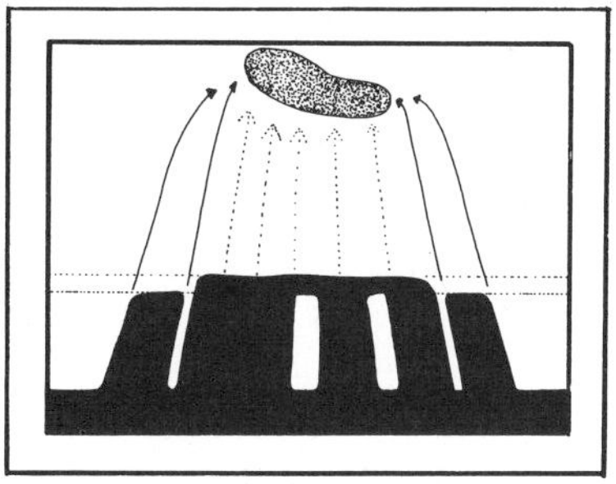

for example, Stonehenge, demonstrate some diagonal and vertical lines, talk about the distribution of light and dark areas and be done with it. But this would not help you at all. There are other pictures of this ancient British monument (by me, by others and perhaps by you) which look quite different, which are composed differently and which feel different. It would be absolutely nonsensical to pick one of these pictures and tell you: this is how to take a photograph of Stonehenge. All those pictures mean something. You would probably like some of them and reject others, because you have your own ideas, feelings and associations concerning Stonehenge. In fact you would probably prefer the photograph which came closest to the one you would have taken yourself.

Realising your ideas

Thinking along these lines brought me to the starting point for my Stonehenge photograph. Before I went there for the first time I had read some books on Stonehenge and looked at postcards, archaeological drawings, etc. This is definitely not my usual preparation for taking a photograph, but I was very interested in Stonehenge even before deciding to go there, chiefly because it is the most ancient looking building or structure I know of. It looks – if you will forgive the Lovecraftian allusions – as if its 'hoary ruins reach far back into the dawn of mankind', steeped in myth and mystery.

Well, to cut a long story short, when I finally visited Stonehenge it was a beautiful day, the sun shone and the place teamed with tourists, wandering around, sitting on fallen stones eating sandwiches, or photographing each other. You can easily imagine that I went away disappointed and without having taken a single picture. But finally, on my third visit, conditions were perfect. It was a cold day in October, the wind blew hard and it rained. Now Stonehenge looked like the place of my imagination. I took a lot of pictures, three of which we will discuss in order to find out what it is all about.

The first one (*50*) shows an overall view of the stone circles under a sky filled with dark clouds. I took the picture almost from ground level for three reasons: a. The horizon had to be as low as possible in order to emphasise the sky. b. The stones were to be rendered very dark (almost as a silhouette), so they had to be isolated from the landscape, which has about the same grey values, and set off against the sky, which is lighter. c. The combination of the 'worm's-eye-view' with the wide angle of the lens (a 21 mm lens was used) makes the stones look like tapering cones with converging lines.

Now let us set off the different parts of the composition against each other and see what they do for the effect of the picture. The diagram (*50a*) shows the elements of the composition and their relation to each other. The continuous line of the horizon close to the lower border serves as a necessary compensation for the sky, which is very low and seems to press downwards. This compensation is intensified by the converging lines indicated by the stones which seem to be surging upwards, except that the movement is stopped twice. First, the line of vertical stones effectively contains all the 'compositional movement' between the horizon and itself. Second, the remains of the upward movement (mainly generated by the stones on the extreme right and left) is absorbed by the dark 'hole in the sky', which is located in the centre of the picture close to the upper border.

Taken separately, these elements of the composition would lend themselves to quite dramatic effects. But as I have shown, they are interlocked and balanced in a way which renders the picture as a whole static and seemingly motionless. This might give food for fanciful interpretations; for example about the forces of nature, represented by the stormy sky pressing down, as opposed to the defying forces of the man-made architectural structure soaring up, and about the equilibrium (and so the timelessness) which has been achieved between nature and artifice. Be that as it may, this picture is satisfactory as far as it goes, but if you think back to what I explained about my intentions, it surely must be classified as a failure, because it does not express what it is supposed to say.

The next attempt (*51*) is a bit more complicated, although it looks deceptively simple. First, consider the relation between the sky and the foreground as shown in diagram 51a. You will find that they are almost alike and symmetrical to each other. Because of this they serve to keep the different elements of the composition together and at the same time they enhance the central part of the picture. Next, have a look at the different lines of the composition (*51b*). You will see that there are no horizontal or vertical lines in the picture, but the diagonal lines are interlocked so as to give a rigid structure for the different pictorial elements.

Finally, the picture contains some irritating elements. These are the almost white clouds, the light grey parts of the upright stone on the left and the small, dark stone which does not fit into the network of diagonal lines and thus becomes the main point of the composition.

The correlation of these features to the impact of the

Compared to illustration 50 this picture of Stonehenge is much more complicated. Apart from the representational aspect, the photograph contains two distinct compositional aspects. The first one concerns the symmetrical planes shown in diagram 51a while the second one is the network of horizontal and vertical lines depicted in diagram 51b.

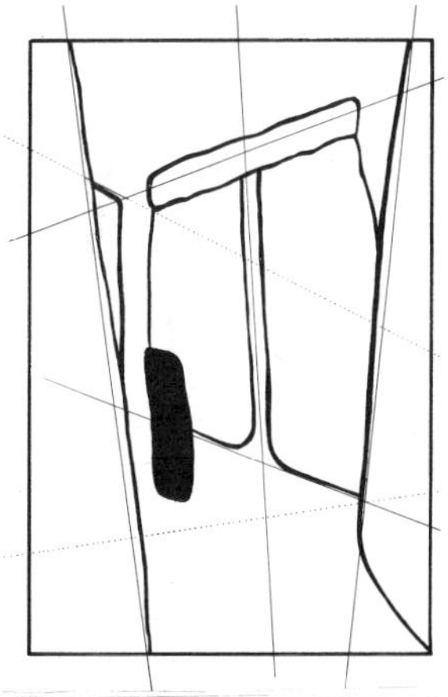

51a

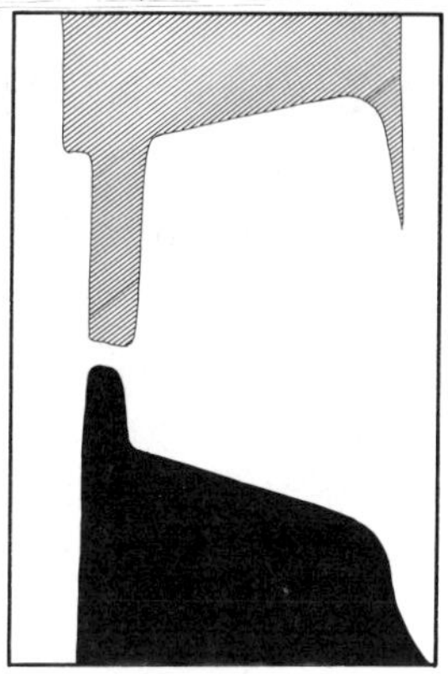

51b

51

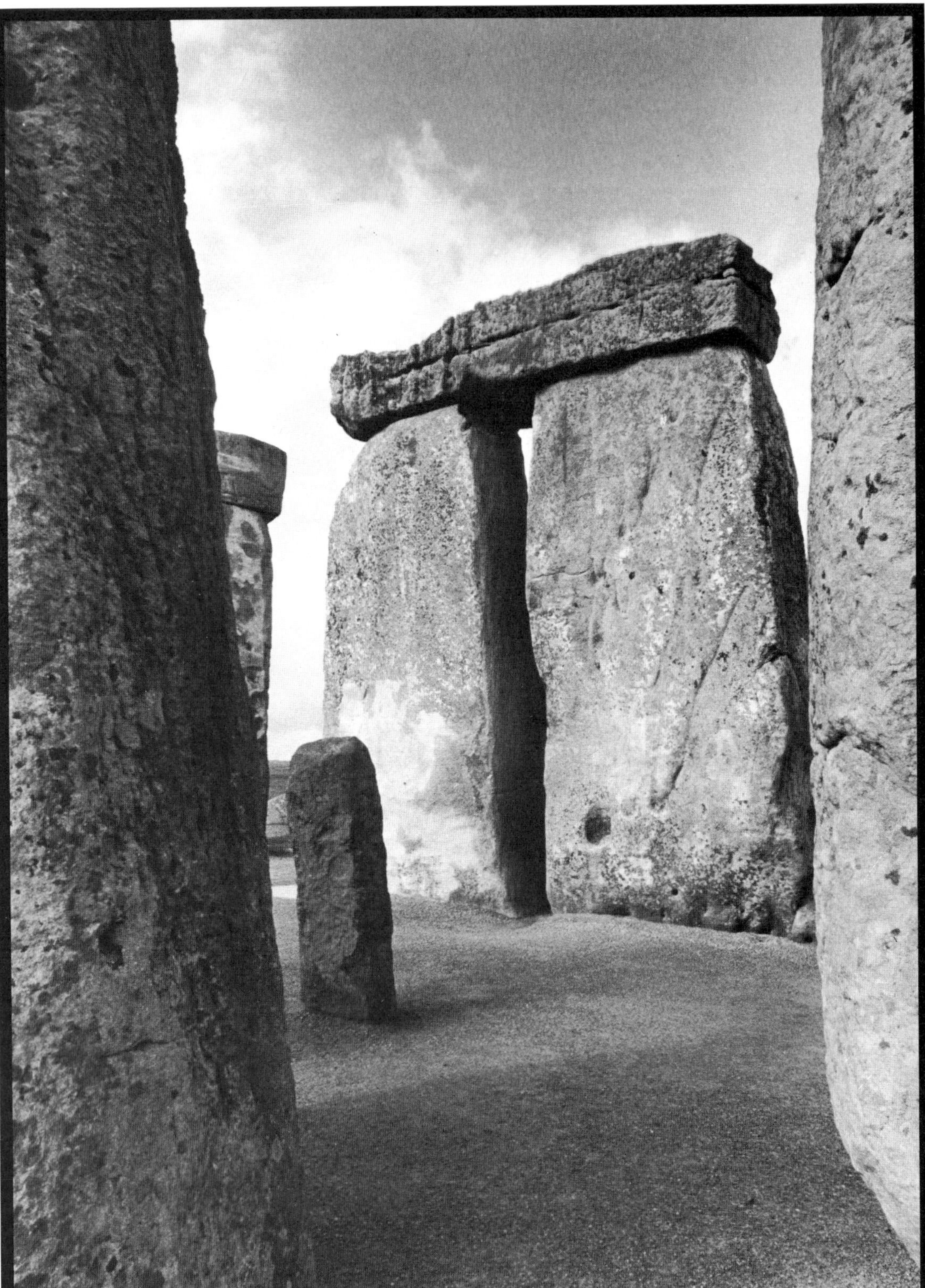

photograph on the viewer now is quite easy to understand. We have a rigid structure as befits the representation of an architectural work. The fact that this construction has nothing to do with what we generally mean by the term 'architecture' is stressed by the exclusive use of diagonal lines. (A picture of a Greek temple with its columns and architraves would surely contain at least some horizontal or vertical lines!) The small stone as irritating element and focal point of interest hints at the fact that the meaning of this structure is at least partly obscure and open to debate, but this is not enough to show the mystical and mythical quality of Stonehenge, which is what I actually wanted to impart to my picture.

Before I go on to the last photograph, however, I want to sidetrack a bit in order to remind you of something which we discussed in Chapter 3. I do not want to give the impression that I walk around poking holes in a canopy of clouds where I need them. And I do not want to pretend that I look at a piece of landscape, measuring diagonals or weighing up portions of sky against pieces of foreground. All that is done by instinct. But these instincts must be trained in order to work properly and one of the best and most reliable ways to do that is to find out why a picture (be it one of yours, one of mine or one by somebody else) does, or does not, meet with your approval. If you create a great photograph and leave it at that, you will not be able to repeat the performance. But if when you get the results of your picture-taking sessions you try to evaluate your pictures as I demonstrate here, you will learn and you will be able to repeat your success or will even do better next time.

The same goes for pictures taken by other people. If you have been told what a photograph is supposed to mean, you can find out whether you believe the realisation to be adequate or not. If you know nothing whatever about a picture, you could try to learn what it really means to you and why it affects you exactly that way. If you do that often enough it will give you the flexibility to react spontaneously to a motif and to find the instinctive approach which serves you best. I know I have already said these things, but I make no apology for repeating them because you should always keep them in mind. But let us return to the business in hand.

The last photograph in this series (*52*) shows what I regard as *my* picture of Stonehenge. Although far from perfect, it contains all the elements needed to express my feelings and ideas on this subject. The composition of the picture is highly complicated. In the following diagrams I just want to show some of its elements and their connection with each other.

Opposite
This photograph of Stonehenge is, to me, the most successful of those shown here, because it perfectly captures my feelings about the place.
Below
52a: the distribution of grey values in three zones. 52b: the compositional movement. 52c: the main lines and weight of the composition.

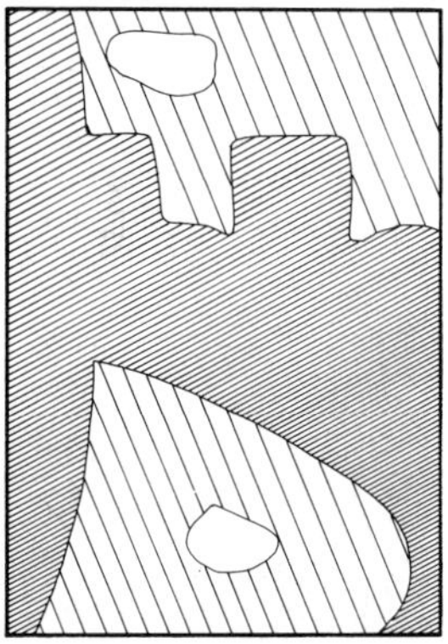

52a

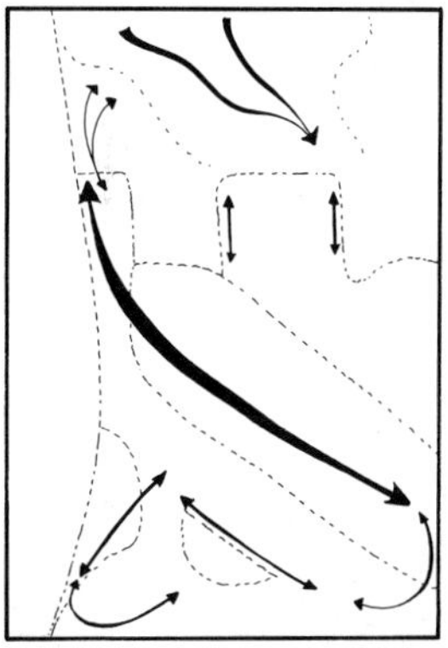

52b

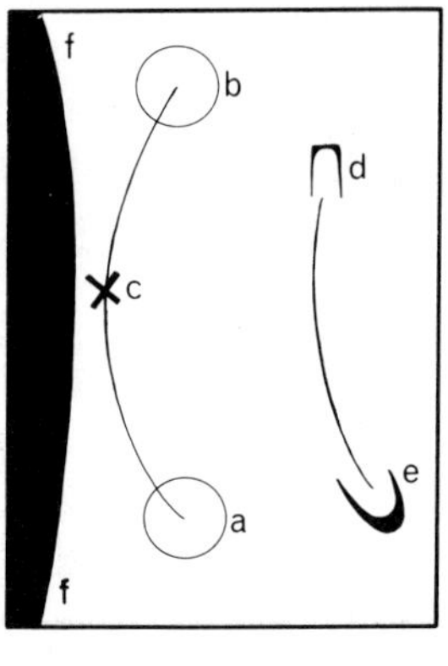

52c

52

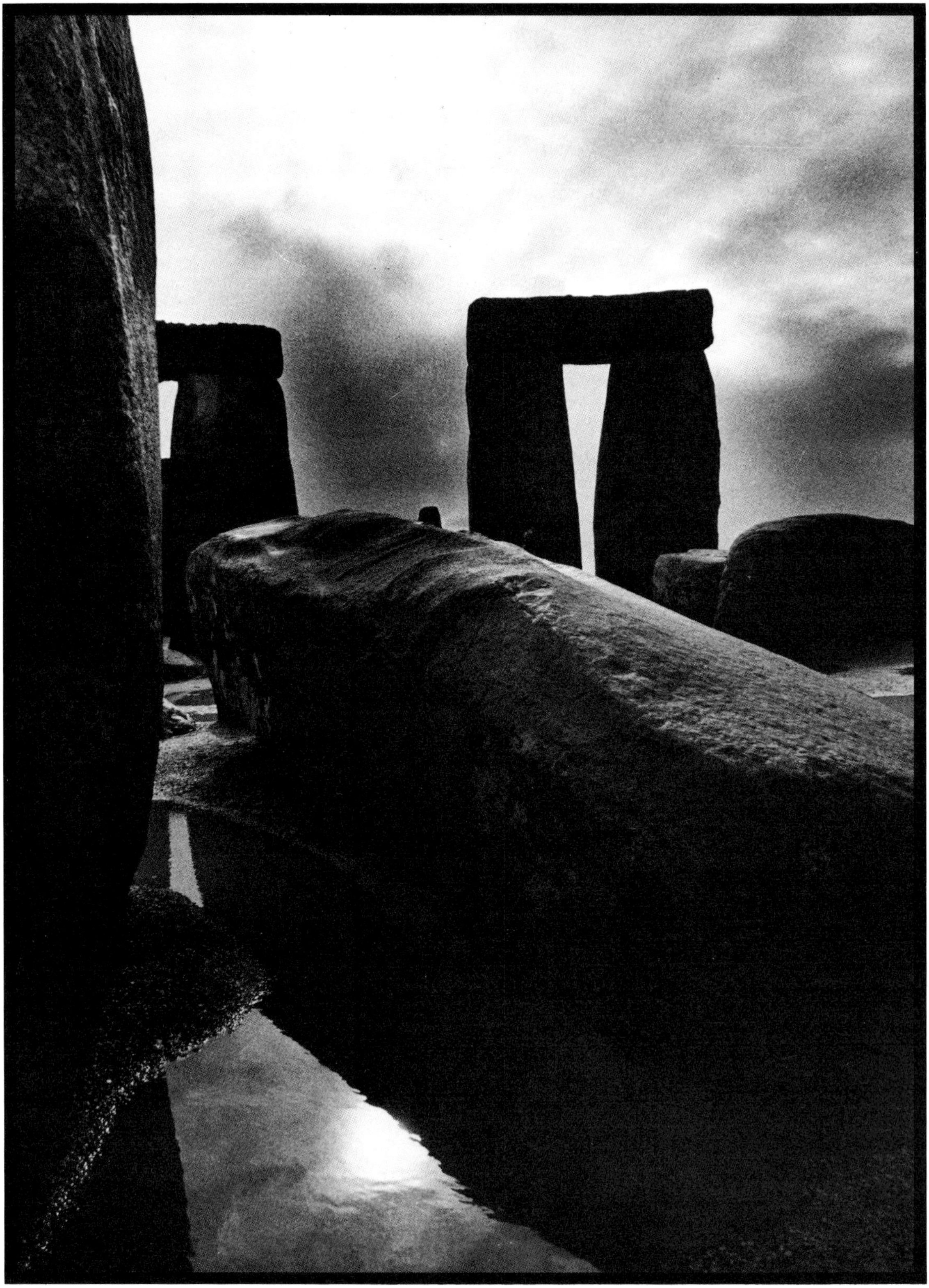

Diagram 52a shows the distribution of light and dark areas. It is quite obvious that the reflection of the sun in the foreground is one of the main reasons for the picture's impact. Not only does it keep the composition together, it enhances the unreal quality of the scene depicted. It would perhaps be going a bit too far to say that the whole structure looks as if it is floating in the sky, but to my eyes the effect is there. This effect is enhanced by the fact that the sun cannot be seen in the sky, but only as a reflection in the lower part of the picture. This is strengthened by the eye-movement induced by the main lines of the composition. The next diagram (*52b*) shows these lines. You will note that the composition is a closed one, although some of the elements are cut off by the frame of the picture. For example, if you start with the diagonal line of the fallen stone in the middle of the picture, your eye-movement will be deflected and led upwards by the dark plane bordering the left side of the picture. The movement is first checked by the horizontal stone on the left and finally halted, reversed and led down to the right-hand side of the picture by the white part of the sky. There it might start again or follow one of the secondary paths of movement, as indicated by the dotted lines in the diagram.

This leads us to the fact that the composition does not have one main point. Instead there are two lines of force as diagram 52c shows: first line: a) reflection of sun, b) white part of sky, c) meeting point of lines of eye-movement; second line: d) point of main contrast black/white, e) darkest part of picture. These double curves are set off against and balanced with the dark curved plane on the left (f).

Analysing the result

Although more could be said about the composition we will get on to the fanciful part of the explanation. I described my intentions concerning this photograph earlier in this chapter. You will remember that I wanted to stress the mystical and mythical qualities of the place. To do this the photograph first of all should be recognisable as being of this specific place. Indeed, the picture shows a very characteristic part of Stonehenge and will be identified correctly by everybody who knows the place. (This is not necessarily so with all photographs; I took some which looked quite nice, but you would have been unable to identify the subject matter.)

Second, when discussing diagram 52a, I have already referred to the unreal quality of the composition generated by the paradoxical distribution of the sky above and below the stones. This effect is strengthened by the other components of

the composition. It is at the same time strong and indeterminate. The strength is provided by the strong opposition of light and dark areas (*diagram 52a*) and the linear and rigid construction of the force lines (*diagram 52c*), while the indeterminate element is introduced by the complicated and interconnected network of eye-movements.

So the picture shows strength and forcefulness together with mystery and elusiveness. It has balance (provided by the composition) although it depicts ruins (in the fallen stone). Its rigid construction hints at a purpose, but no clues as to its nature are given. In short this photograph is a representation of my feelings, ideas and associations connected with Stonehenge and, with a bit of luck, it might strike you the same way.

'Contraction' and 'expansion' of an idea

Having reached this conclusion, let us retrace our steps and consider what we actually did – apart from discussing some pictures. We started with an idea which I wanted to represent in the form of a photograph in order to get it across to you. This should actually have started you on a comparison of our ideas on this subject. The idea which I chose for this demonstration is not the only one possible in connection with Stonehenge and it is also very personal. If you wanted to photograph Stonehenge you might, for example, start with the idea of showing its geometrical construction, which is said to be closely related to astronomical and chronological factors – and you would come up with quite a different set of pictures.

But whatever you do, regardless of your starting point and your results, the basic procedure is always the same: if you start with a preconceived idea, you will get to your result by a process of photographic elimination. You will discard all aspects of your subject which do not conform with this idea. Instead, you will try to stress and enhance those which will serve to get your idea across. This process might be called 'contraction'. One motif or theme (and each motif) would lend itself to a multitude of possible pictorial realisations. If you start with a preconceived idea you will have a field of possibilities which you will have to narrow down – and that is usually done by the time-honoured process of 'trial and error'.

This description of the process of 'contraction' implies, of course, that there is a second way of doing things. There is – it is the process which is called 'expansion'. Expansion means that if you are confronted with a given subject you might not have just one idea about or one impression of your motif but a multitude of them. One motif can easily contain different or

even contradictory elements. If so, some thought is required. The average amateur photograph is generally taken without these considerations and then is a failure because of this. If you see a motif which strikes you as interesting, unusual or beautiful, you cannot just take a picture and hope for the best. You will have to find out first exactly what it is that took your fancy. It might be one thing: a feeling, an idea, a mood, an association. Or it might be a combination of factors, it might be an affinity or a contradiction between two or more elements, or it might even be something entirely different. But whatever it is, you will have to find out first and shoot afterwards. All this is covered by the term 'contraction'.

If, on the other hand, you are unable to pin down your emotions and thoughts to one thing, you would have to divide your motif into its different elements and make a picture for each of those. This is what I called the 'expansion' of the subject matter. You will then realise each of these separate possibilities by a process of contraction. So the general and final approach to taking a picture is by contraction; by elimination and reduction until the final result is achieved. But more often than not a motif consists of more than just one aspect, and then each of those should be explored. Before talking about the photographs which I have chosen to illustrate these processes, I would like to give a purely hypothetical example. If you see a collection of photographs of New York, or any other metropolis, you will probably always find a particular theme (and perhaps you have already photographed it). This typical picture consists of an old, dilapidated house, set off against the immaculate and immense structure of a skyscraper. This theme actually consists of three parts. First, the old house, which is probably quite an interesting theme in itself; second, the skyscraper, and third, the juxtaposition of these opposites. Each of these themes would require different handling and whether you take all of them or just one, is simply a question of your intentions.

Contraction – a practical application

This treatment applies to the three photographs which we are going to discuss next. They show three different views of the small English harbour of Mullion Cove, near The Lizard in Cornwall. Diagram 53 demonstrates the spatial relation between the three themes, it shows the positions of the different things depicted and the viewpoints used. If you look closely at the first photograph (*54*) you will be able to discern the mast-head of the sailing-boat on the right and the pier-head on the left. But

Opposite
This photograph of Mullion Cove in England deals with an apparent disparity in the impressions made on me by this place. It looks very old and dilapidated on the one hand and well-kept on the other. How I tried to transform this impression into a picture is explained on page 88.

Bottom
The placing of the main elements of photograph 54 is shown here. Note how the main dividing lines of the horizon and the railing divide the picture into four equal parts.

Below
The viewpoints for the next three photographs and the relation of their elements to each other. Illustration 54, for example, was taken from point a.

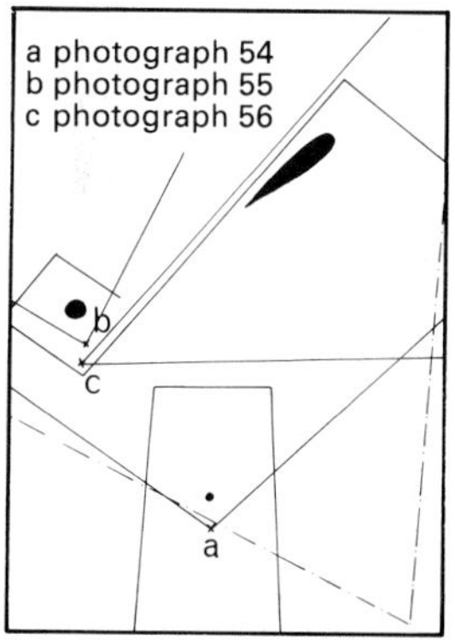

53

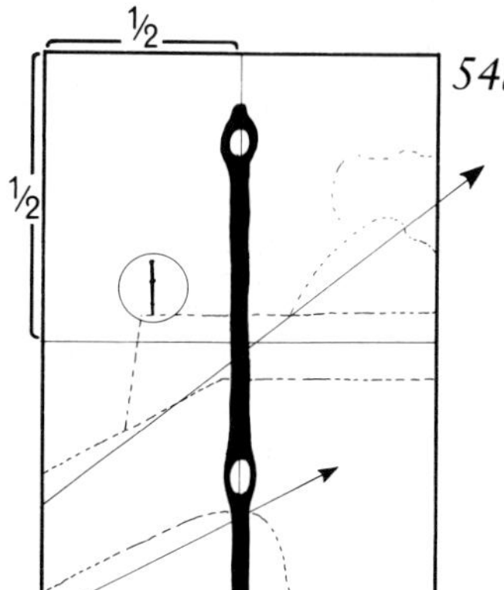

54a

54

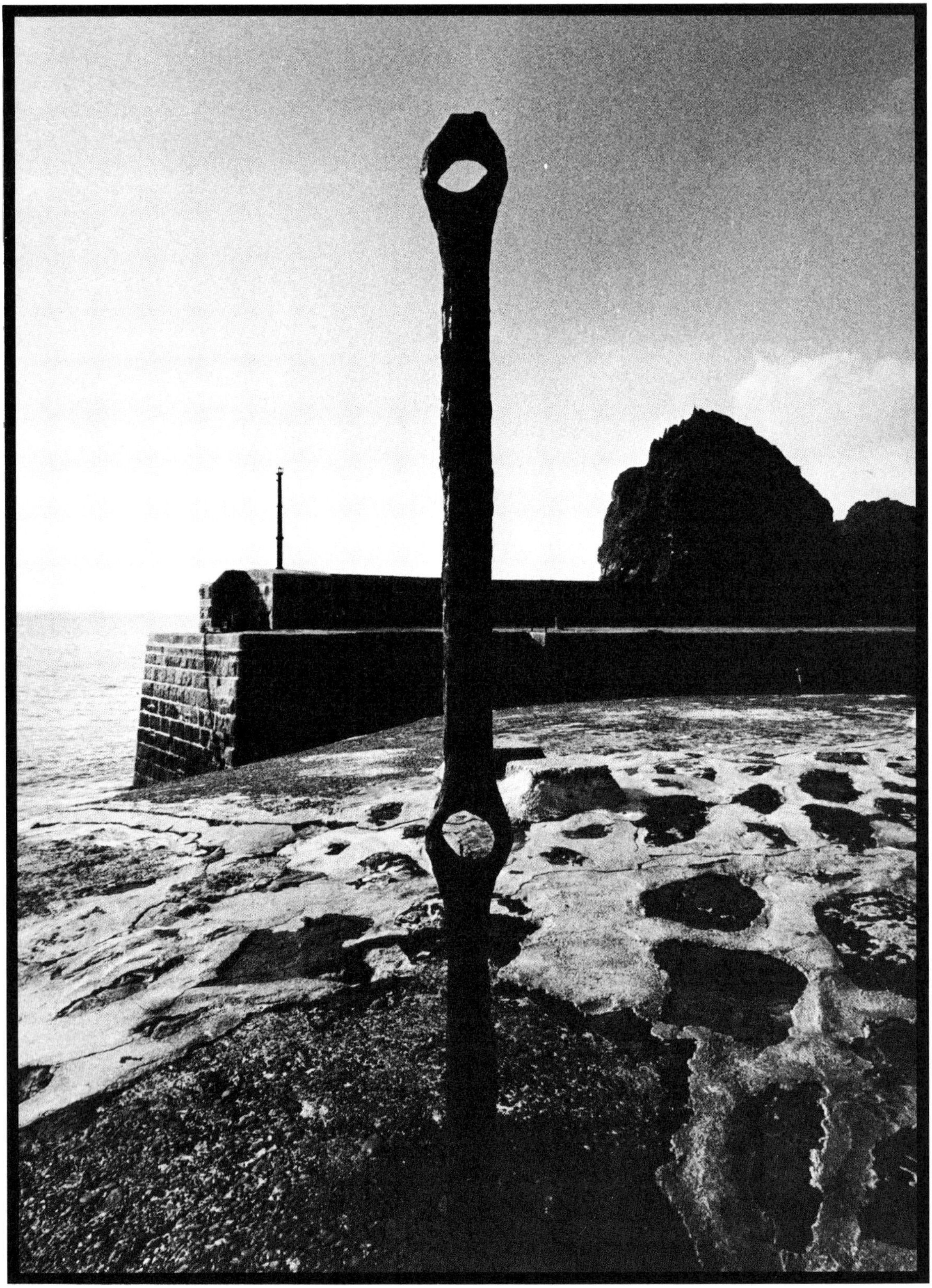

55

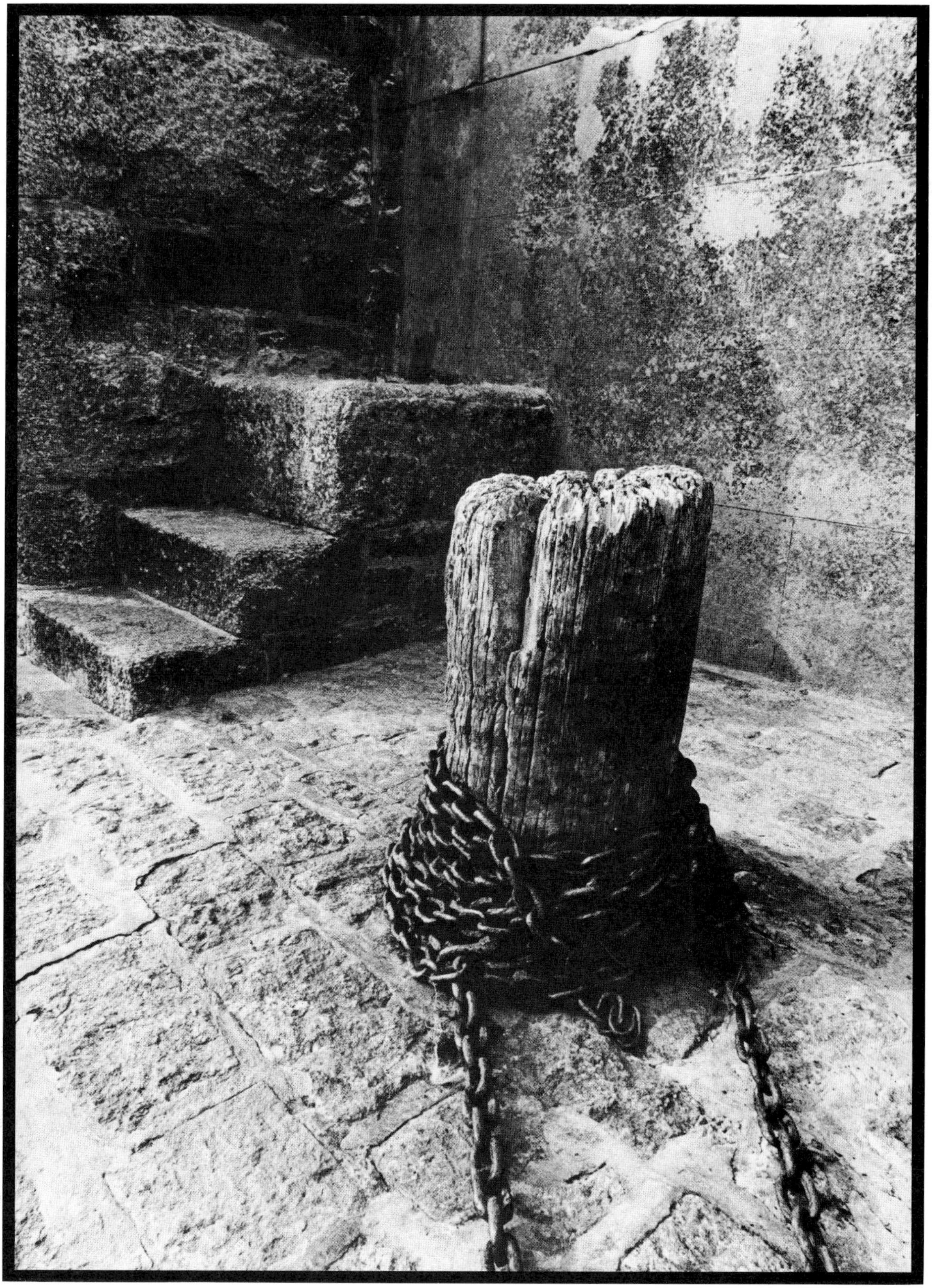

all this is actually beside the point, I just wanted to show you the relation between the different parts of the theme and to demonstrate the fact that you could indeed include all of them in a single picture. The dotted line in diagram 53 shows the angle of view.

I spent some hours at the place and had the opportunity to watch a lot of people taking pictures. All of them – without a single exception – shot an overall view of the harbour, similar to that indicated in the diagram. All of them took away a dull and insignificant photograph. I know that for sure, because out of curiosity I tried the shot myself.

Now, having concluded these preliminaries, let us discuss some alternatives. First of all I was struck by a curious discrepancy between the overall appearance of the place and the look of its individual parts. Everything was quite old and dilapidated. For example, the piece of old iron railing which forms the main part of the first photograph (*54*) was rusty and no longer served a definite purpose. By contrast, the pier on which it stood was well maintained and kept free of litter. This general air of being 'immaculately groomed' combined with the decayed appearance of the individual parts is easily explained. On the one hand Mullion Cove is very old, on the other hand it is under the care of the National Trust, and in consequence is well preserved.

The next consideration was how to compress the atmosphere which was characterised by this dissimilarity into one photograph. My attempt at a solution is shown in 54. Although the actual height of the iron railing which forms the main part of the motif was not more than two feet, it looks enormous and massive. This was achieved by getting very close to it (about one foot away) and by choosing a viewpoint about one foot high. The use of a wide-angle lens (21 mm) enabled me to isolate the railing from the background and to enhance the impression of great size (compare Chapter 5). This main element is contained in an absolutely rigid overall composition. The line of the railing and the horizon each bisect the picture-plane so as to divide it into four equal parts (*54a*), while the broken diagonal lines formed by the piers, the rock and the clouds are effectively balanced by the lamp-post on the upper left. This lamp-post does more to the composition than its size might suggest. First it echoes the main vertical line of the composition, displaced to the left. Second it has quite an impact because it represents the point of main contrast (almost purely black-and-white).

These means of composition not only serve to stress the

The second view of Mullion Cove deals with another of its aspects. Here I tried to show both the massive construction of the harbour and its protective function. Accordingly the composition is much 'tighter' and more 'hemmed-in' as 55a shows.

55a

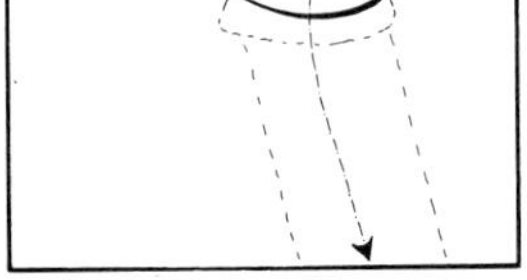

disparity mentioned above, they also emphasise another aspect of the atmosphere which I connected with this place. I have already stated that the harbour of Mullion Cove is very old. In fact it is so old that it looks strange to our modern eyes, which are used to entirely different types of harbour. Furthermore it is almost deserted, and its picturesque surroundings tend to stress the mysteriousness, aloofness and the feeling of displacement which to me seemed to belong to it. So I tried to express my feelings for the place by the 'unnatural' quality of the composition, in particular by emphasising the spatial relationship of the things depicted, the distortions of size and the exaggerated contrast stressing the unusual lighting of the scene. (By now you surely must have noticed that I am always attracted by those qualities of things which are unusual and out of the ordinary – which is not a bad photographic policy. If you have a preference of any kind, it might as well serve as the starting point for a consistent photographic 'oeuvre'.)

But the scenery also lent itself to other interpretations. The harbour, although very small, was massively built; its function as a shelter against the forces of nature was an equally dominant feeling which demanded quite a different photographic realisation. Picture 51 shows a spot which is completely sealed off by the walls and the stone base. The composition is equally self-contained: the diagonal line formed by the three steps (*55a*) is blocked off by the vertical landing. The slightly diagonal upwards thrust of the wooden post is stopped and reversed by the contours of the shadow and the landing. At the same time the diagonal placement of the wooden post neutralises most of the force of the three diagonal steps. There is only one opening to the outside world – the line formed by the meeting point of the wall and the steps, extended through the wooden post and the chain (dotted line in the diagram). This connection, however, is very small, because most of it is counterpointed by that part of the chain which is wound around the post. All these factors tend to give the viewer an impression of quietude and remoteness.

This leads on to the last example (*56*) which also contains these elements – but in quite a different interpretation. The appearance of seclusion is undoubtedly there, but it is connected with another aspect of the scene. In the preceding photograph the seclusion was shown as a self-contained state of equilibrium. Here the viewer is almost irresistibly drawn into the picture. His eye is directed by the converging lines of the composition away from the open and light grey part on the right-hand side and away from his precarious viewpoint (*56a*) to the composition's

Emotionally speaking, the last picture of Mullion Cove contains aspects of both the preceding interpretations. Therefore it is much more complicated compositionally (56a) and probably takes a bit more time and effort to understand completely.

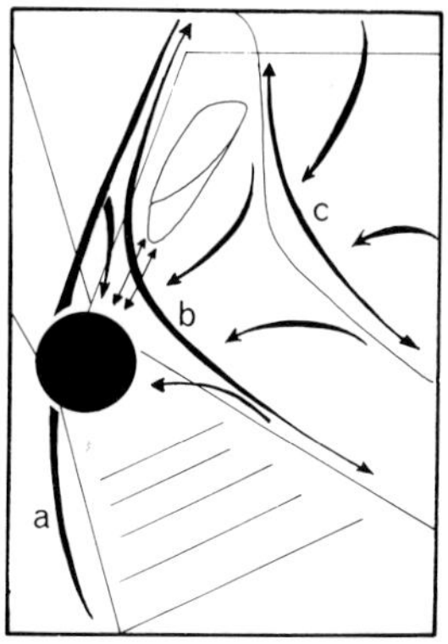

56a

56

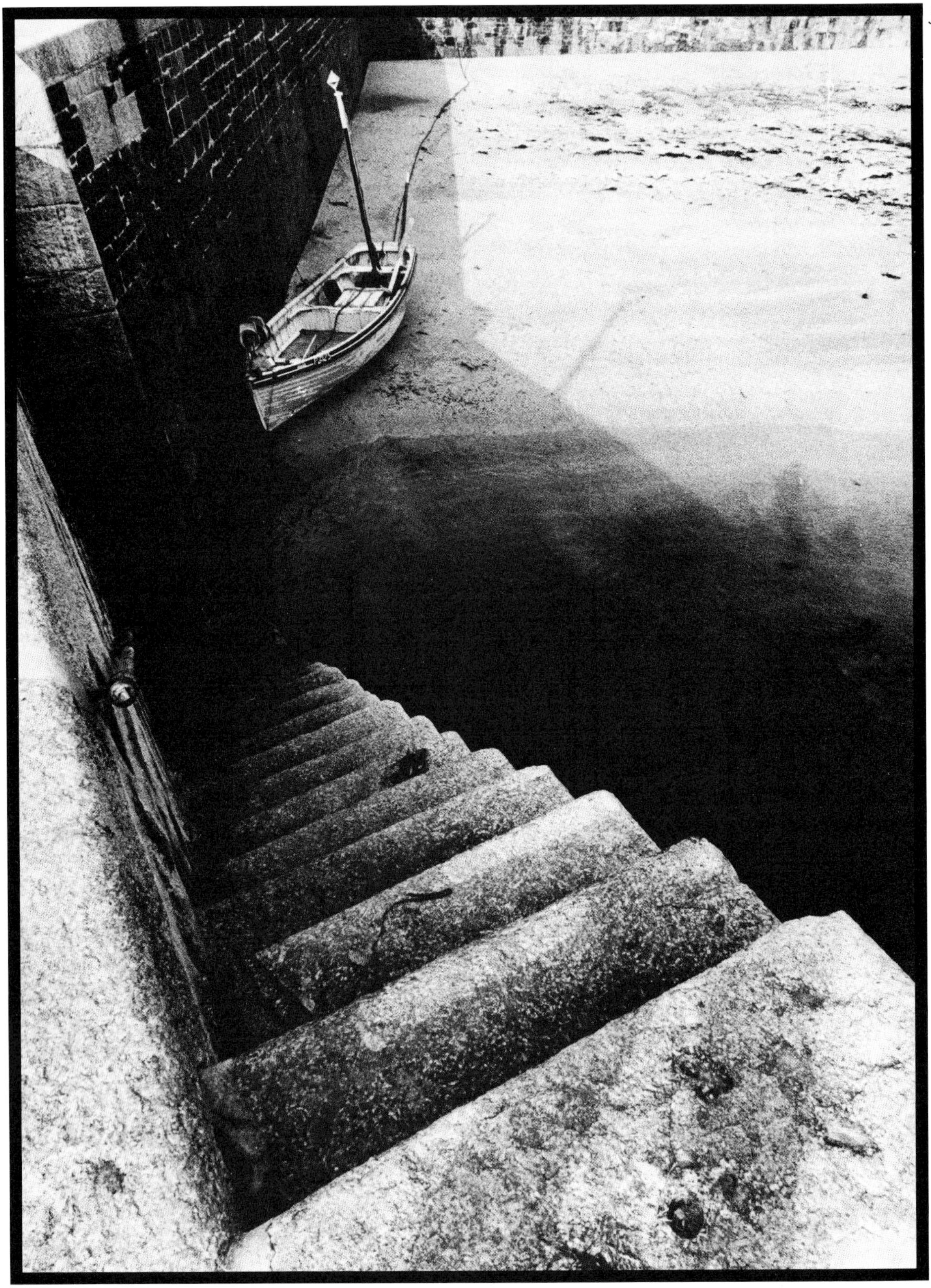

main point. This is nothing but the black hole, indicated in the diagram by the black circle. This part of the composition is effectively 'fenced in' by the three curves a, b and c. Even the lines formed by the contour of the boat point to this spot.

On the other hand, the main interest of the subject lies in the boat itself. That is why the attention of the viewer is drawn back and forth between boat and the black hole. This enhances the irritation provided by the strange spatial relationship of the different walls and stairs. (Please note: the camera was not tilted at all, but pointed straight down into the basin of the harbour.) A part of the interpretation of this composition I see in the fact that seclusion is not necessarily associated with quietude and tranquility as in the preceding photograph. It could just as well be associated with an active property which serves as a kind of magnet, irresistibly attracting the viewer.

Contraction as an aid to composition

Be that as it may, I hope I have convinced you that one motif more often than not has different aspects which have to be represented in different photographs. If you isolate these aspects and then optimise each one in a single photograph, you will be able to create pictures which are much more compelling and impressive than unclear and muddled overall views. You must always keep in mind that, normally, the viewer does not know your intentions. If you want to say or express something, you have to state it as simply and as expressively as possible. If you do not do that, the viewer will not be able to interpret your picture. So, first try to find out why you want to shoot a certain photograph. If there are several reasons, take a separate picture for each of them. Second, try to compose your picture so that all its elements add to your intentions. Do not forget that each detail does something to the viewer (he reacts to it consciously or subconsciously). If the picture contains details or compositional forms which do not conform to your intentions, the viewer will be irritated and confused.

This brings us to a very safe and simple rule beyond all considerations of 'expansion' and 'contraction'. The rule states: 'If you are not satisfied, do not shoot – or at least do not show your photograph'.

9 The Impact of Different Types of Composition

We have seen in the preceding chapters that you are not entirely free to compose a photograph just as you want, because you generally have to work with the material which the reality of your chosen subject offers you. On the other hand you will have a large number of variations at your disposal. In general, the amount of things you can do with (or to) a given subject is limited only by your imagination and your technical skill.

You will, however, soon find out that for any photographer there is only one way to create a specific picture. This may sound like a paradox, but it really is not if you keep in mind our discussion about the two sources of a photographic image. We stated that reality on the one hand and the photographer's personality, expressed in his vision, on the other are bound together by the means of composition to form the picture. That means two things. First, that no two photographs of a given subject will be alike if they are taken by different photographers. Second, that for you as just one photographer (provided that you do not have a split personality) there will be one way – and one way only – to realise your vision.

So what do we get out of this? The preceding chapter ended with the statement that you should be clear about your pictorial intentions. I tried to show that you should realise your vision with precision and clarity so as to get it across to the viewer of your photographs. Now we just have to go one step further by realising that there will be only one picture which will really meet your requirements – that is provided that you do have definite intentions. If you just play around – which is a delightful thing to do and very instructive besides – there is no way of telling what kind of meaning and message you will get in your photographs and how they will be appreciated by the viewer (and by yourself).

The question now is: Provided that you have chosen to take a photograph of a given subject, what kind of shape is it going to take? Or, in other words, what kind of composition are you going to choose for the realisation of your ideas? This is the point where nobody can really help you. I cannot tell you: If you have this or that kind of subject you will have to choose

57

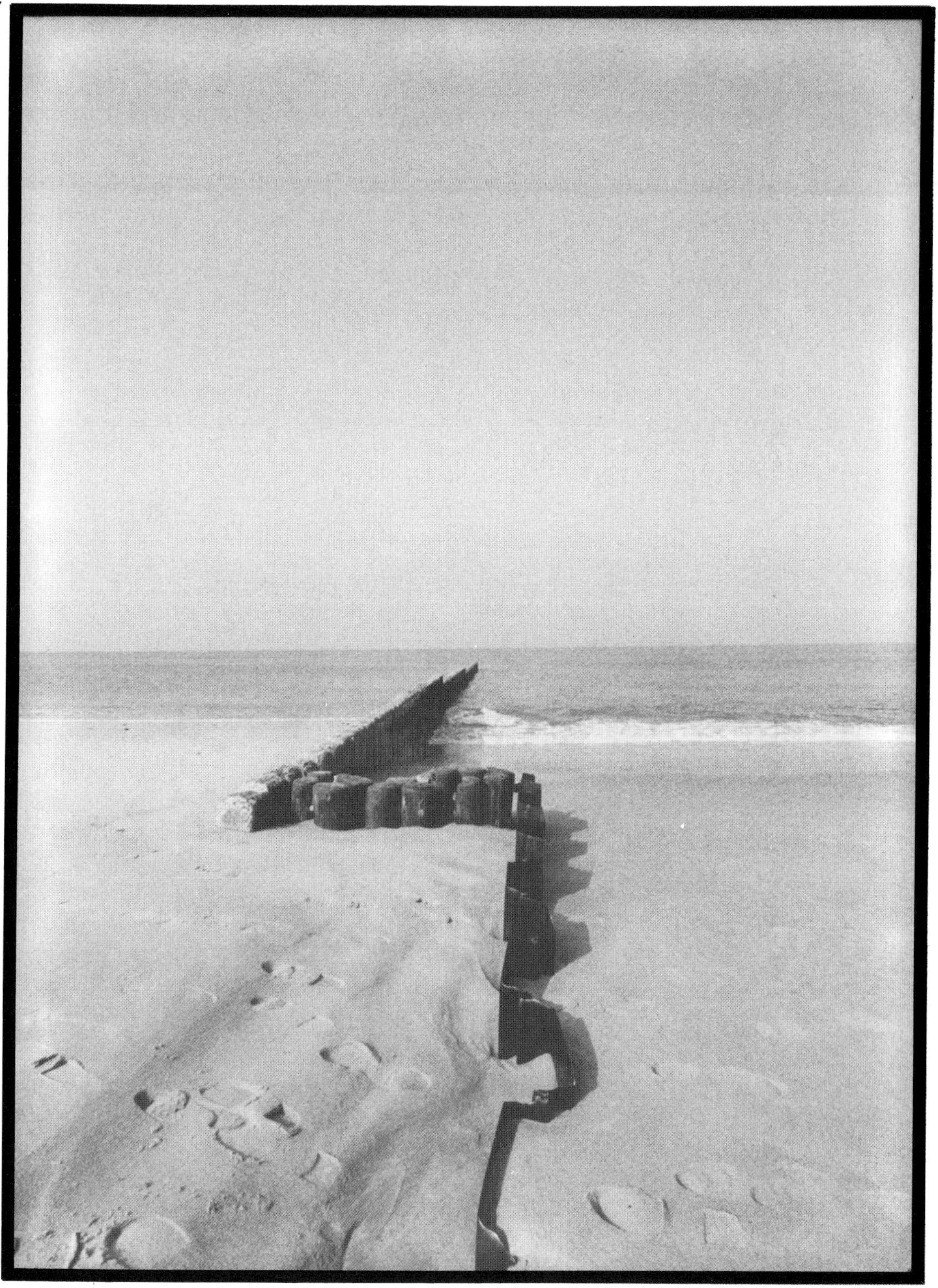

this or that kind of composition. It cannot be done because the kind of composition which you will have to choose depends entirely on what you want to say and how you want to say it. But fortunately this is not quite a complete impasse. Although you will have to make your own mistakes and so learn from them, I can at least show you what I did in certain situations. In this way you might be guided by my example or even learn to avoid the mistakes which I made.

In making your decision about what kind of composition you want you have two basic possibilities: you can either try to make your photograph as simple and visually bold as possible in order to arrest the attention of the viewer immediately; or you can make your photograph complicated so that it will slowly 'unfold' to the viewer. A third – and not so basic – approach would be to aim for a photograph which appears superficially simple and bold, but is actually 'deep' and complex. Each one of these ways has its own advantages and disadvantages which I will discuss with the help of the following photographs.

Opposite
This picture (taken on Sylt in West Germany) proves that so-called compositional 'mistakes', like bisecting the picture plane with the horizon, are sometimes the strongest point of a photograph. If you aim at rigidity and simplicity, the composition of your photograph by necessity must reflect it, that is, it too must be rigid and simple.

Below
Another example of a composition which exactly quarters the picture plane (compare with diagram 54a).

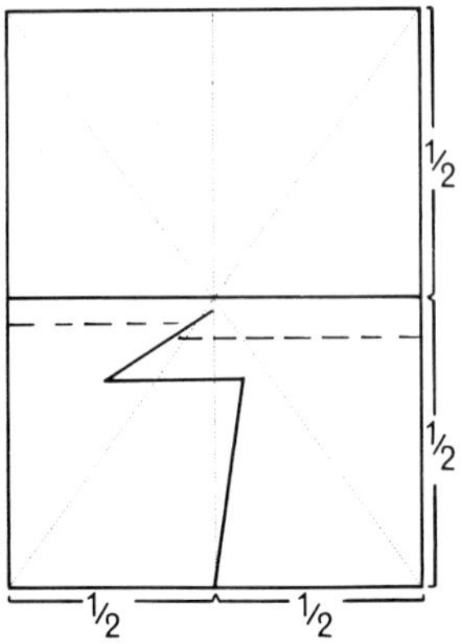

57a

Signal-effect compositions

The first picture (*57*) shows a breakwater on the isle of Sylt in the North Sea. This is quite a well-known spot – not in itself, but because it is some kind of meeting point on what might be termed a jet-set-nudists-bathing-beach. Although this is one of my more successful prints I have never been able to find out whether people buy it because of that or because they really like it. Be that as it may, I have chosen this picture as an illustration of an extremely simple composition. If you look at diagram 57a you will find that the horizon divides the photograph into parts of equal size. The lower part is again divided into two equal sections (defined by the extreme ends of the breakwater). Almost exactly half of the breakwater is on the left-hand side, the other half on the right-hand side of the photograph. The upper half is completely empty.

Before going any further with the interpretation of this picture it might be interesting to find out whether it is possible to make a photograph which is even simpler than this one and compare them. If you look at 58 you can easily see that the answer is both 'yes' and 'no'. The answer is 'yes' insofar as it is possible to make an even simpler image. But at the same time the answer is 'no' because this photograph does not have any impact at all. As far as subject matter is concerned, both photographs have almost exactly the same content. Even the composition of both pictures is so closely related as to be

almost exactly alike. The only difference is that the breakwater in the second photograph runs in a straight line parallel to the vertical picture-frames (*58a*), while it forms a kind of ornamental zig-zag in the first one.

If you agree with me that the first photograph really does have an impact on the viewer while the second one does not, we could reach some interesting conclusions. It is generally stated that some of the 'golden rules' of composition have to be used everytime a photograph is taken. We have already seen in the first chapters of this book that this concept is quite wrong. The photographs now under discussion stress this point. Illustration

58a

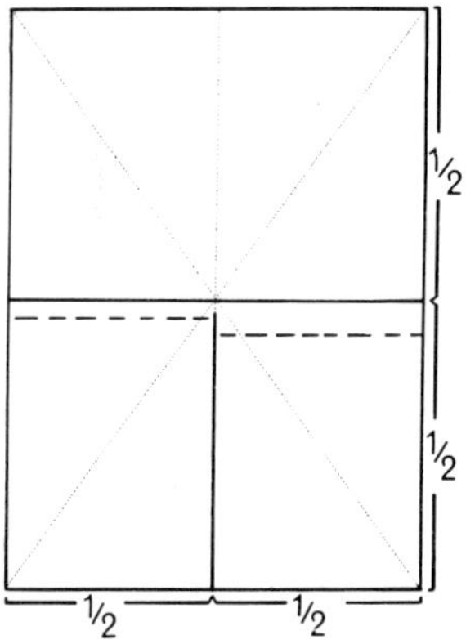

58

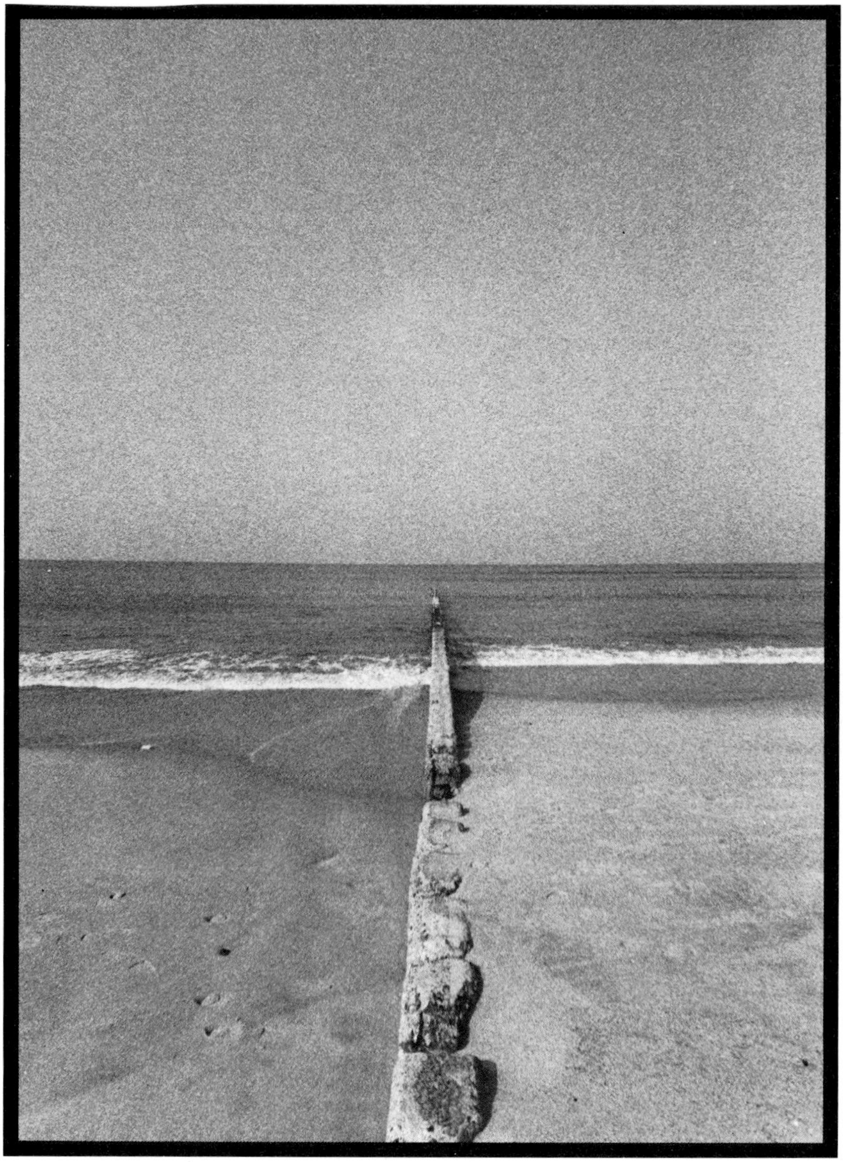

Above and left
If you compare this picture and diagram to the preceding one, you will notice that rigidity and simplicity can be carried too far. If the composition is too simple, it tends to be come boring and uninteresting.

Opposite
The last of this set of three pictures shows the other extreme: the composition is very complicated and convoluted (compared with the other examples). To me this has not enhanced the impact of the photograph, which in turn means that things have been carried too far in the other direction, without anything being gained.

58 seems to show that the horizon really should never divide a photograph into two equal parts and that the main part of the subject should not be placed in the exact centre of the picture, because this results in an uninteresting and/or boring composition. The first illustration (57), however, shows that this is not necessarily true. The photograph follows the same principles of construction, but it is not only compelling, it even draws its main impact from its rigid and allegedly un-compositional construction. What makes this photograph interesting is actually something very small and easily overlooked: it is the zig-zag form of the breakwater and nothing

59

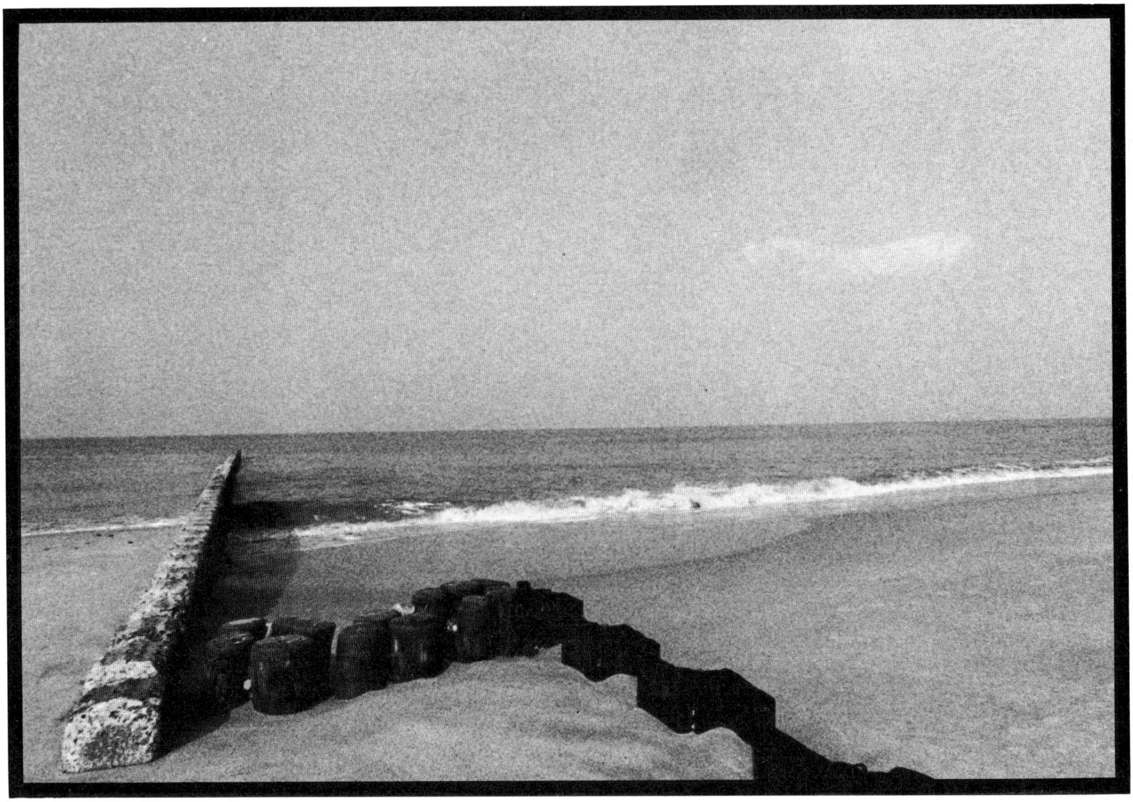

59a

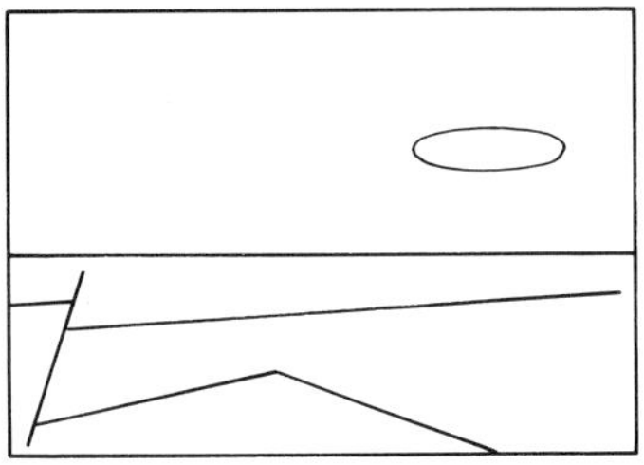

else. If you have a small thing like that which you want to bring to the attention of the viewer, you have to stress it as much as possible. You cannot do this in the context of a complicated or hard to follow composition, because it will be lost on the viewer. But if you keep your composition simple and straightforward a small deviation from it gains dominance and importance.

I would like to prove this with the next photograph (*59*), which shows the same breakwater as in the other pictures, but seen from a completely different viewpoint. Compared to the other two photographs its composition is fairly complicated because a lot of blank space is counterbalanced against the convoluted form of the breakwater, which is placed well off centre (*diagram 59a*). In contrast to 58 this photograph is decidedly not boring. But in my opinion it is nothing but a show-off, it demonstrates that I really was able to make a satisfying composition out of seemingly imbalanced and contradictory elements, although compared to the first photograph it does not succeed.

When I took these photographs the scenery was peaceful, wavelets lapped the sand, the breakwater snaked into the sea and everything was dominated by a blue and empty sky. The overall impression was one of quietude charged with an almost magical (or surreal) air of expectancy, like a stage before the appearance of the first actor. So the thing to do was to walk the small path between an absolutely static and boring image on one side (as represented by 59) and the convoluted but meaningless formality on the other side in order to express the precarious equilibrium described above. If you are aiming for an ambivalent photograph like this one you should take into account that the narrower the path between these extremes the more successful the finished photograph will be – if it succeeds at all.

Now, to return to the starting point and take stock of the situation. When I took these photographs, I was greatly impressed by this scenery without being able to say what exactly impressed me and why it did so. That is why I took a lot of pictures (apart from the three shown here). When making the enlargements, I finally decided that I liked the first one (*57*) best because it seemed to me to contain the essence of the place. Trying to work out why this was so, I came up with the thoughts (or, if you prefer, the rationalisations) which I have described. If I had thought about it before taking the first photograph, just one would have been enough – or I might have formed an even better solution on the spot.

All this seems to stress two points: First: you know by now that composition does not mean the tasteful arrangement of diverse pictorial elements on photographic paper. Everything you do when composing a picture has some meaning – and that is what you should be concerned with. Second: there are no safe rules in composition: what is regarded as wrong or boring by some people might be used by you to form a strong and compelling image – if you know how to go about it. Indeed, rules are a framework placed around successful existing work in an attempt to account for its effectiveness.

This business of knowing what to do and how to go about it does not necessarily imply a great deal of thinking and planning by the photographer. It all depends on what kind of person you are. Some people do it by instinct, others think long and hard about it and a very few people know nothing at all: they just shoot and come up with a perfect picture every time. But apart from these lucky few (I have never met a person like this myself, but they are said to exist) we all have to work at it in order to achieve something noteworthy. And that means that you should start thinking about the composition of photographs taken by yourself or by others if you are dissatisfied with them or just want to get better.

Complex compositions

The next illustration (*60*) is a case in point. It shows part of the fortifications of Mont St Michel in Brittany and when I took this photograph I did not think about it at all. I saw the thing, took a shot and when I printed it later on it came out exactly as I had visualised it. Much later, when I began to plan for this book, I started to wonder why I liked this picture and why others did, too. I then found out that this seemingly simple photograph has a composition which is so complicated and well balanced that I could never have got the thing together if I had tried to think it out beforehand. (That is why talking about the composition of a photograph is usually a case of being wise after the event. But getting wiser helps, whenever it happens.)

The composition of the photograph looks austere and powerful – as befits the representation of fortifications of such size and age. This has been achieved mainly by the distribution of compositional elements and the placement of the light and dark values. There is no continuous grey scale, instead we find three well defined zones. First the pure white and unstructured sky in the upper part of the picture (*60a*) which is oriented to the left. Second, the middle-grey zone in the lower part of the photograph, which is oriented to the right. And finally, the dark

grey and partly black zone which runs like an inverted 'z' from the lower left- to the upper right-hand corner. All this is kept together by a set of analogies. The middle-grey sand corresponds to the roof of the tower, while the white sky finds its counterpart in the almost structureless white upper part of the stone. At the same time, the black bulk of the tower on the right-hand side is counterweighted by the black part of the stone on the left.

This set of analogies serves as a rigid base for the movement which is introduced into the picture by the 'z'-form of the dark main structure (see the black arrow in 60b). Although this movement is quite strong, it is effectively contained within the picture-frame because the white part of the stone and the pinnacle of the tower provide definite points for the beginning and ending of the movement, while the black parts of the composition on the right and the left (the hatched part in 60b) effectively keep it from getting out there. All this comes together to form a powerful and deceptively simple looking image.

Now let us compare this composition to that of the first photograph in this chapter (*57*). This first photograph looks simple and uncomplicated – and that is exactly what it is as we discovered by looking at its composition. In my opinion it is an image that could well be thought out before it is done – provided that you know what you want to do! But I think that this would never work with a relatively complicated composition, such as that in 60. If I had had to work this one out beforehand, I would surely have been so muddled and

Opposite
This turret, photographed at Mont St. Michel in France, illustrates a kind of composition which is not nearly as simple as it looks at first sight.

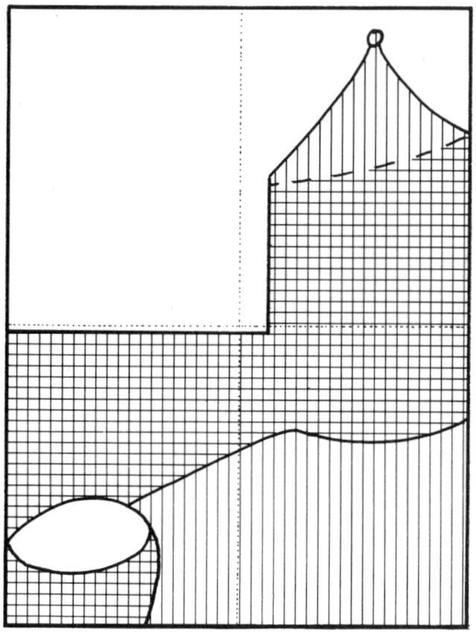

60a

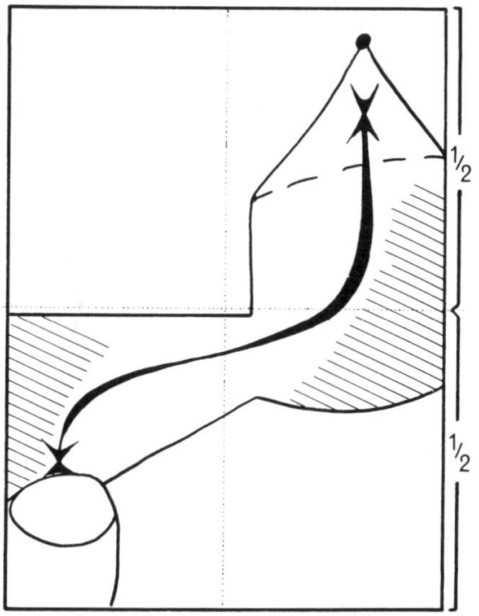

60b

Far left
The main planes of the composition of illustration 60 are defined by their different grey values, which are concentrated in almost symmetrical parts of the picture plane.

Left
The main lines and weights of the picture and the bisection of the picture plane by the horizon.

60

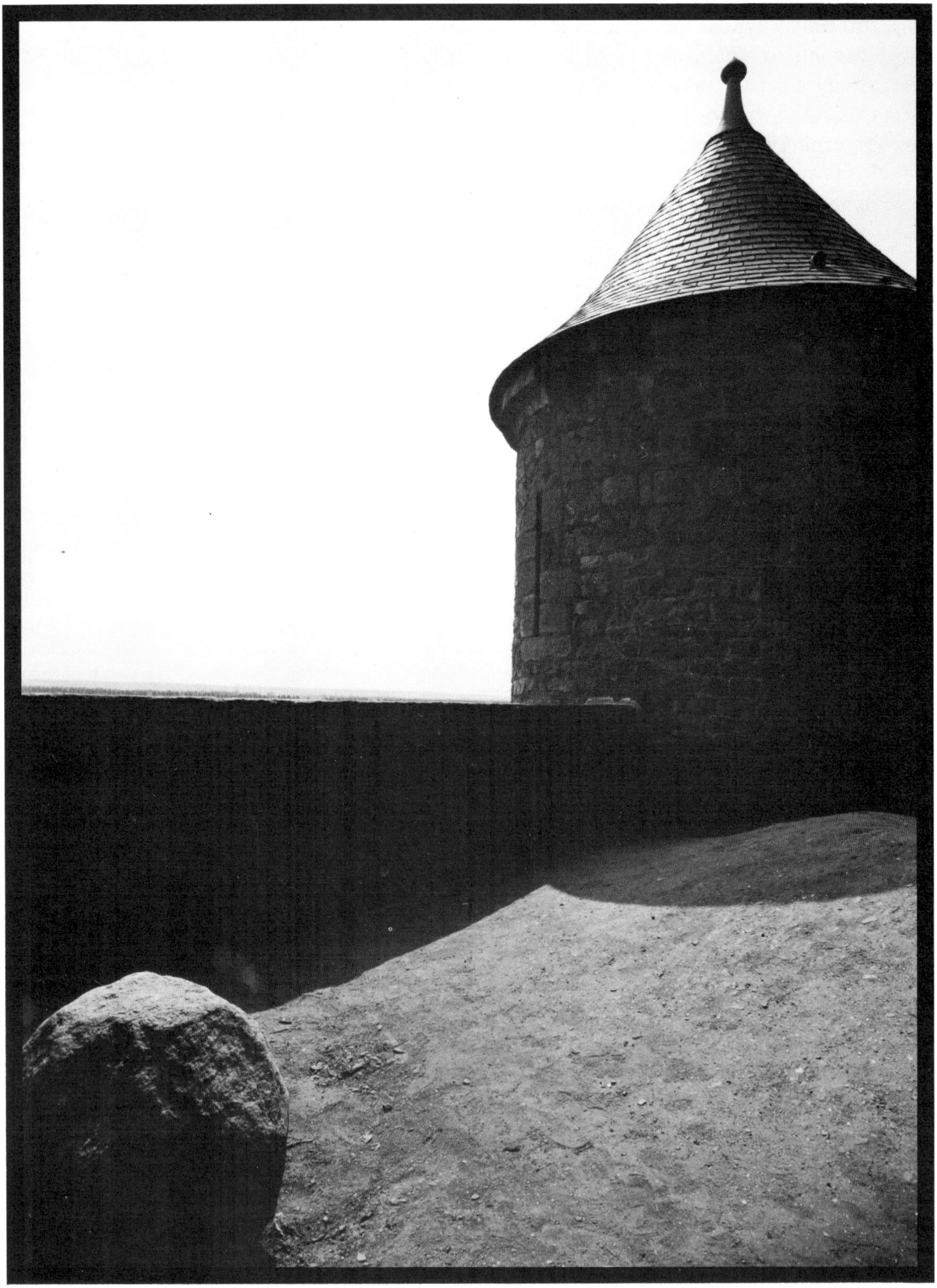

61

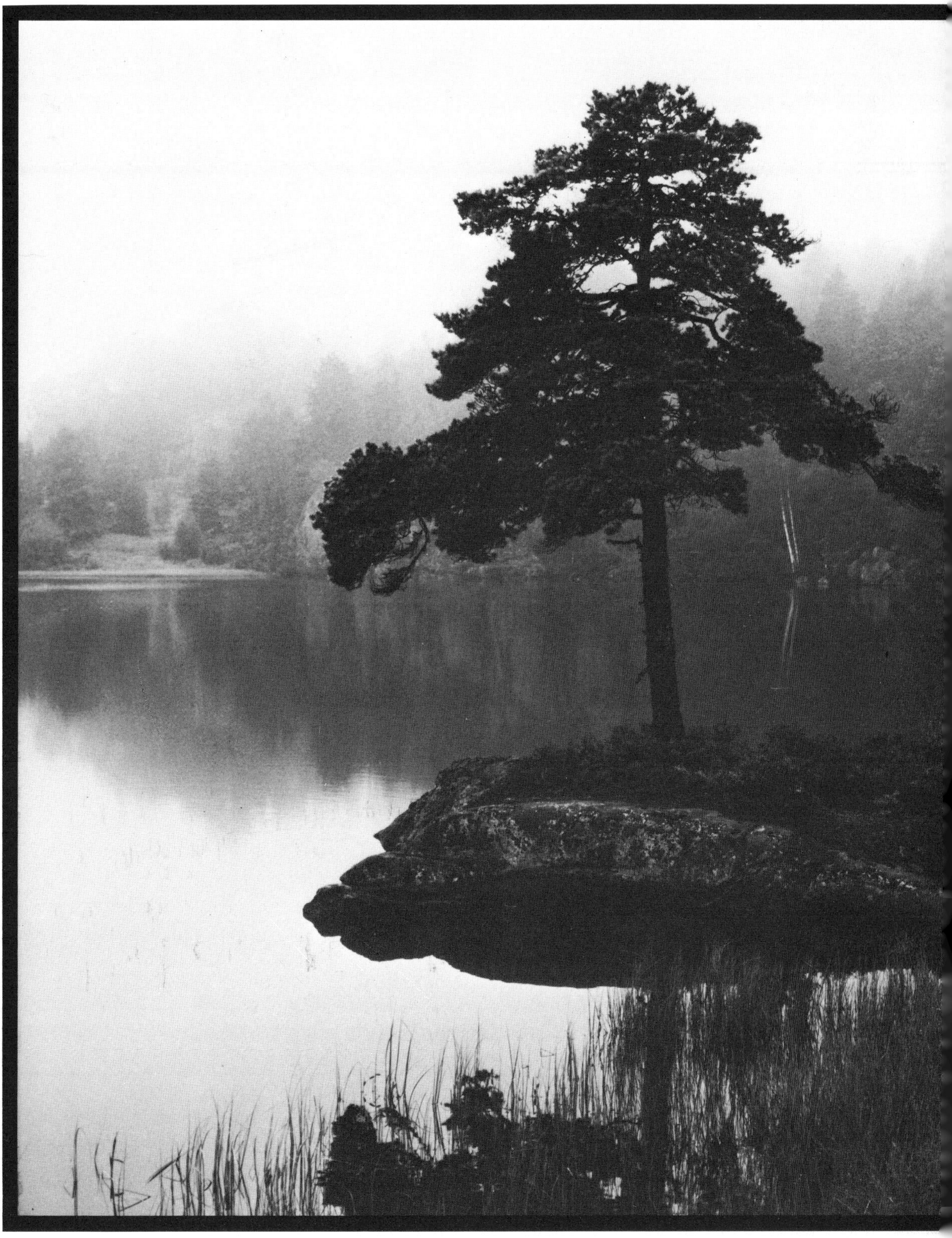

of subject matter or composition) which allows the viewer to make contact with the picture and which gives him a basis for his dealings with it.

The basic approaches to composition

Thus we have two basic approaches to making photographs which are visually appealing and/or intellectually and emotionally moving. Each of these approaches can be realised in different ways. If these concepts are new and unfamiliar, you may find them a bit confusing and the following diagrammatic summary may help you to sort out what we have discussed so far.

This diagram is far from complete, but it shows the principle of the thing. I suggest that you extend and amend this list according to your own ideas and preferences and check some photographs against it. You would, for example, find that photograph 57 belongs to categories I/A and I/C, it is a positive example. Illustration 58 is classified as a failure: it belongs to I/A and I/B, which cancel each other out, so that we are left with nothing worth talking about. On the other hand pictures 60 and 61 both belong to II/B and II/C and come out quite well. And so on . . .

If, however, you want to try this kind of ploy with some of your own photographs, you will soon find that a chart like this does not really work. Photographs and their perception form such a very complex field that formalised tables and foregone conclusions will lead you nowhere. The diagram and categories which I have tried to formulate are intended to give you a starting point for your own thinking and evaluation of photographs – nothing more.

Another look at illustration 61 will persuade you that there really is more to the question of composition than we have so far discovered. Although we have described the various parts of the overall composition and some of their interactions, this does not solve the question of why this kind of composition attracts the viewer and why this attraction is maintained once he has appreciated the photograph.

A question such as this is extremely difficult to answer because it touches upon psychology and physiology as well as the sciences and philosophies of aesthetics. But the following very simplified example will give you an idea of what it is all about. If you look closely at illustration 62 you will see either the drawing of a goblet in white on a black background or you will see the silhouettes of two faces in black on a white background. What you see first or what you see most easily

distribution of the scenery seem to coincide completely. But this photograph is, nevertheless, as carefully composed as the other examples in this chapter. Diagram 61a shows the main elements of the composition. The dark form of the tree is situated just left of the centre of the picture-plane. It seems to be pushed even more to the left by the open-ended oval of trees and other vegetation (indicated by the hatched area in the diagram). This movement is reversed by the V-shape formed by the tree and its shadow. The final rigidity of the whole composition is provided by the downward thrust of the lines formed by the rock and by the counterpoint of the small black form with which the shadow of the tree is safely 'anchored' to the lower border of the picture.

In the preceding chapter we discussed the same principle of composition, that is, a composition whose overall appearance is one of static rigidity, while a lot of movement (of the compositional variety) goes on between its well counter-balanced parts. While composition of the kind shown in illustration 57 lives by sheer force, this one does it through ambivalence.

This is an interesting and highly important point: if you try to make your photograph simple and visually bold, you are sure to catch the attention of the viewer immediately. But the question then arises: how long will the interest of the viewer be held by your picture? More often than not you will find that photographs which appear fine at first glance are disappointing when you look more closely at them, because apart from the initial surprise there seems to be nothing more or nothing 'behind' them. On the other hand you will find another category of photographs which are highly interesting and intriguing, although they offer the viewer no obvious way of making contact with them.

If they were failures, 57 would belong in the first category and the last one in the second. Each of these categories offers you a potential way in which to realise your pictures, but you should keep in mind that both have their disadvantages. The kind of 'signal effect' photograph shown in illustration 57 needs something more to retain the interest of the viewer once it has been caught. This 'something more' could either be an underlying formal complexity of composition or it could be an intriguing and/or moving thought or feeling, both of which would draw the viewer to a longer and closer look at the picture. On the other hand the 'no-approach' photograph, which belongs to the second category, would need a kind of visual handle in the form of some bold or intriguing detail (be it

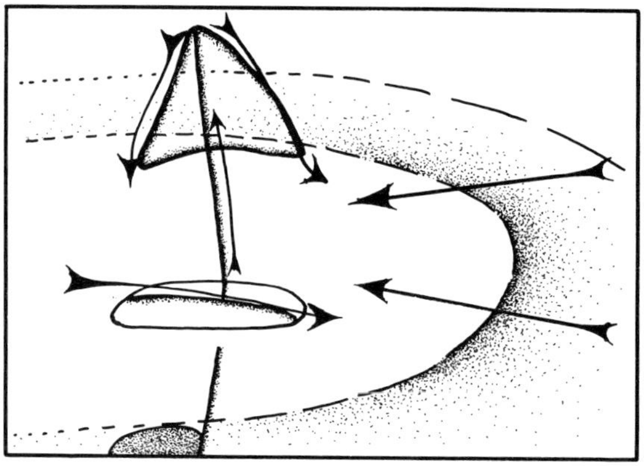

61a

The main parts of the composition seem to show a very complicated relationship between its various parts. That appearances can be deceptive becomes immediately clear if you look at illustration 61.

confused that in the end I would not have taken a photograph at all.

Again that leaves us with the question: What do you get out of all of it? The answer should be obvious by now, but it really is one of the most important points in this discussion and so we will return to it time and again. I have already stated that I cannot furnish you with a set of rules which you just have to apply to your subject in order to create a great masterpiece. If that were possible, everybody would be a great master and there would be no sense in doing photography. But what I can do is to suggest methods of approach which enable you to find out what makes pictures work (or not, as the case may be). If you use these as you are meant to, you will be able to say more than just the usual 'I like this one' about a photograph. And this in turn will enable you to take better photographs in the end, because it all adds to the field of experience upon which you consciously or subconsciously draw when actually taking pictures.

With that sermon still ringing in your ears, we will look at some more pictures. So far we have dealt with two: a simple-looking one which really was simple in its composition and one which looked deceptively simple yet was actually quite sophisticated in construction. But both photographs look as if someone had arranged their elements carefully and according to some preconceived plan or idea.

'Natural' compositions

Now we are going to deal with an entirely different approach. If you look at illustration 61, a landscape in southern Norway, you will probably not be able to detect any effort at composition at all, because all the elements of this picture seem to fall quite naturally into place. If you want to detect the underlying composition you will have to look closely, because the (artificial) structure of the composition and the (natural)

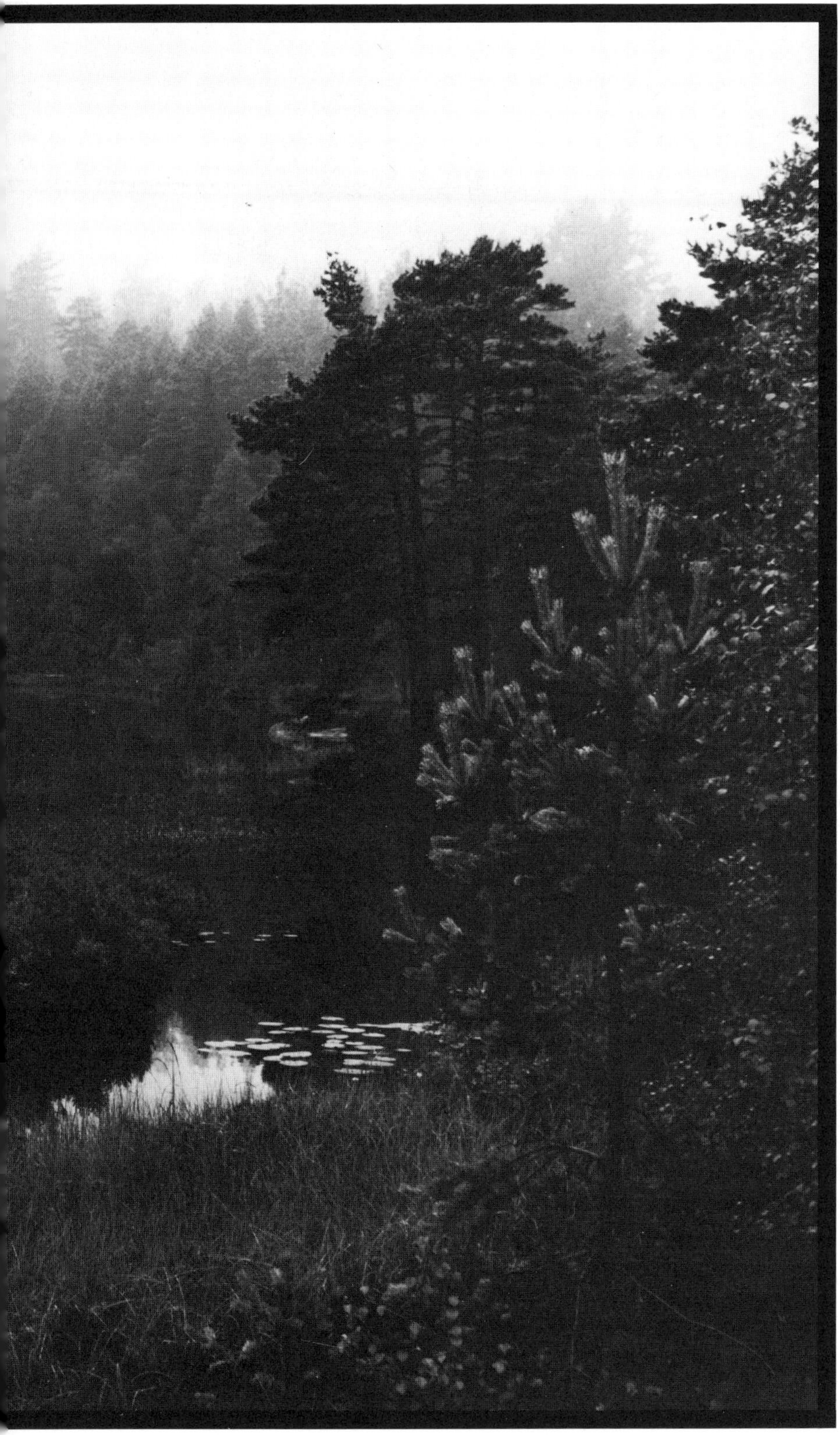

The very close interplay of lines and planes in this 'composition' were not carefully created by the photographer. They were there and fell into place quite naturally.

I *signal-effect-photograph*	II *no-approach photograph*
visually bold, simple composition, easy to grasp, fig. speaking: leaps at the viewer	no obvious clues to formal construction, meanings difficult to locate, because no easy access is given
quickly exhausted, because it offers no "resistance" to the perception of the viewer	offers scope and variety, lots of material for the imagination and food for thought

THESE POINTS CAN BE EVALUATED DIFFERENTLY:

leaves everything to the imagination of the viewer, free association	channels imagination and associations, narrows field of possible interpretations
empty formalism, has nothing to offer beyond some visually out-of-the-way configurations	its complexity always leads to new discoveries and renews the interest of the viewer indefinitely or over a long period of time

62

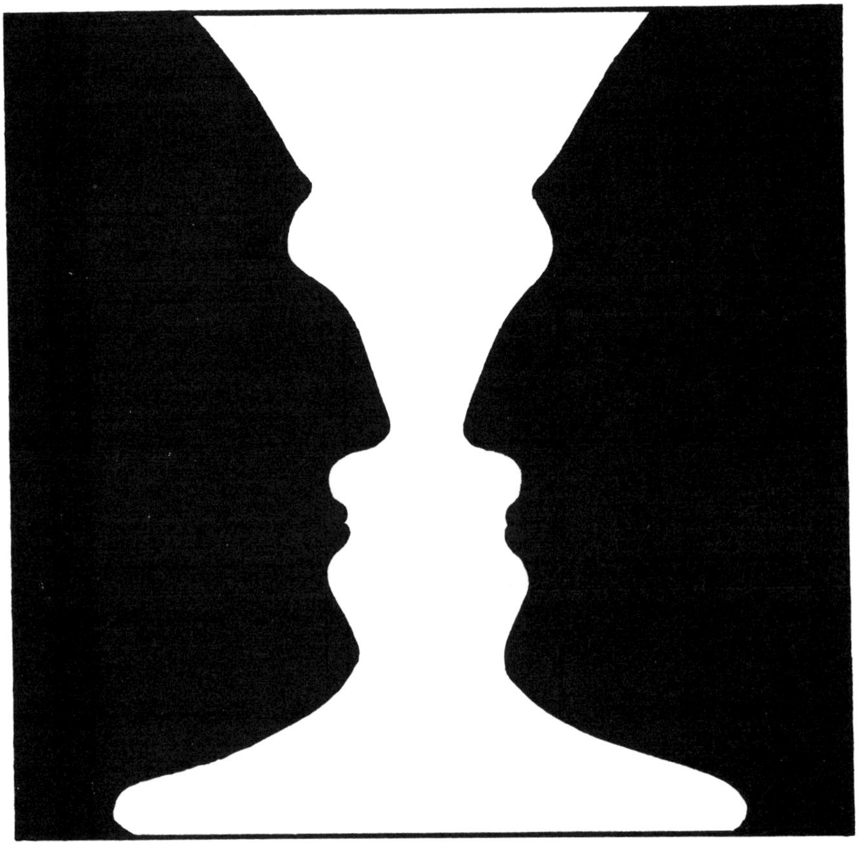

The ambiguous response to this kind of drawing cannot be resolved once and for all. Although you can force yourself to see either the goblet or the two faces, which aspect strikes you first may change when you have another look.

63

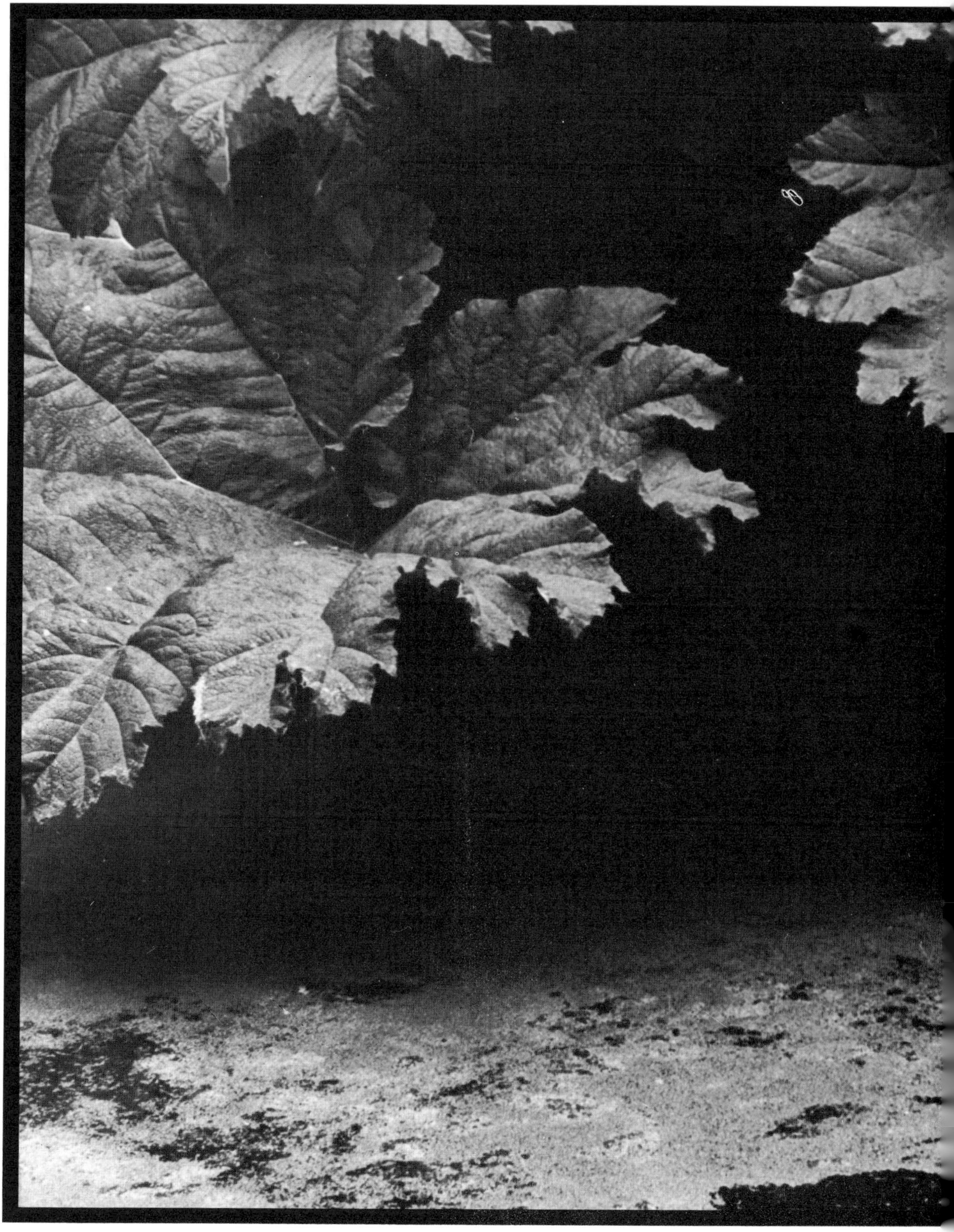

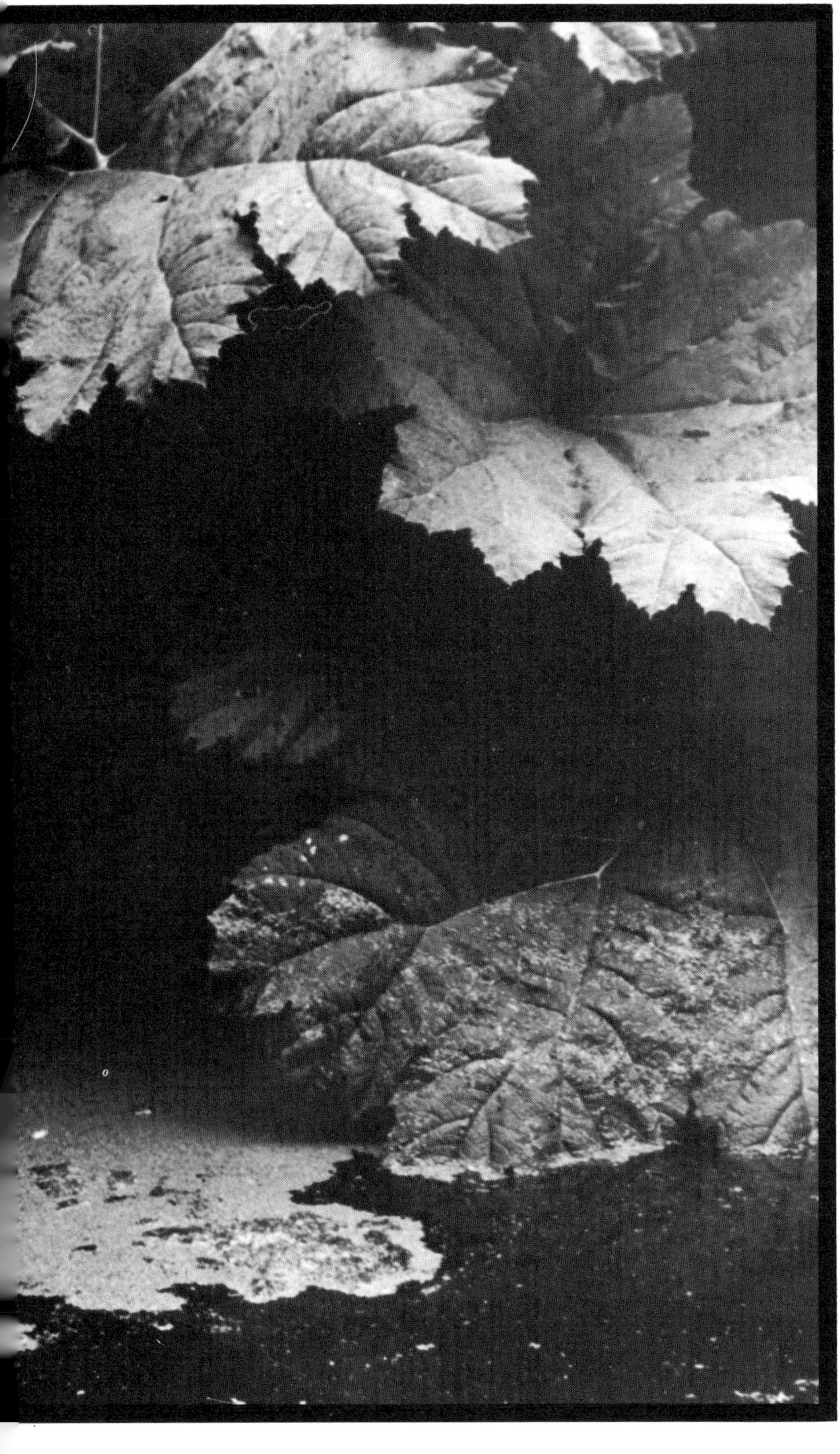

These leaves are organised into an exceedingly simple composition by the framing and the exposure, which resulted in the central black part of the picture.

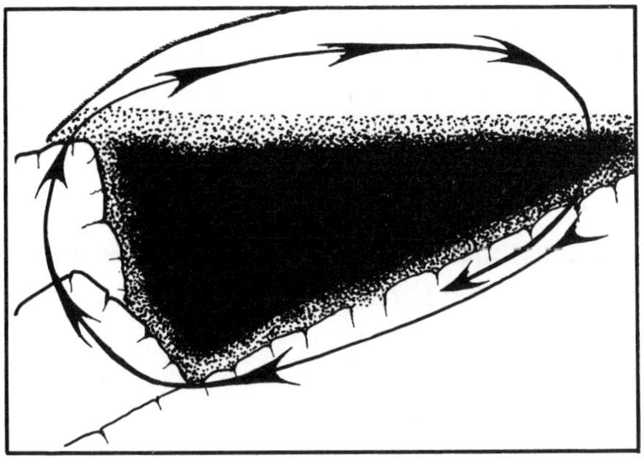

63a

The simple and uninterrupted clockwise compositional movement of 63 (preceding pages) originates from the framing of the leaves around the black hole.

depends on your psychological make-up and on the scope of your associations. But whatever it is, you will not be able to get rid of one of the two 'interpretations' of the picture. This insoluble ambiguity makes it interesting or, to be more accurate, is its main and only point of interest.

If you now return to illustration 61 and its composition, you will find that the relation of its elements to each other form the same kind of ambiguous pattern as that discussed above. They provide an optical paradox which cannot be solved or reduced to a static and finite pattern. This means that a composition based on these principles will always offer new 'resistance' to the viewer and will retain his interest in a way that "goblet face" did not.

Of course there are other levels in a photograph which could provide you with similar effects, for example certain aspects of a subject, but as we are looking at photographs from the compositional point of view, I will content myself with giving two examples which will give you an idea of these other possibilities.

The composition of photograph 63 is extremely simple. As shown in diagram 63a, the gaze of the viewer is forced into a kind of constant movement around the centre of the picture. The path of this motion is defined by the diagonal line of the leaves leading from left to right, by the 'steps' provided by the leaves on the right-hand side leading downwards and by the border between the black and the middle-grey zone in the foreground. The main part of the composition is the black 'hole' in the centre of the picture-plane, while the actual subject matter has been arranged along its borders. This provides us with the two key elements for the understanding of this photograph. First there is the ambiguous composition in a very simplified form and second, the unusual distribution of the subject matter itself.

It should be obvious that a combination of subject and composition which produces a black hole as the main point of interest, leads to a photograph which exudes a general air of mystery. Or, putting it more bluntly, what the viewer is interested in when looking at this photograph is the structure and arrangement of the leaves. But because of the arrangement described above he is forced to take into account the black hole as an important part of his visual experience. Although this probably happens subconsciously he is left with an irritant which not only provides the interest in this photograph, but helps maintain it because of its ambiguity.

The first photograph in this series (*61*) worked in this way because of its composition. The second one (*63*) worked as a result of the combination of subject matter and composition. The final photograph in this chapter provides us with an example which works chiefly through its subject. If you look at illustration 64 and the accompanying diagram (*64a*) you will see that the composition of this photograph is as simple as that of the preceding one. The three dark areas form a triangle – the castle, the rope and the rock on the right-hand side. This again provides us with a perpetual motion from one main point to the next. But this time the real mystery and interest is provided by the subject matter itself. The composition provides you, the viewer, with a close connection between a castle, a piece of rope and a formation of rocks. But what does it mean? The answer will probably remain hidden or it will change as the viewer changes his mood and, with it as a point of reference, his associations.

With that we really took a plunge into the difficulties and complexities of composition. If you feel a bit lost the following summary may help.

Summary

First: The photographer has the opportunity of choosing from an almost unlimited number of possibilities if he wants to create a specific picture.

Second: If, however, he has clear and well defined intentions, only one of these possibilities will really work for him.

Third: These possibilities can be divided into two basic groups: a) the 'signal-effect' photographs and b) the 'no-approach' photographs.

Fourth: A 'signal-effect' photograph is a picture which immediately arrests the attention of the viewer because it depends on or consists of a simple and visually bold element which, figuratively speaking, jumps at the viewer. On the other

64

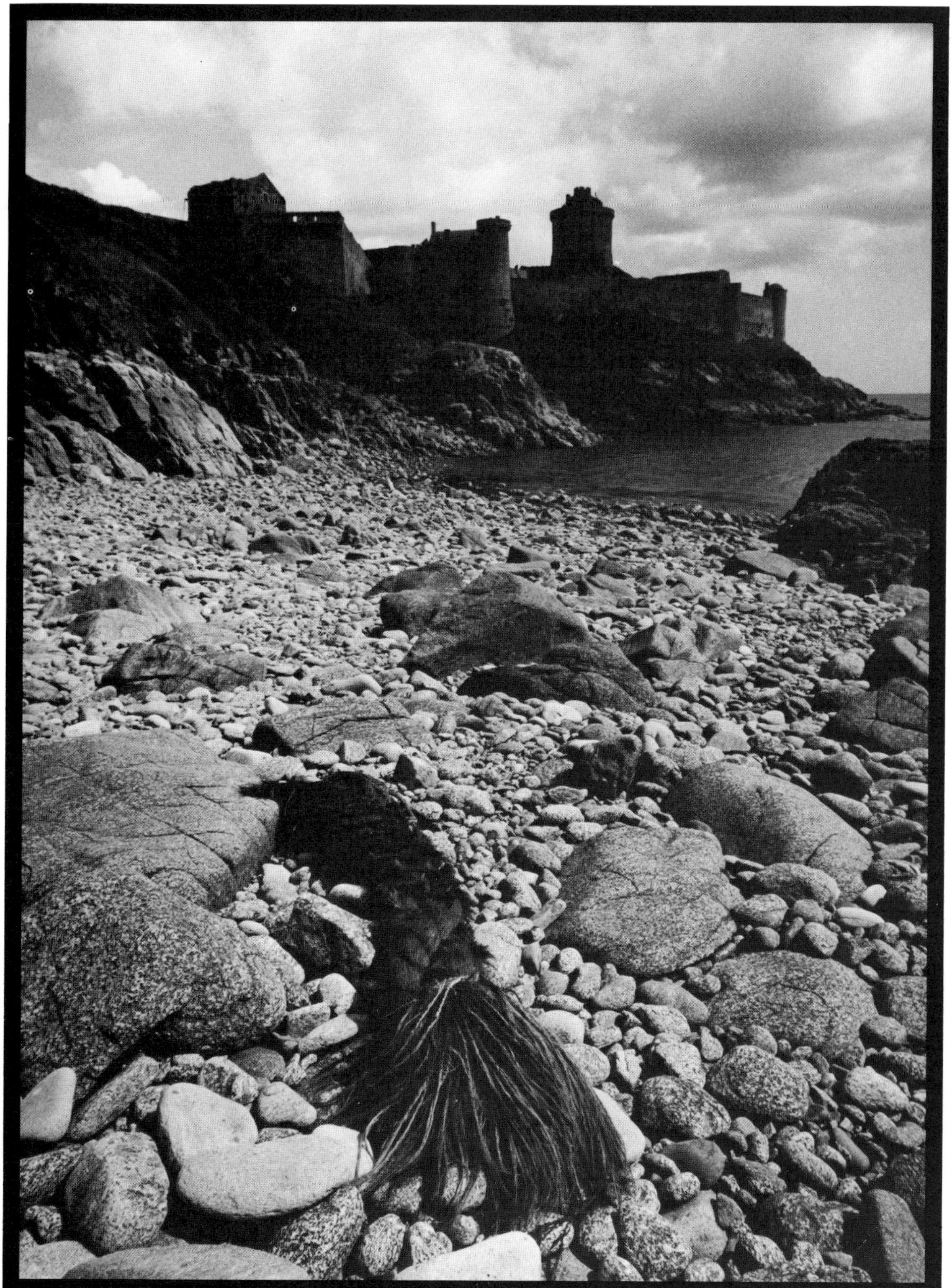

Opposite
The photograph of Fort la Latte in France looks fairly complicated. But the diagram (*right*) shows that the underlying composition consists of only a few easily recognised elements.

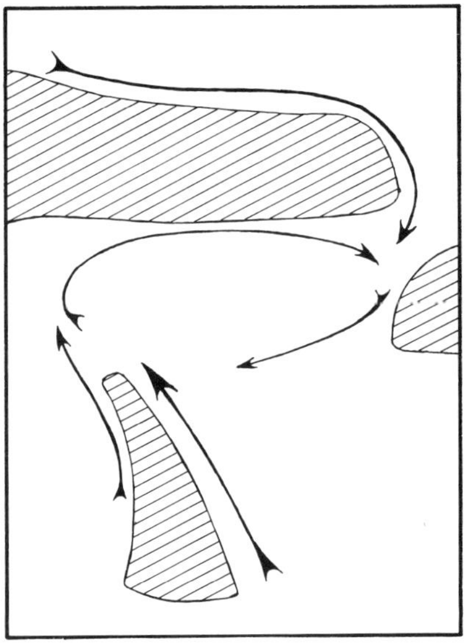

64a

hand, a 'no-approach' photograph is visually complicated and self-contained. It offers the viewer no clue or pointer for his approach.

Fifth: If realised purely, neither of these principles will provide you with satisfying results. A signal-effect photograph will be exhausted quickly and offer no more interest to the viewer if it contains no other levels of composition and/or meaning than the 'signal' itself. The viewer of a no-approach photograph will not even start to deal with it either visually or intellectually if it does not provide him with an 'opening' in the form of some obvious and appealing element of the subject or composition.

Sixth: Whichever of these basic possibilities is chosen, there are some ways to enhance the interest of the viewer even further. The principal one is to choose an ambiguous composition or an ambiguous combination of subject matter and composition.

Seventh: The ambiguous photograph provides the viewer with a visual and/or intellectual paradox. Because this paradox cannot be solved or reduced to clearly defined elements, interest in the photograph can be maintained indefinitely or at least for a prolonged period of time.

10 Aids to Composition

So far we have dealt with composition without regard for the more practical difficulties, which we are likely to meet more often than not. In contrast, for example, to a painter, you are not entirely free to do what pleases you, because a photographer to some degree is bound by the properties of his subject. Telegraph-poles, lamp-posts, traffic-signs and the like, are cases in point. They are often placed by some kind authority just where you do not need them – photographically speaking. If you meet an obstacle like this the easiest and safest way out is not to shoot, or, if you did, at least not to show your photograph. The viewer judges you by your photograph and not by your intentions. That is why you should never show a photograph if you have the slightest reason to be dissatisfied with it – and unwanted telegraph-poles or unlooked-for traffic-signs are surely reasons for being discontented with a photograph.

But apart from the 'no-shot' rule which is always safe, there are other ways and means to circumvent problems of this kind. The best way to deal with unwanted elements in your subject is to try to incorporate them into the photograph, and giving them a meaningful part in the composition. Of course, this is easier said than done and it might even require you to change your original intentions completely. But as long as you keep an open mind you can get away with almost anything.

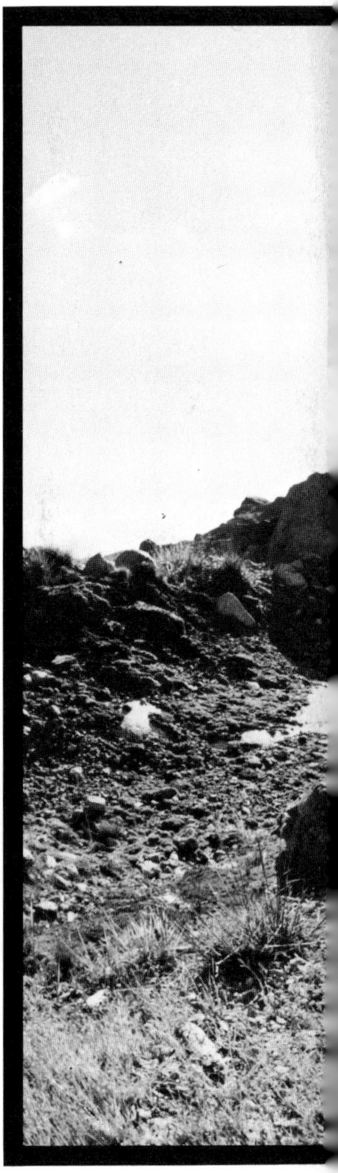

Fish-eye lenses
The first photograph in this chapter should give you an idea of what can be done. Illustration 65 shows a road in Norway which, although lonely and far from any settlement, was frequented by heavy lorries. My first idea was to show a stretch of road with a lorry on it, seen from the side. I tried it on Polaroid (see Chapter 12) and it did not work out as I had hoped.

Next I changed my viewpoint so as to get an oblique view of the road. That was when the beacon poles obstructed my view of the road. First I was at a loss what to do, but then I came up with the idea which you see realised in the

Curves caused by the use of fish-eye lenses can be very useful for creating an interesting composition. The curved pole on the left is the mainstay of this composition. A straight rendering, as made by a 'normal' wide-angle lens would not have given an interesting composition at all.

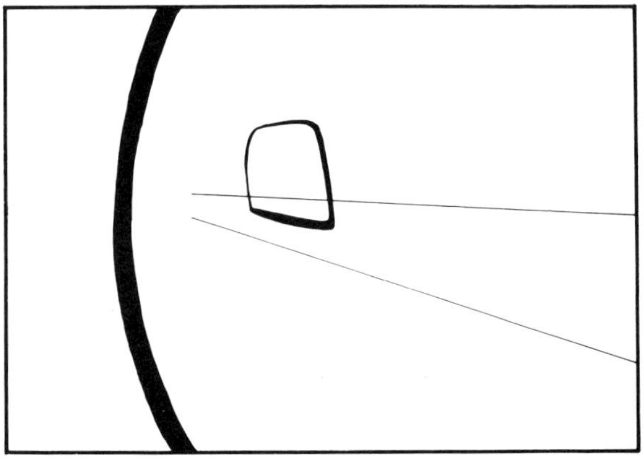

65a

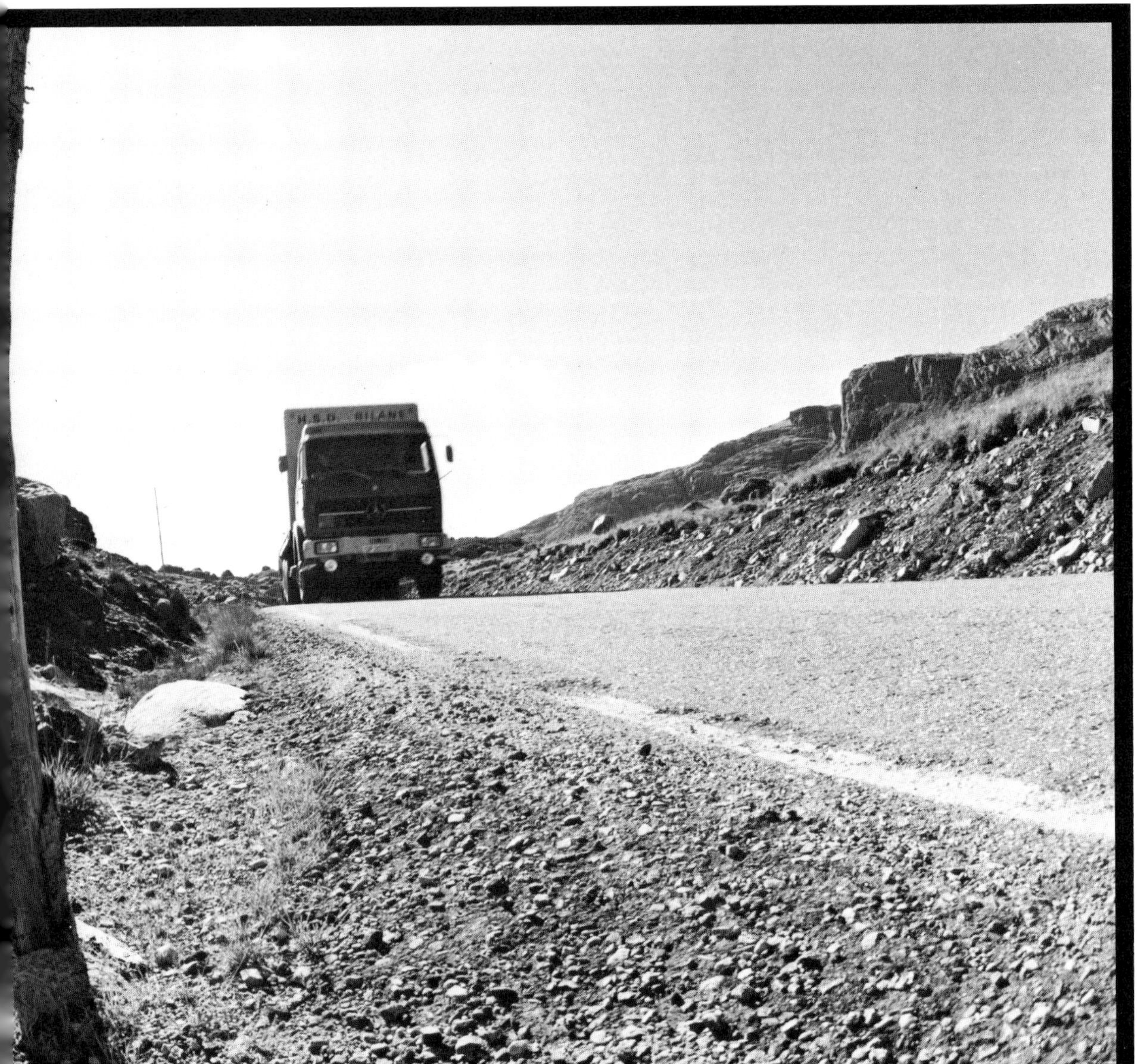

65

photograph: I changed the lens to a moderate fish-eye (37 mm on a 6 × 7 camera) and incorporated one of the poles into the foreground of the picture by positioning myself very close to it.

I think the result is quite convincing. The beacon pole and the road form a kind of bow-and-arrow arrangement (*diagram 65a*) which gives a strong impulse of movement to the lorry in the background. This impression of movement is enhanced by a very slight amount of unsharpness in the lorry itself (due to a relatively long exposure). I hope you will agree with me that what, at first, seemed to be an obstacle to the photograph which I wanted to take, turned out to be its strongest point. So do not give up if you run into difficulties of this kind, in my experience there is generally a way around them.

The interesting thing is that this photograph was made possible by the use of a fish-eye lens. You can easily imagine that a rendering of the beacon pole as a straight line would have resulted in an uninteresting composition. That leads us to the next point. In my opinion fish-eye photographs usually depend upon an eye-catching effect without giving anything more to the viewer (refer to our discussion in the preceding chapter!), but judicially applied, the fish-eye lens can be a great help in finding a strong and convincing composition which it would otherwise have been impossible to achieve.

Many people own a fish-eye lens, but most of them no longer use it because it now seems outdated and unfashionable. But the flood of fish-eye photographs which overwhelmed us a few years ago proves that most photographers did not know what to do with it. They applied it without regard to its great compositional possibilities, instead heading directly for its special effect, which really gets exceedingly boring after you have seen it a dozen times if there is nothing more to support and enhance it. But however it may have been used, we should regard the fish-eye lens as a valuable photographic means of achieving very special compositional effects – as long as it is used according to its possibilities and limitations. In order to give you a better understanding of what can be done with fish-eye lenses, I will show you some more photographs, but again I hasten to add that there is no substitute for your own experience.

Illustration 66 gives you an example of the use of a moderate fish-eye lens on a 35 mm camera (focal length: 16 mm). When you first look at this picture you may not notice that it has been taken with a lens of this kind. That is easily explained. You know that all lines reproduced in a fish-eye photograph run straight as long as they pass through the central

Opposite and below
Sometimes a subject almost forces you to use a fish-eye lens. This one begged for its curved lines to be exaggerated by such a lens. Nevertheless its perspective looks almost normal because some of its important lines are straight, which is due to the peculiar perspective rendering of fish-eye lenses.

Bottom
All lines in a fish-eye photograph are completely straight, as long as they go through the centre of the picture plane.

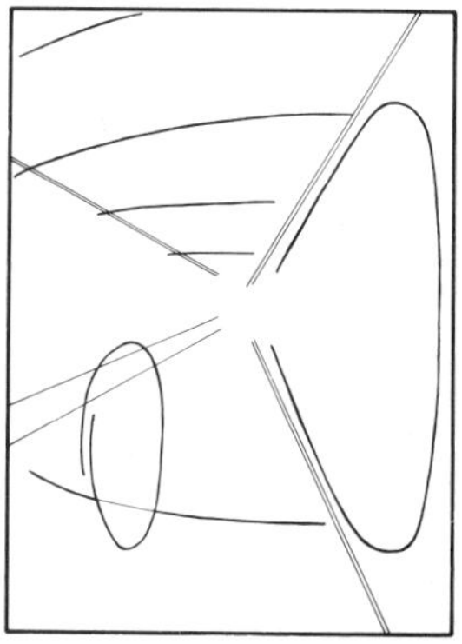

66a

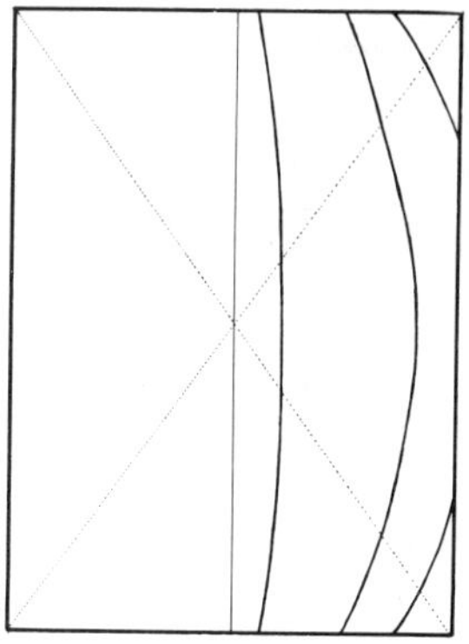

67

66

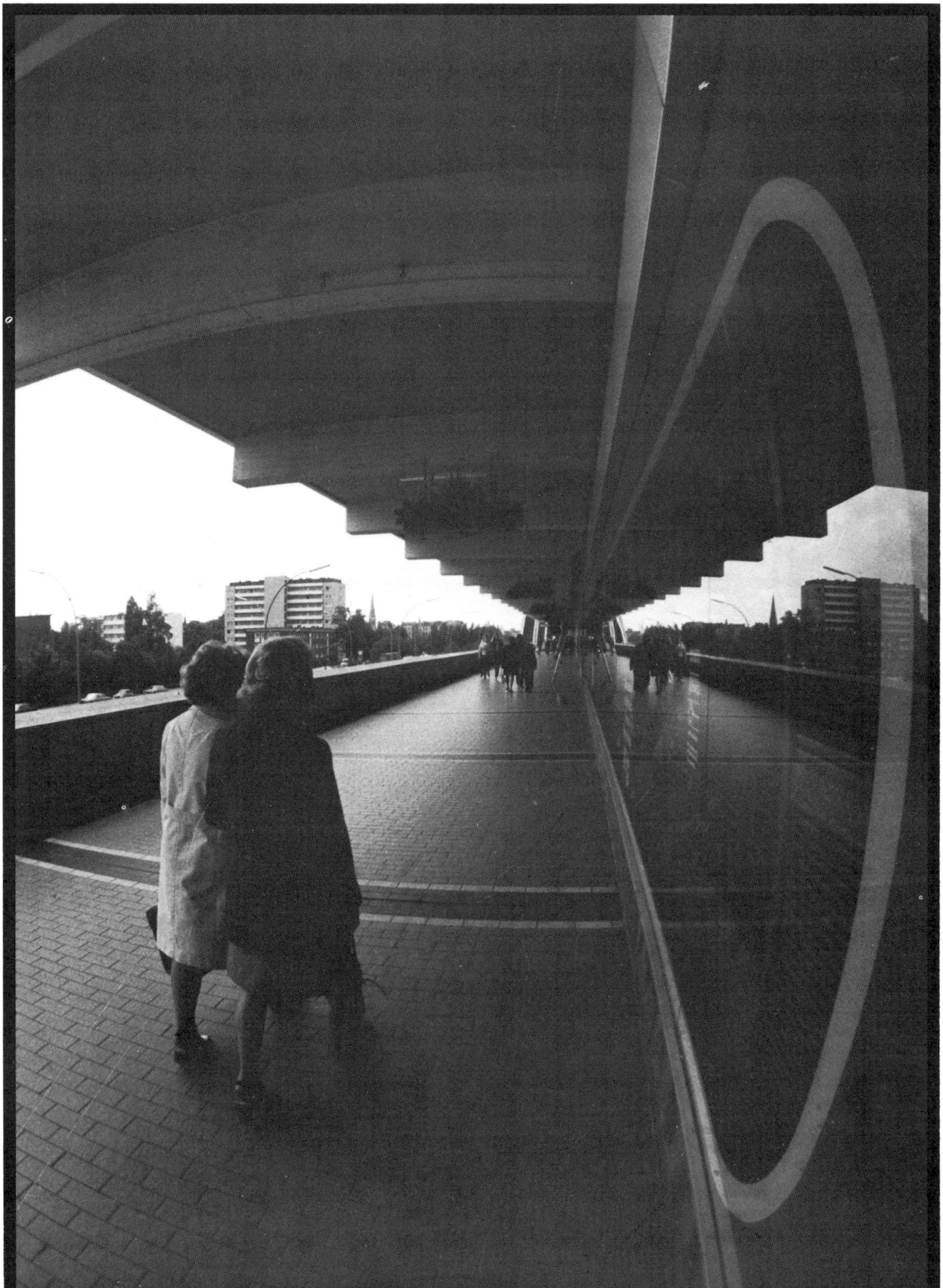

68

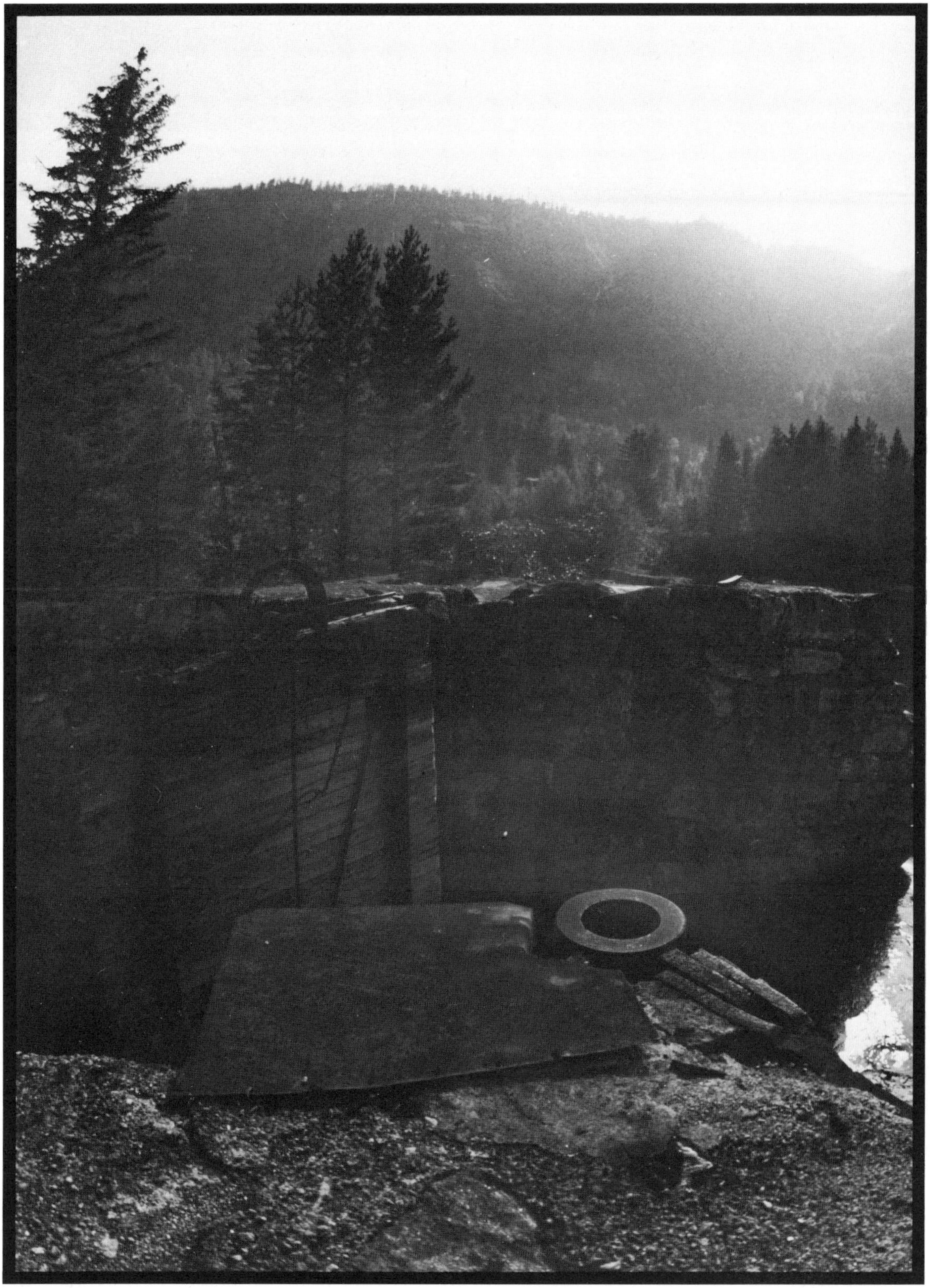

If you have a problem in finding a convincing compositional relationship between straight and curved lines in a subject it always is a good idea to try a fish-eye lens as I did here (37 mm lens on 6 × 7 camera). This kind of effect works best if there are no buildings, because strongly curved walls look rather startling, although curved tree trunks, for example, are much less noticeable.

point of the picture-plane. If they do not pass through the central point they are reproduced as curves, the curves being the more pronounced the closer they are to the edge of the picture (*see diagram 67*). As you can see by referring to the photograph (*66*), this fact can be used to arrange the compositional elements of a picture according to your wishes. The lines which provide the photograph with its central perspective (double lines in diagram 66a) run almost exactly through the central point of the picture and are accordingly almost straight. This fact has been disguised by some cropping on the right-hand side, so that they are off-centre in the finished enlargement. (Please note: If you want to do this kind of thing, you must frame your photograph accordingly when shooting. You should not leave it to chance because you then might not have enough space left for cropping.)

The concrete girders in the upper part of the picture are another interesting feature. The first one appears to be curved, while those in the distance look almost straight because they are much closer to the central point. But the most interesting thing in the photograph, and the main reason why I used a fish-eye lens for it, is the ornament painted on the shop-window on the right. It actually was an exact semi-circle which I could not fit into the composition at all, but the perspective distortion provided by the fish-eye lens gives exactly the amount of deviation from the right-angled picture frame which was needed to guide the viewer's gaze into the depth of the photograph.

As far as the other elements of the composition are concerned, it should be quite obvious by now that the horizontal lines formed by the concrete girders and the stripes across the pavement slow this movement down, while the form of the two shoppers in the foreground draws the gaze of the viewer back. I shall not go into these aspects of the composition in detail because I just wanted to indicate some of the possibilities for intelligently applying the fish-eye lens.

The next photograph (*68*) demonstrates the same kind of approach with a different subject. It shows a disused and partly destroyed sluice in Norway, photographed with a 37 mm fish-eye lens (6 × 7 camera). Here the compositional problem was to find a convincing relationship between the round form in the foreground and the straight lines of the trees and the sluice itself. Instead of aiming for a rigidly rectangular construction and the resulting juxtaposition of the circular and the rectangular forms, which it would have been quite possible to do, I tried to give a more continuous impression and blend the different elements of the composition into a less dramatic but

The easiest way to reduce the grey values of a subject is to photograph against the light (contre jour) as here. Nevertheless, the range of grey tones was reduced to two different grey tones and black without any additional manipulation.

more consistent unity. The best and easiest way to do this was to use a fish-eye lens because the typical fish-eye effect is not so strongly visible as to make the viewer painfully aware of the optical trick.

This leads us to quite a good rule-of-thumb for the judgement of fish-eye photographs. If the effect of the fish-eye distortion sticks out like a sore thumb, the photograph did not succeed. If, on the other hand, the effect looks like an almost natural part of the overall composition, and consequently is integrated into it, the fish-eye lens has been used successfully as an instrument of composition.

Apart from the fish-eye lenses discussed here there are other special-effect lenses and cameras which change the 'normal' rendering of perspective. There are, for example, lenses which give cylindrical perspective distortion and panoramic cameras with moving lenses. I will not discuss them here because most people do not have equipment of this kind, so to discuss them would be superfluous. It is fair to say, however, that they may be used in ways similar to those described for the fish-eye lens. But let me add a word of warning: you can use everything to take photographs with (that is, of course, as long as it provides you with some kind of picture), but in my opinion you should never aim solely for an optical effect. It is better to integrate optical effects into the photograph. Or, to put it more bluntly, everything you do, including the use of optical effects or other technical tricks, should add to the mood and/or meaning of the photograph which you want to create. This is what I wanted to demonstrate with the fish-eye pictures shown so far and it applies equally to the rest of the photographs in this chapter.

Another difficulty which you will often meet is that your subject matter contains too much detail. Whether you want to show a bold and simplified image or stress some particular aspect of your subject – the problem is how to reduce the wealth of detail which, under normal conditions, would be recorded on your film. Surprisingly, there are many ways of dealing with this kind of problem.

Contre jour

The easiest way to suppress detail and to simplify the composition is to take pictures against the light (*contre jour*). In extreme cases you will get black silhouettes set off against a white background. These always look striking, but are generally no more than an eye-catcher. But if you use this kind of lighting with a bit of moderation, the resulting photographs can look much more interesting – for example illustration 69. This

photograph has not been manipulated in any way. It is a straight enlargement on grade three paper from a normally developed 400 ASA film. Nevertheless, the grey-scale of the subject has been reduced to three values which symbolise the different distances between the parts of the subject and the camera (and with that, to the viewer). In a 'normal' rendering this photograph would just have shown a confusing mass of trees, and I can think of no other photographic way of showing the order in an apparently disordered subject like this.

But for other purposes there are other ways to make use of backlight. One of these is shown in illustration 70. Backlight creates long and heavy shadows, which can easily be employed as an interesting and intriguing part of the composition. This nude, photographed on Fuerteventura in the Canary Islands, had been placed on a slope of sand which was bordered by an outcrop of very dark rocks. This provides an interesting composition as diagram 70a shows. The shadow under the body has the shape of an arrow-head, thus giving a basic upward movement to the composition. This is further enhanced by the 'S'-form of the body itself. But the whole movement is checked by the almost black wedges of rock on the left and the right.

Each time I see this picture, I cannot resist the temptation to associate the form of the irregular shadow thrown by the body with that of a fluttering cape, which of course enhances the impression of movement even more. But apart from these fanciful touches it is easy to see that the shape of the shadows and the direction in which they fall are really the most important single contribution to the overall effect of the photograph – not only because of the formal configuration described above, which provides us with the framework of motion, but also because the relatively big dark or even black areas of shadow make for a bold and simplified image.

These are only three examples of ways in which light and shadow can be used for the composition of photographs. It really is a great pity that so many photographers are content to value lighting only according to its brightness. That is, they are satisfied if there is enough light to take a photograph and consequently they do not see the value of the quality of the light (and the shadows), which after all is much more important for the effectiveness of the photograph.

When taking pictures you should always try to understand the relationship of the lighting and its associated shadows to the subject, because very often you can solve compositional problems or add to the effectiveness of your photograph by waiting for the light to change. This, of course, is quite difficult

70

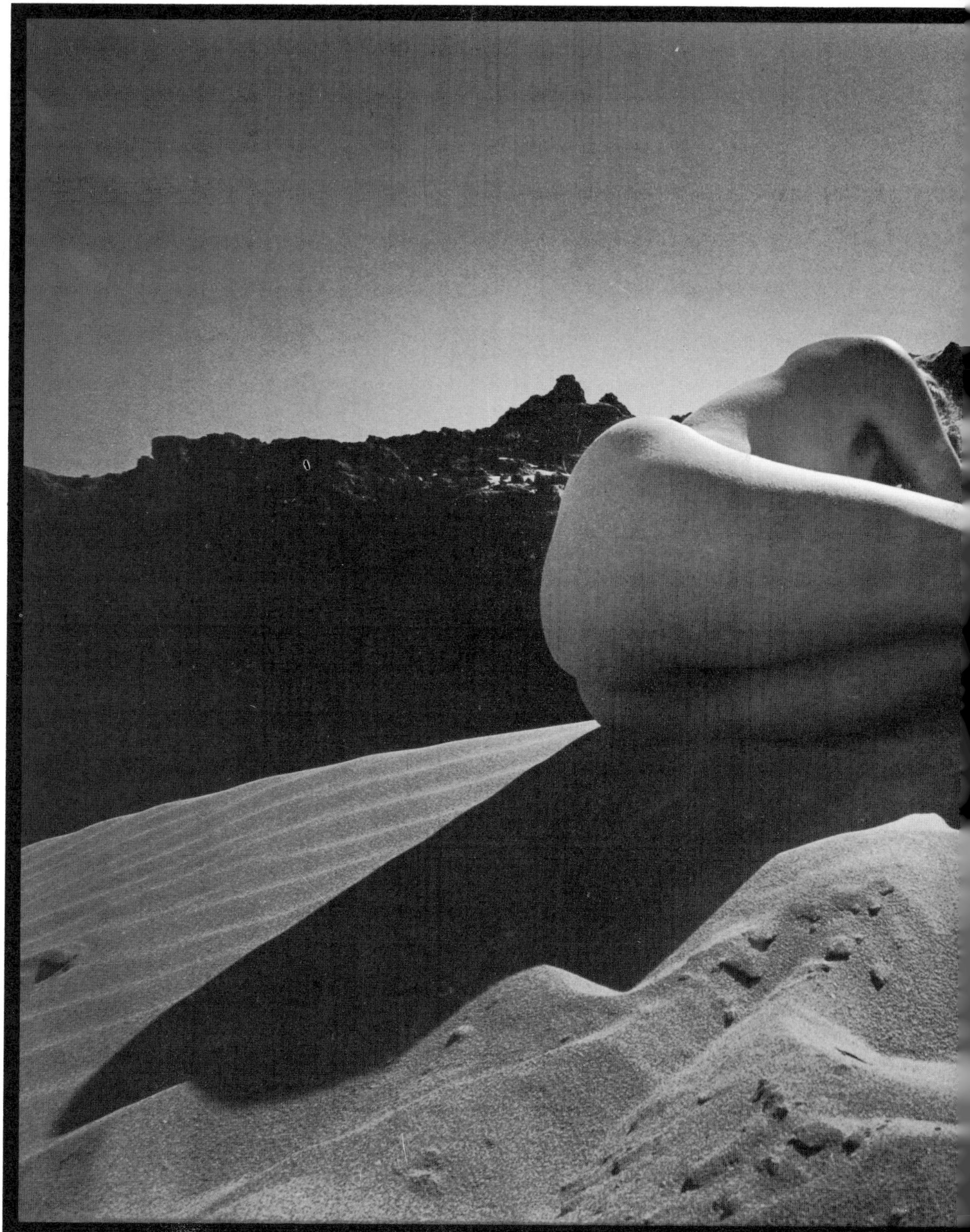

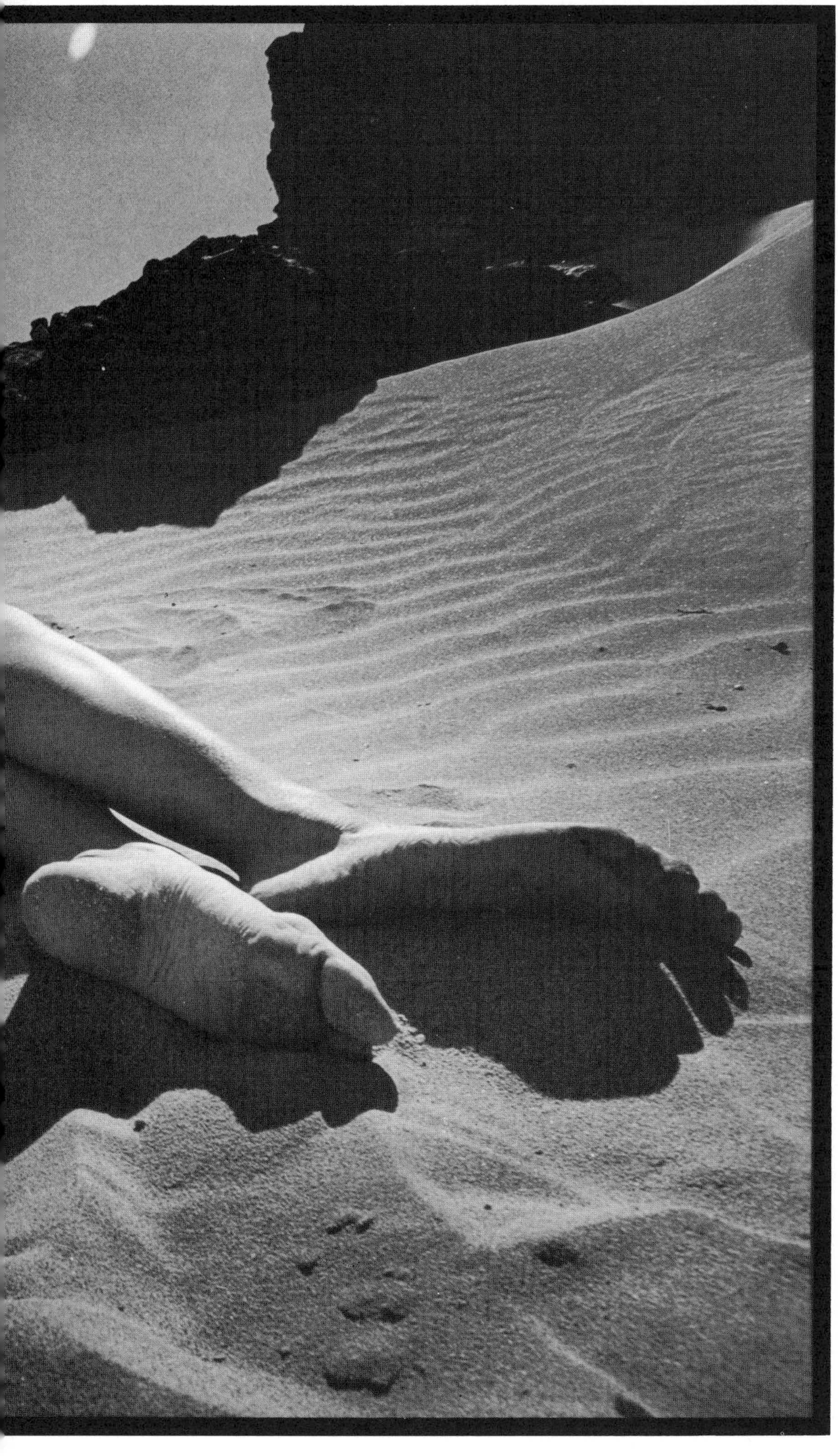

If done conventionally, the nude offers little scope for original composition. For example, contre jour light is normally used in order to stress the outlines of the body. Here the main purpose was to emphasise the shadow thrown by the body, which is a very important feature of the composition (see 70a next page.)

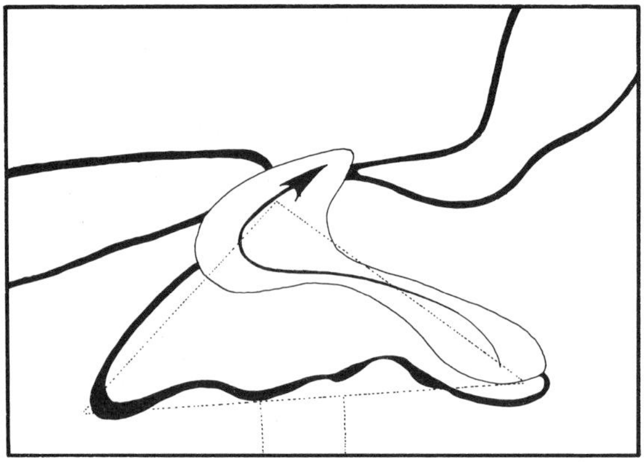

70a

The importance of the shadow in 70 (previous page) is clearly shown. It is the basis for the upward thrust of the compositional movement.

to do, because you must be able to visualise how your subject will look under different lighting conditions. Careful comparisons of enlargements of the same subject taken under different lighting conditions will show what worked and will give you clues for future work. (You might want to refer to Chapter 7 and the discussion of the effect of different lighting conditions on a single subject.) I introduced the question of lighting here because it offers a way of suppressing unwanted detail in the subject. There are other possible ways of doing this which I will discuss next.

Snow and fog

Snow and fog not only offer lots of interesting subjects in themselves, they also work as great simplifiers. They reduce otherwise complicated and perhaps formally confusing landscapes to simple lines and planes in a limited range of greys or colours, thus making it possible to photograph subjects which otherwise might pose insoluble photographic problems.

If, however, you want to use meteorological conditions such as these in your compositions, you should add a great deal of patience to your photographic equipment – or else you just have to depend on luck. For example, to get illustration 71 I had to wait more than two years until exactly the right amount of fog came together with adequate lighting conditions. Fortunately this subject is close to my home, giving me the opportunity to go and try for a picture every time we had fog or a thick haze. You can see that the fog divided the different objects into three well defined planes by assigning each of them a separate section of the grey scale according to their distance from the camera. In addition, the last plane, which forms the background, slowly dissolves into a featureless light grey on the right-hand side of the picture, thus adding a slight amount of depth to the otherwise backdrop-like appearance of the composition. It should be obvious that this kind of photograph could never be taken without the fog – and that is why I regard it as a 'compositional aid'.

When using fog in your pictures you are not entirely dependent on nature, because you can influence the effect of the fog to some degree by the choice of lenses of different focal lengths. The next photograph (72) was taken at the same time and at almost the same place as 71, but I used another lens for it – a 100 mm lens on a 35 mm camera for the first photograph and a 17 mm lens for the second one. If you compare these two photographs, you will find that their impact on the viewer is quite different, although both show the same kind of subject photographed under the same meteorological conditions. Technically, this difference is caused by the lenses. If you use a long focal length lens, the distance to your subject is usually much bigger, compared to the use of a wide-angle lens. As a result there is a greater quantity of fog between the camera and the subject when you photograph with a long focal length lens. This in turn leads to the conclusion that you can enhance the fog-effect with long focal lengths and diminish it with short ones. In addition to this the backdrop-effect is strongly pronounced by the use of longer focal length lenses, while the use of wide-angle lenses leads to a gradual merging of grey values (or colours), which gives an entirely different impact to the photograph.

All these nuances can, and should, be employed as a means of composition when aiming to give a definite mood and/or meaning to your photograph. By your choice of lens you can enhance those properties of your subject which you want to stress, while suppressing others. Accordingly you should never be satisfied with the obvious when you first meet a new subject; in my opinion a good photograph is even worth waiting a year or two for if you cannot get it in any other way.

This applies to winter photographs as well. Apart from the fact that the winter offers a variety of subjects in itself, it can, like fog, be used as an aid in composition. Snow and ice reduce the complexity of landscapes, while stressing their graphic and formal features. Photograph 73 is a case in point. It shows a subject which you would probably never look at twice if you saw it under normal conditions. But hidden behind its ordinary facade it has an underlying quality of order and tranquility which is brought out by the snow, because it eliminates everything superfluous and enables us to see directly what we could otherwise only guess at. I have not included a diagram for this photograph, because the reduction of the grey scale to an

71

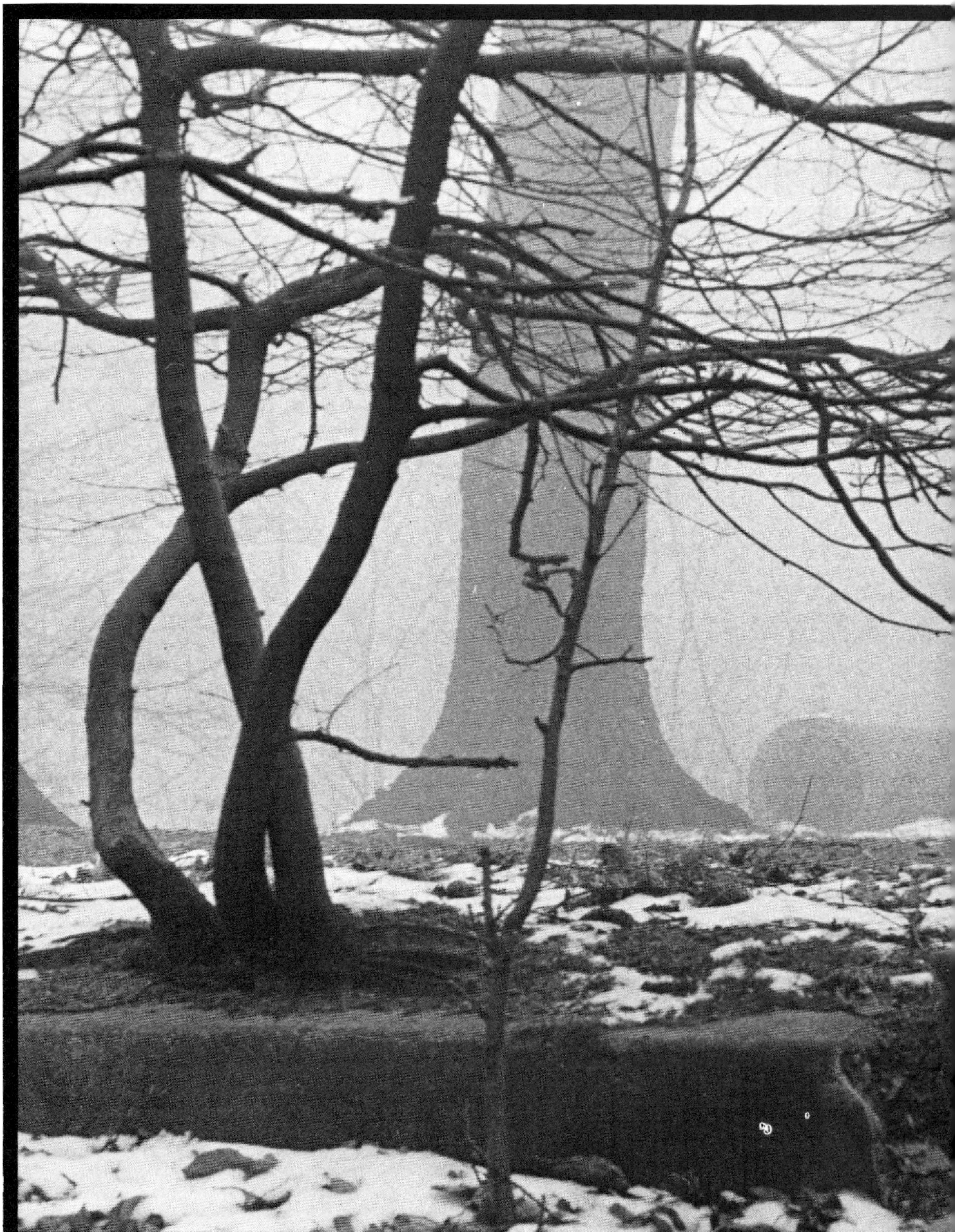

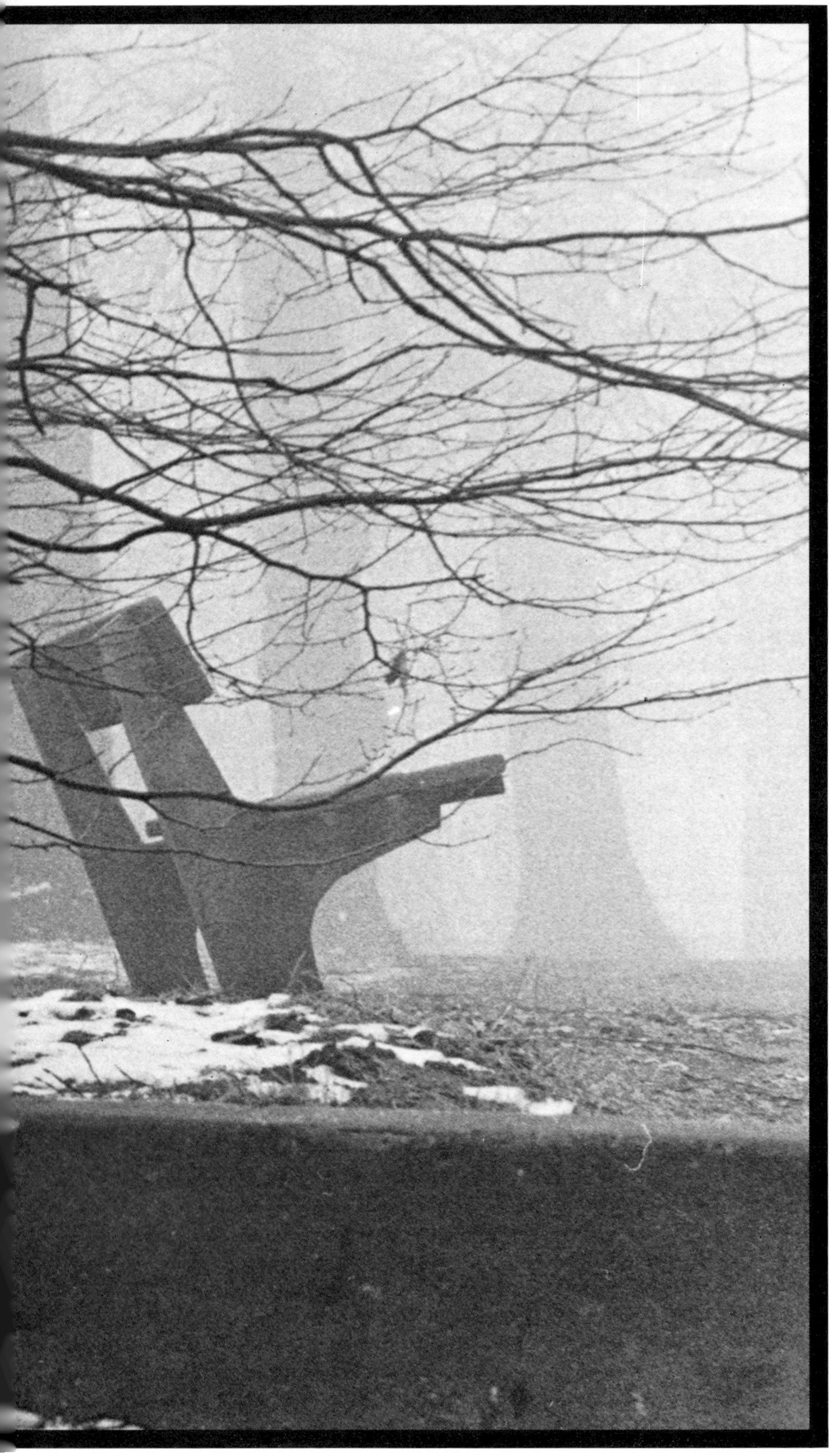

Fog can be regarded as a 'compositional' aid, because it can drastically change the formal properties of a subject, the most obvious of these being the separation of distances. The appearance of fog-covered distances can be influenced by the choice of focal lengths. Long focal lengths (100 mm lens in this case) usually mean greater photographing distances, so that there is more fog between camera and subject.

72

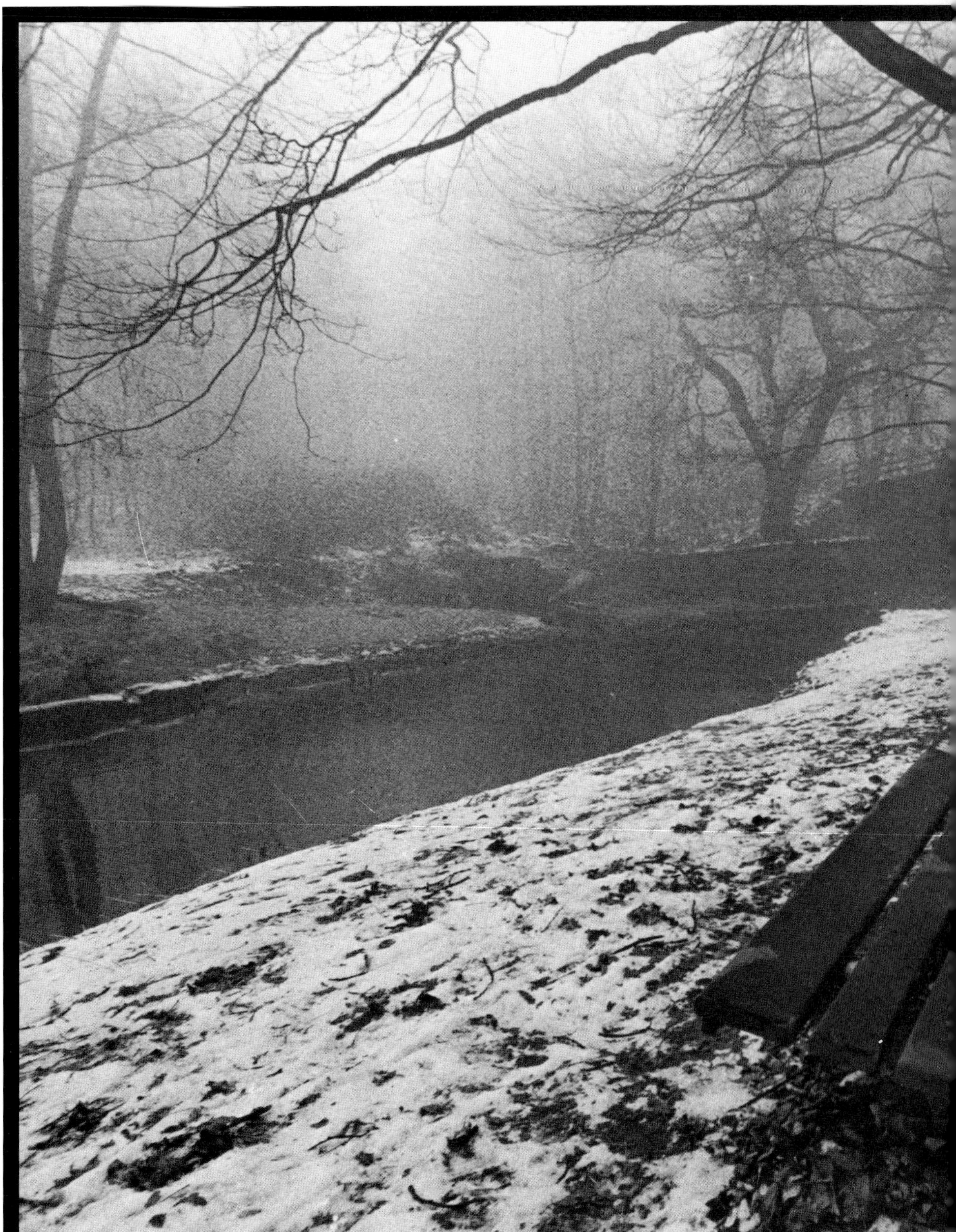

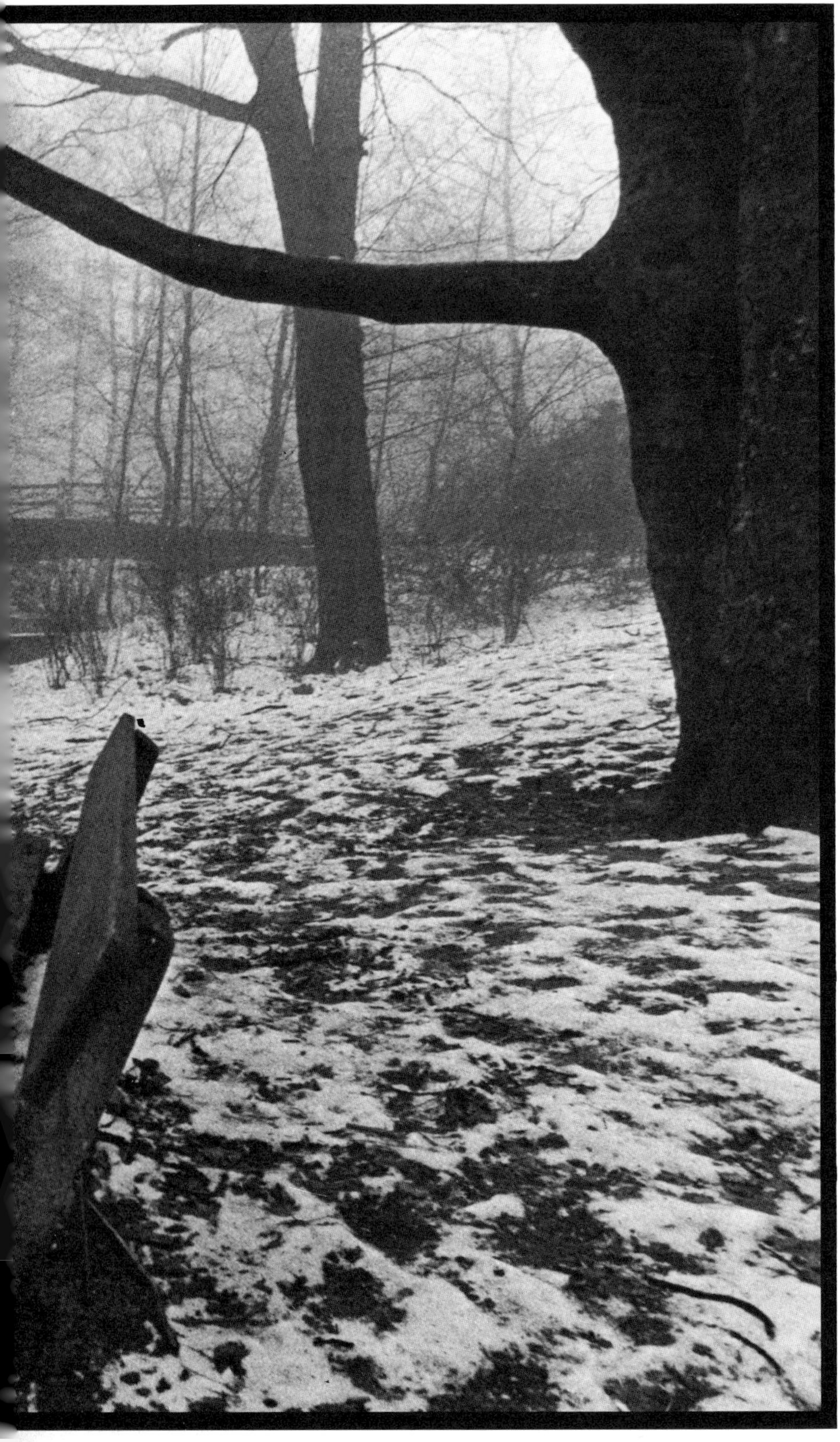

The use of a short focal length usually implies that you get very close to the main part of your subject, so they are less affected by the fog than the more distant objects. This allows you to adjust the impression of fogginess according to your compositional requirements.

73

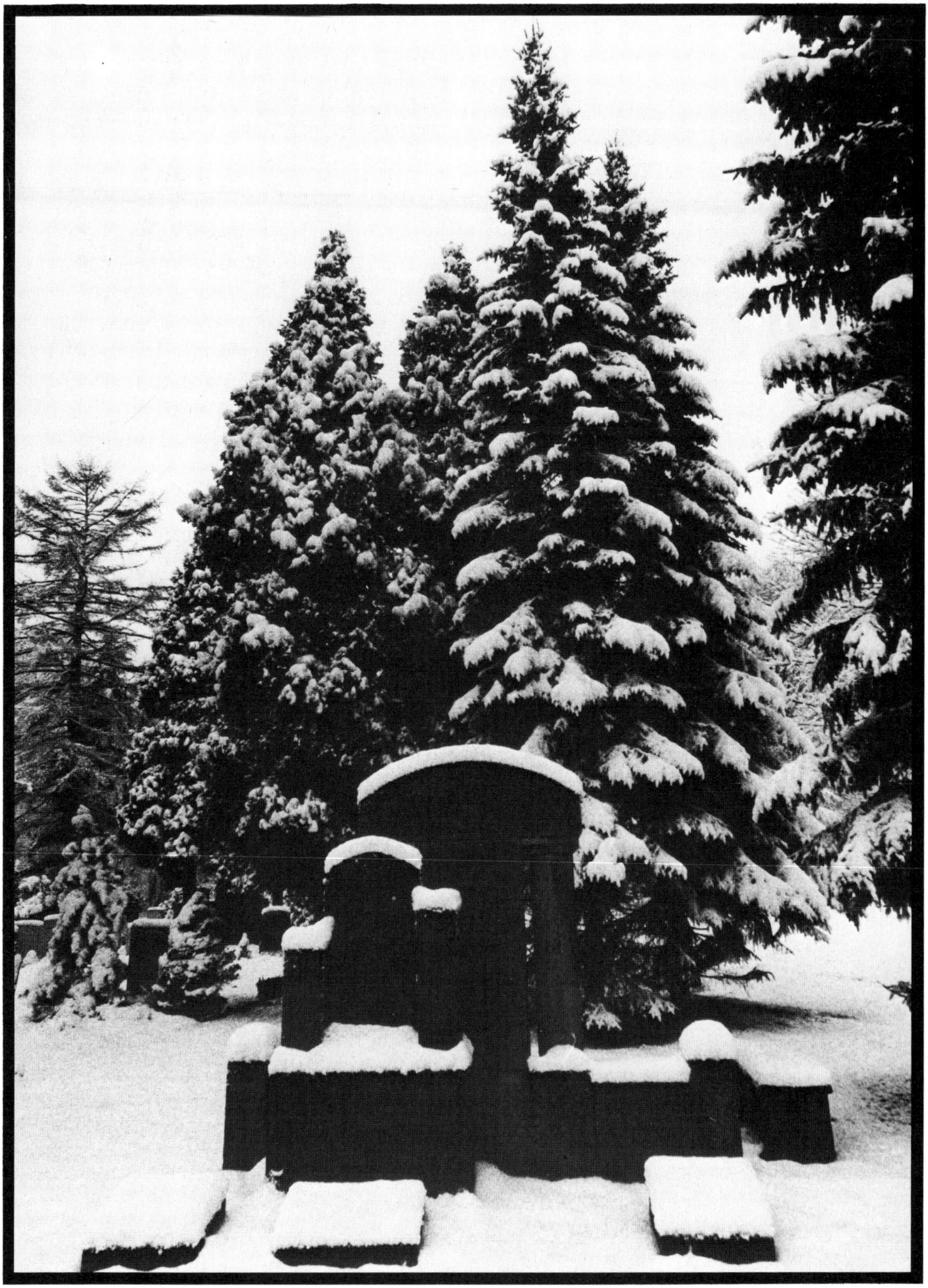

Snow is the great simplifier of nature. It reduces the amount of detail and the grey scale (or colour) of your scene, thus allowing you to arrive at simplified graphic pictures.

almost purely black-and-white contrast and the resulting clarity of the forms and lines gives the picture itself a diagram-like appearance. It is this immediate visibility of the underlying structure of a normally disordered subject which makes it interesting to the viewer.

The compositional possibilities shown in these examples should lead you to think about subjects long-term, at least as far as they are static and easily accessible to you. Compositions which you cannot realise now might be feasible later on – and even if you have nothing definite in mind, you should try different photographs of the same subject under different conditions, because it will sharpen your sensibility or feeling for the inherent photographic qualities of various things.

On the other hand, if you are one of the more impatient types, who cannot wait for nature to change, you might want to try one of the technical approaches which offer similar solutions to your photographic problems.

Graphic films

One of the most widely practised approaches to the simplification of compositions is the use of graphic films. If you want to work along these lines, you have two basic ways to realise your pictures. First, you can use orthochromatic films, with extremely hard gradation, directly in your camera while shooting your photographs. Second, you can take your pictures in the usual way and then copy them on to graphic films later in your darkroom.

It is easy to say which method you should use if you know exactly what you want to do and if you know the properties of the material you want to use – you should use graphic films on the spot. On the other hand, if you are not quite sure about your intentions (and if you like messing around in the darkroom) you should choose the second method.

But let me add a very personal point of view concerning the whole range of graphic experimentation in photography. To experiment this way is, in my opinion, no solution to bad photography. If you have a failed photograph there is no way in which you can improve it afterwards. If you have something to say, say it in the way which you think best, but never forget that the way to realise a really good photograph is a continuous one. That means that if you want the best possible results, each step in the process should be optimised according to your intentions and abilities. Practically speaking, it means that the negative which you make must be planned for the desired final result irrespective of the method you choose. (You will find

74

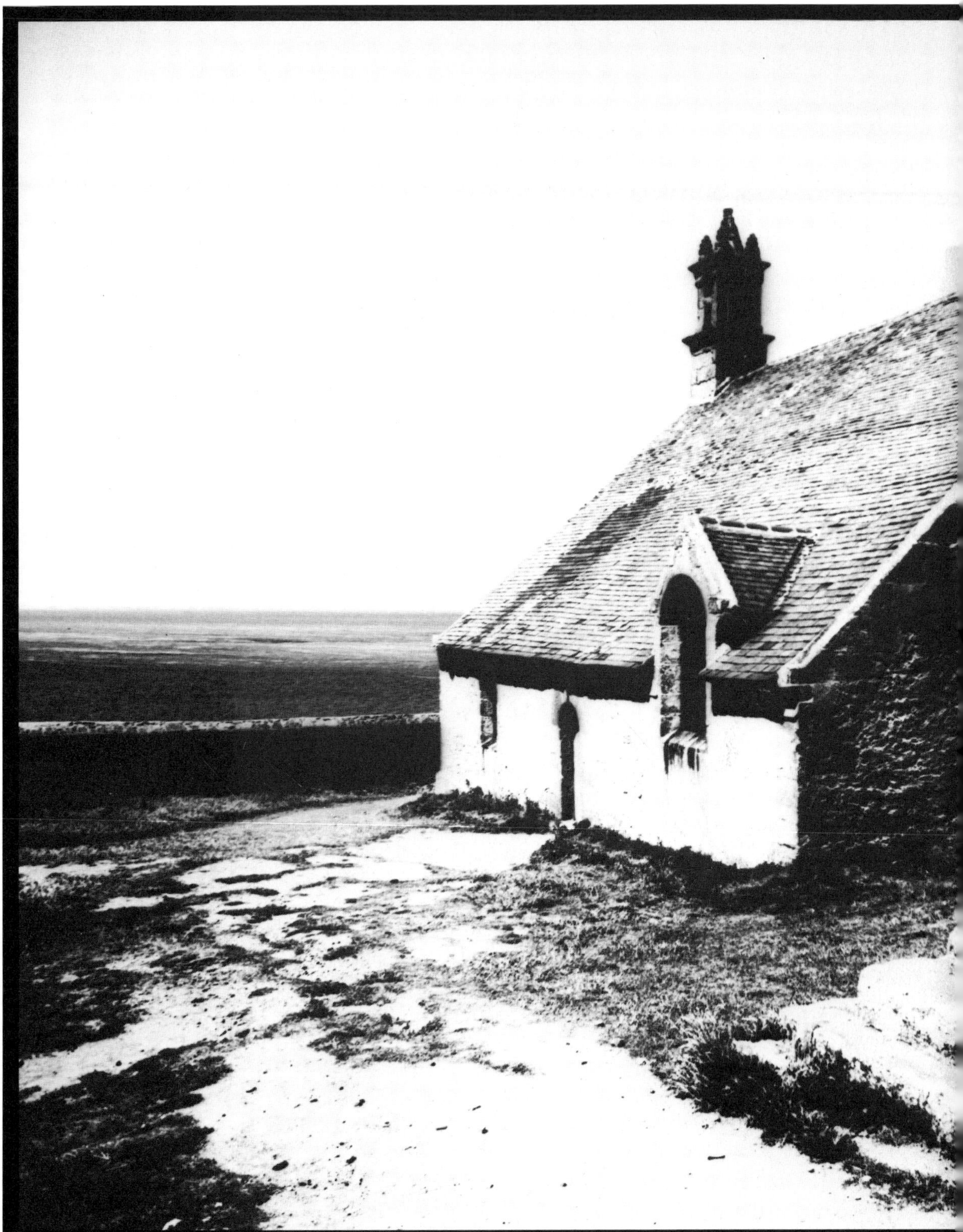

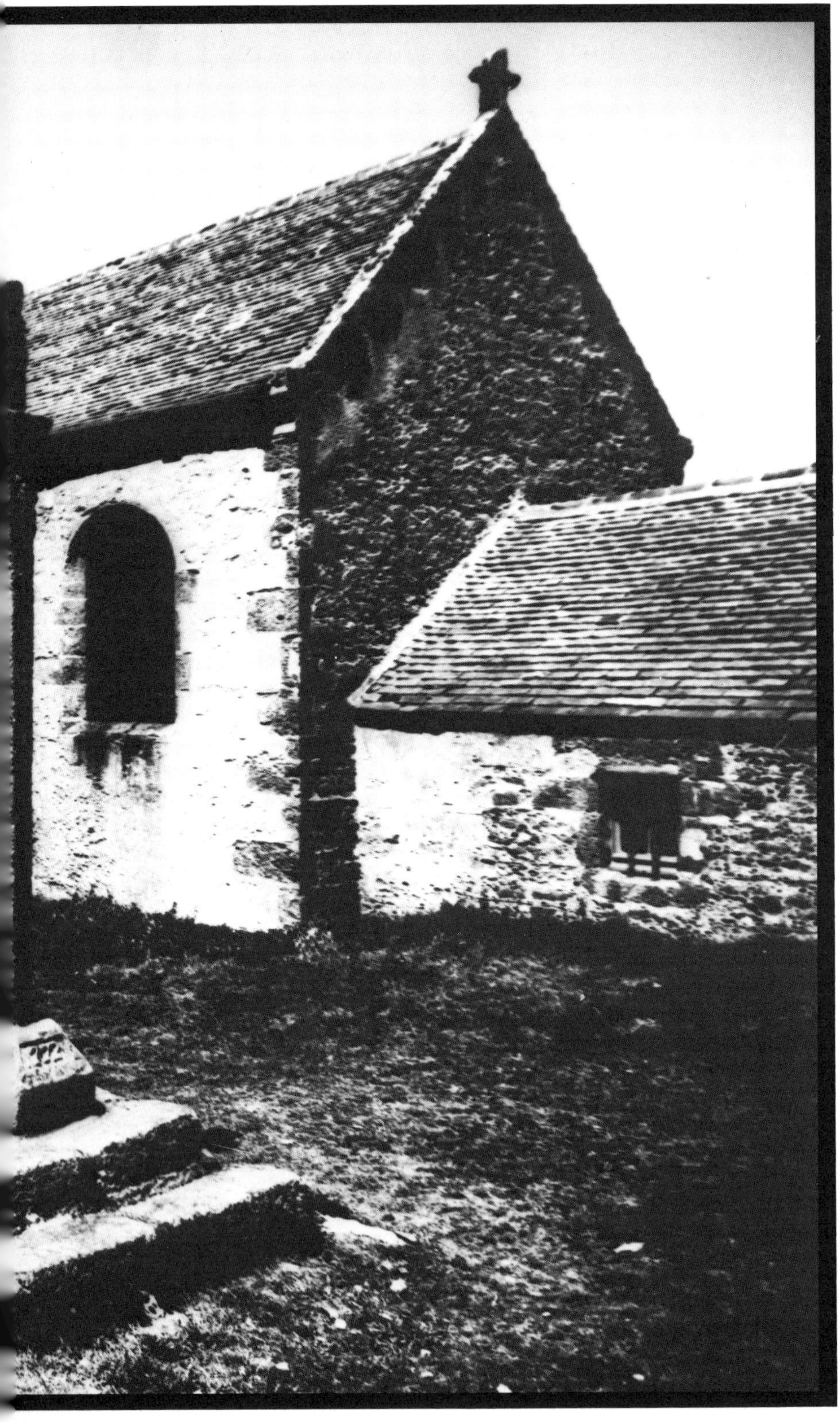

Apart from natural means of simplifying the composition of a picture (like snow and fog, 71–73) there are also some photographic ways of doing it. One is to use graphic films for subjects which would usually require a half-tone rendering, as here. I also took this French church on a high-speed film (next page) so that you can compare the different effects.

75

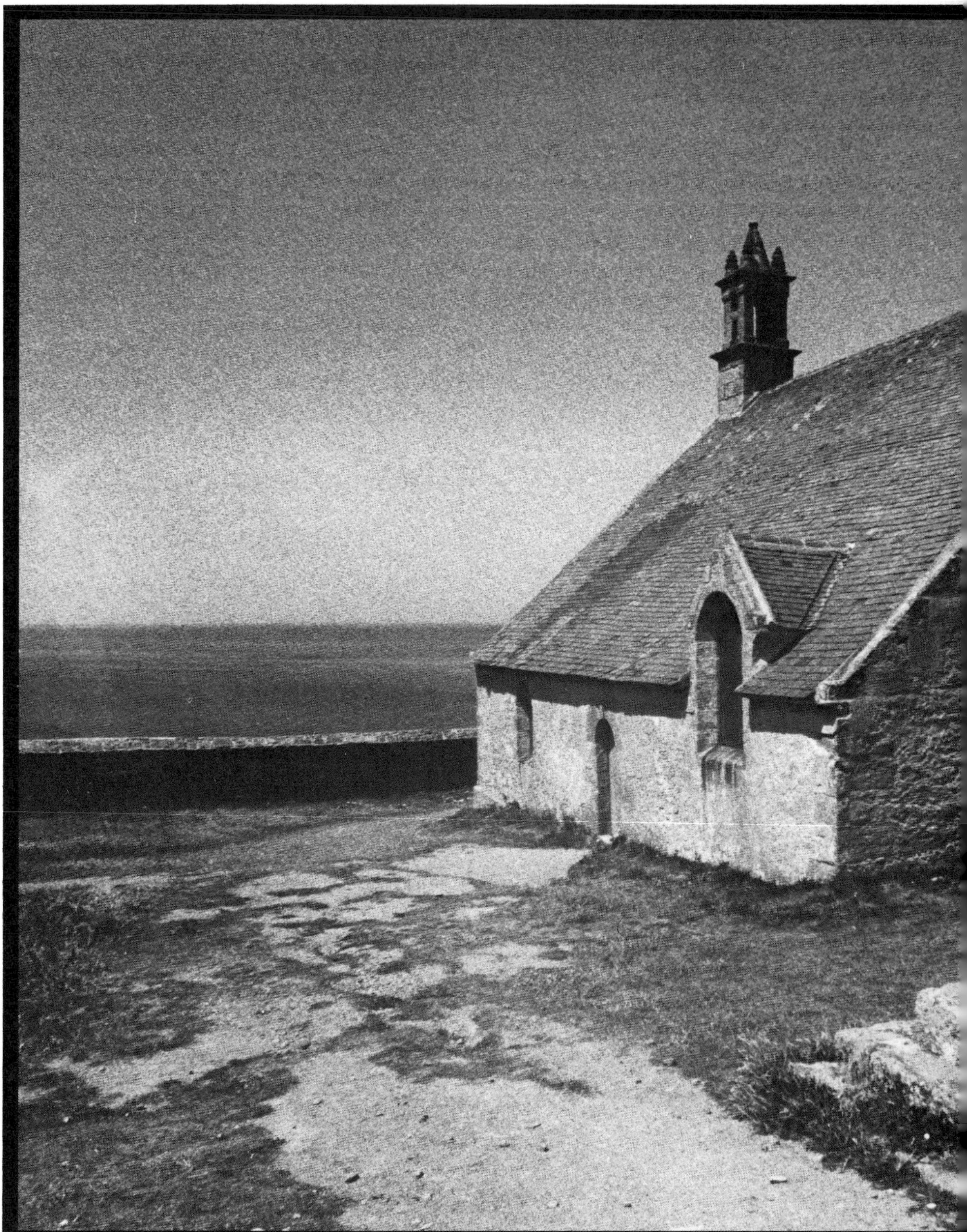

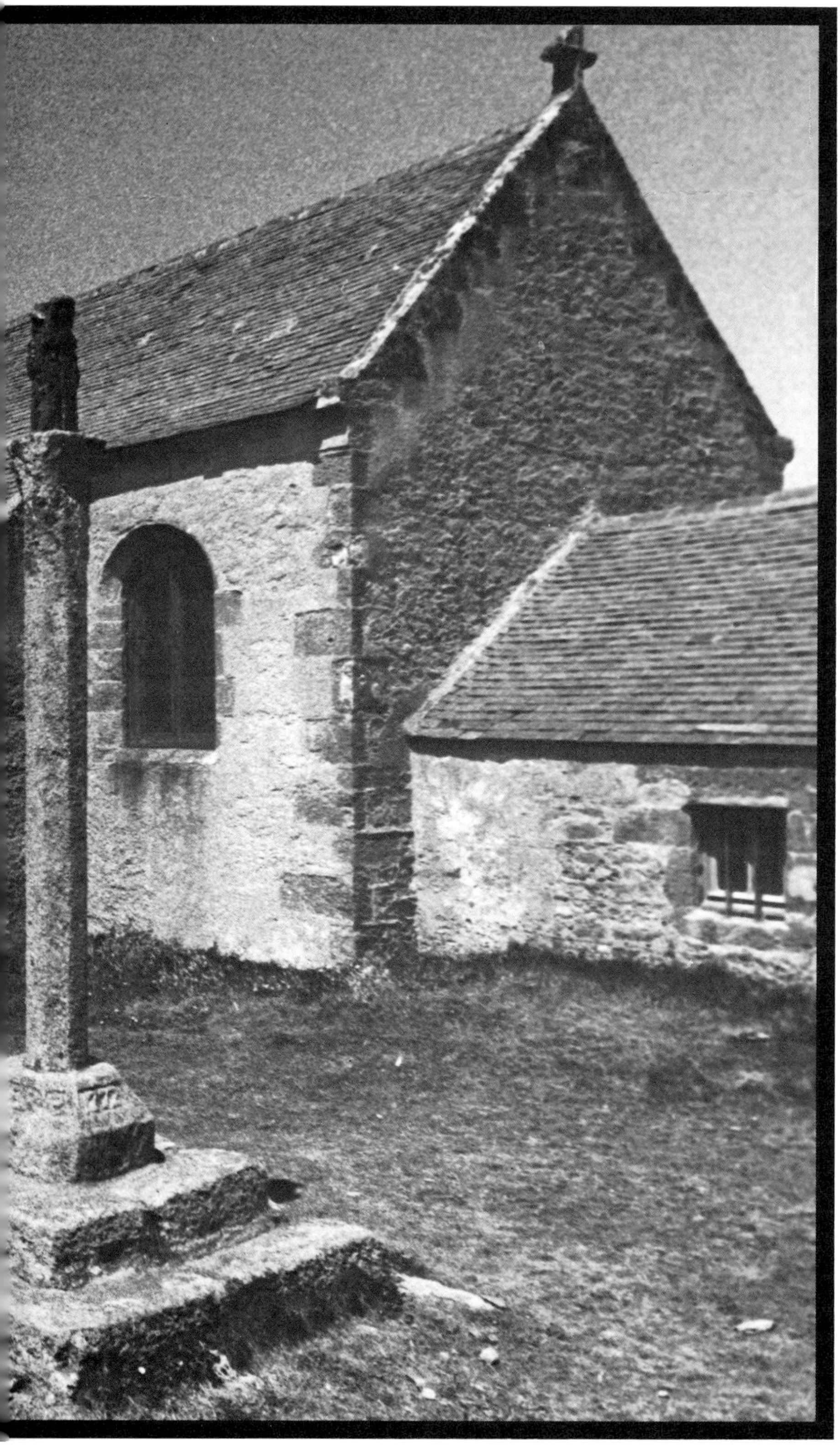

Compare this with 74. It is an example of the suppression of photographic detail by using a high-speed film (400 ASA). It is obvious that no detail smaller than the accumulation of grain can be shown. You can therefore influence the suppression of detail by developing the film for an increase or a reduction in the coarseness of the grain structure and by cropping.

some more thoughts on these questions in Chapter 13.) That is why I prefer the use of graphic films in the camera, when aiming for bold black-and-white compositions. I will explain the basic procedure for this kind of work, but if you want to know more about the practical side of the appropriate darkroom techniques you should refer to the available technical manuals, because here I am only concerned with exploring the compositional possibilities of the technique.

As examples of this kind of work I want to discuss two photographs of the same subject, a church in Brittany, France, which were taken at the same time, but which were realised with entirely different films (graphic film 'Agfa-Ortho-Professional' and normal 400 ASA film). The first photograph (*74*) was taken under fairly strong light with graphic film. You can see that the original grey scale of the subject has been reduced to broad expanses of almost purely black-and-white areas, giving a bold and simple image. In order to show what really happens to a subject if you treat it this way, I have included a similar shot of the same church, taken in the same light but recorded on 400 ASA film.

What is much more important than the actual technical differences of the rendering of the grey scale, is the different feeling or mood which is produced by employing these technical principles. The first picture, taken with graphic film, draws its impact from the overall structure of the subject. The different planes are partially dissolved into pure white, which gives the picture its 'eroded' look – and this word 'eroded' was the reason for my decision to use this kind of film on this subject.

As photograph 75 shows, the building is made of local stone and is overgrown with lichen and creepers so that it blends naturally with its surroundings. This impression is enhanced by the erosion of wind and water and century-long use. On the other hand it is, by its very existence, a defiance of the forces of nature and historically, in times of trouble, such buildings were used as sanctuaries by the people of the neighbourhood.

As I saw no way of combining these ideas into one picture I tried instead to separate them and came up with the two solutions shown here. The first one deals with the apparent contradictions in the building – between the aspect of erosion and the impression of strength and durability. The second one is more concerned with the unity between nature and the man-made structure. When I looked at it this way, the decision to use the special technique described above came quite naturally and the results seem to me to be equally convincing (although you, of course, might have a definite preference).

If we return to our starting point, you will now understand why I stated that the decision to make use of this kind of technique results in a composition with special properties, which should be used in accordance with your intentions.

I would, however, like to give you some advice on the use of graphic films, because your influence on the rendering of the subject is much greater than you might at first suppose. The separation of tones into pure blacks and whites is not automatic. It depends on two factors, which you can at least partially control. The first one is the exposure time chosen (meaning the assumed speed of the film) and the second one is the lighting. If you shoot in very strong light you will get results whose overall-appearance will resemble that of illustration 74, that is, a juxtaposition of broad expanses of black and white. If you look more closely at this photograph, you will see that the rendering of detail is entirely different in the shadow-areas (for example the gable-ends of the building). This shows that you will get more detail and smaller areas of black and white in diffuse lighting instead of the bolder and more graphic division of the picture-plane in direct light. As indicated by the illustration, you can to some degree combine both effects in one picture by the choice of the right exposure time. (A few experiments with one or two films will show you what can be done much better than any rules or tables which I could prepare for you.) All this offers a great variety of ways in which to realise your ideas and allows you to choose with accuracy the right amount of abstraction which you need for the purposes of your composition.

Everything we have discussed so far in connection with these films also applies to all other photographic tricks and special techniques. Whatever you do, whether you choose a special lens, use an unusual film or employ any other of the endless possibilities for achieving photographic effects, it always has a direct influence on the composition of your photograph. You should be sure to remember this in order to make the most of your work.

Creating your own subjects

If, however, none of these possibilities appeals to you, you are not necessarily out of business. If everything else fails, you can at least make your own subject matter, which leaves you every imaginable freedom to create the composition of your photograph exactly as you want it. This is the practice in studio photography, especially still-life photography, where you can

(and should) arrange everything down to the last detail, including, of course, the lighting.

But you are not necessarily stuck indoors if you want to arrange your subject matter yourself – it can even be done in landscape photography. To show you what I mean, the last two photographs in this chapter are from a series on which I have been working for about three years. I will not go into great detail, but it is a very particular art form, combining both the landscape and *objets trouvé* which interest me. The point which concerns us here is that the main feature of photographs 76 and 77 is the sculpture which has been especially made to be photographed, at the same time bearing in mind the compositional possibilities of the photographic process. The size of the structures depicted is a good example of what I have done. It is nothing that the viewer could possibly know or recognise, that is why he must guess the size guided only by his experience of and with photographic representation.

The dissatisfied photographer has a last resort: he can make his own subjects, even in landscape photography. This peculiar combination of *object trouvé* and landscape probably shows the compositional possibilities of viewpoint and focal length better than a 'natural' subject would, because the actual properties of the object depicted are unknown to the viewer. He must rely on compositional information in order to guess at size and proportions.

In fact, the real size of the structures depicted is between 8 and 10 inches (20 and 25 cm), but most viewers instinctively believe them to be much bigger. This is the result of the judicious application of some compositional conventions. First, extreme wide-angle lenses (mainly 17 mm) were used in order to exaggerate the size of the foreground (see Chapter 5). Second, the viewpoint was close to the ground, giving the kind of view which is generally associated with much bigger structures, and third, the 'objects' themselves were designed to look as monumental as possible. These elements of the composition combine to give an overall impression to the viewer which depends more on the compositional elements than on the real properties of the subject – and so this extreme case throws some light on a photographic principle: To compose or make a composition means to create a picture, or – in the terminology of J. R. R. Tolkien – a photograph is a product of subcreation by virtue of its composition.

Summary

In this chapter I have used very different photographic examples to show how you can extend the range of what is usually done in photography and so achieve really original work. Apart from seeing some examples of what can be done and discussing how it was achieved, you should have learnt one thing: everything you do when taking pictures becomes part of the composition – and each detail of the composition, however small it may be, has its influence on the viewer of the photograph, be it on a conscious or subconscious level.

76

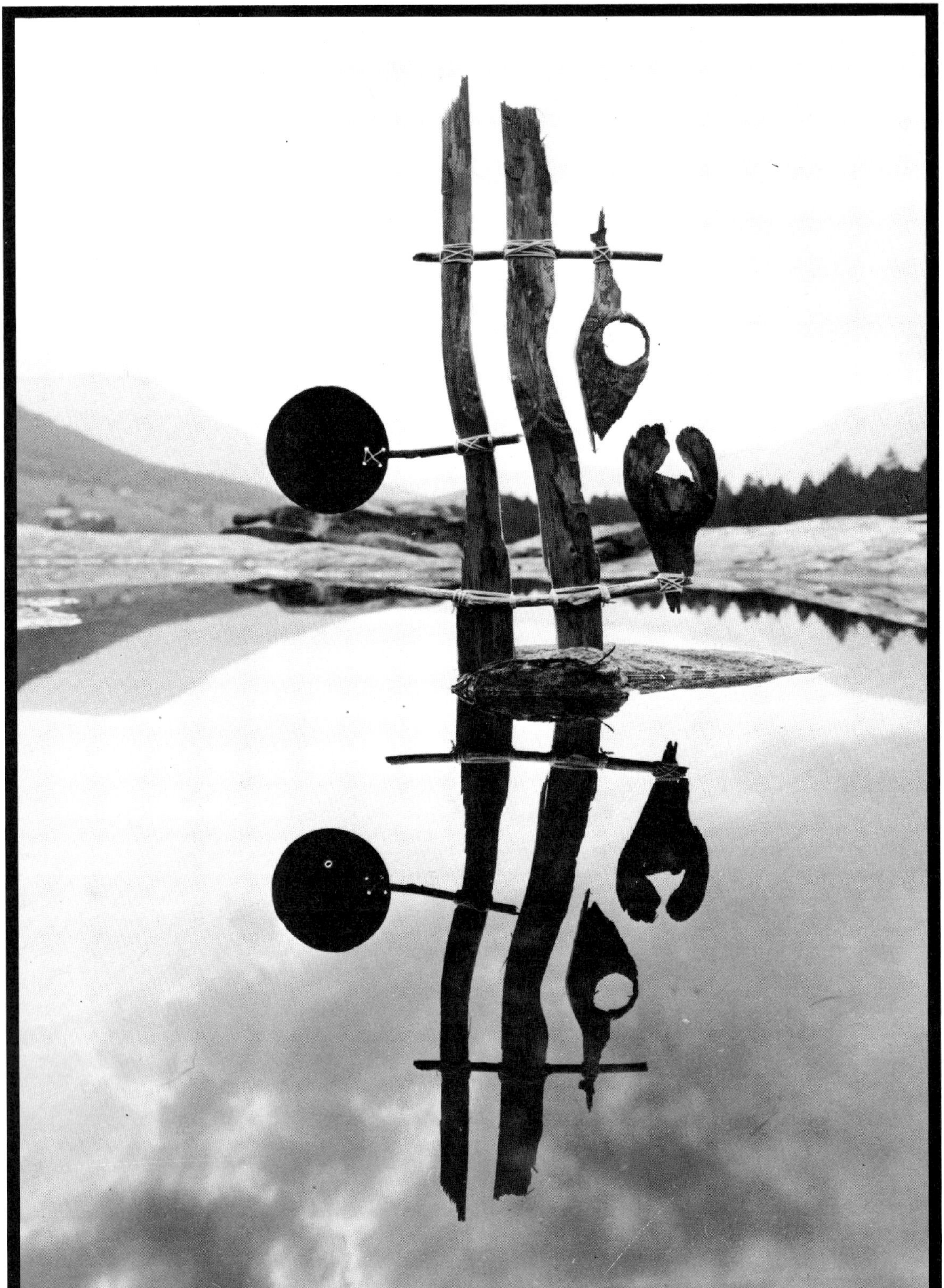

77

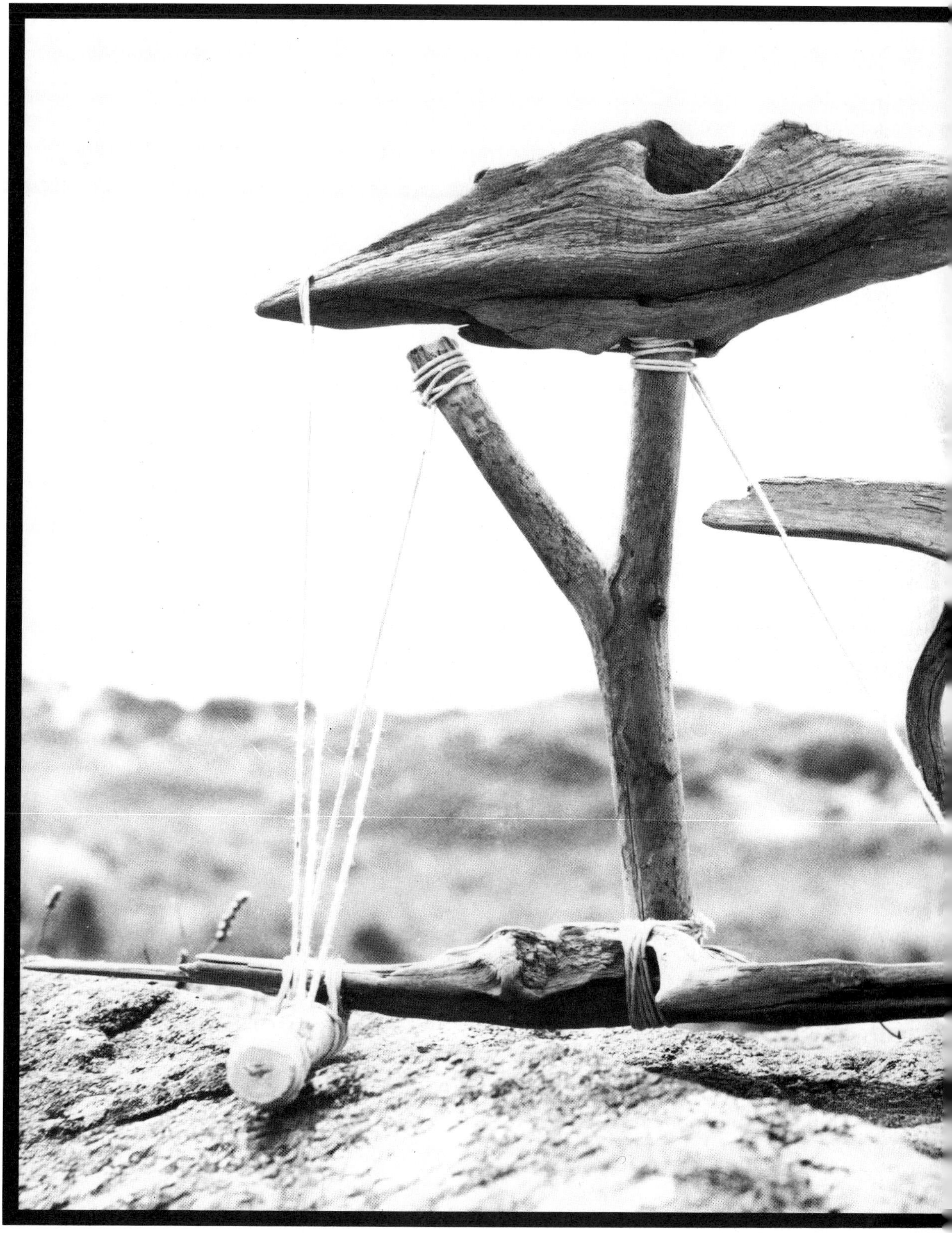

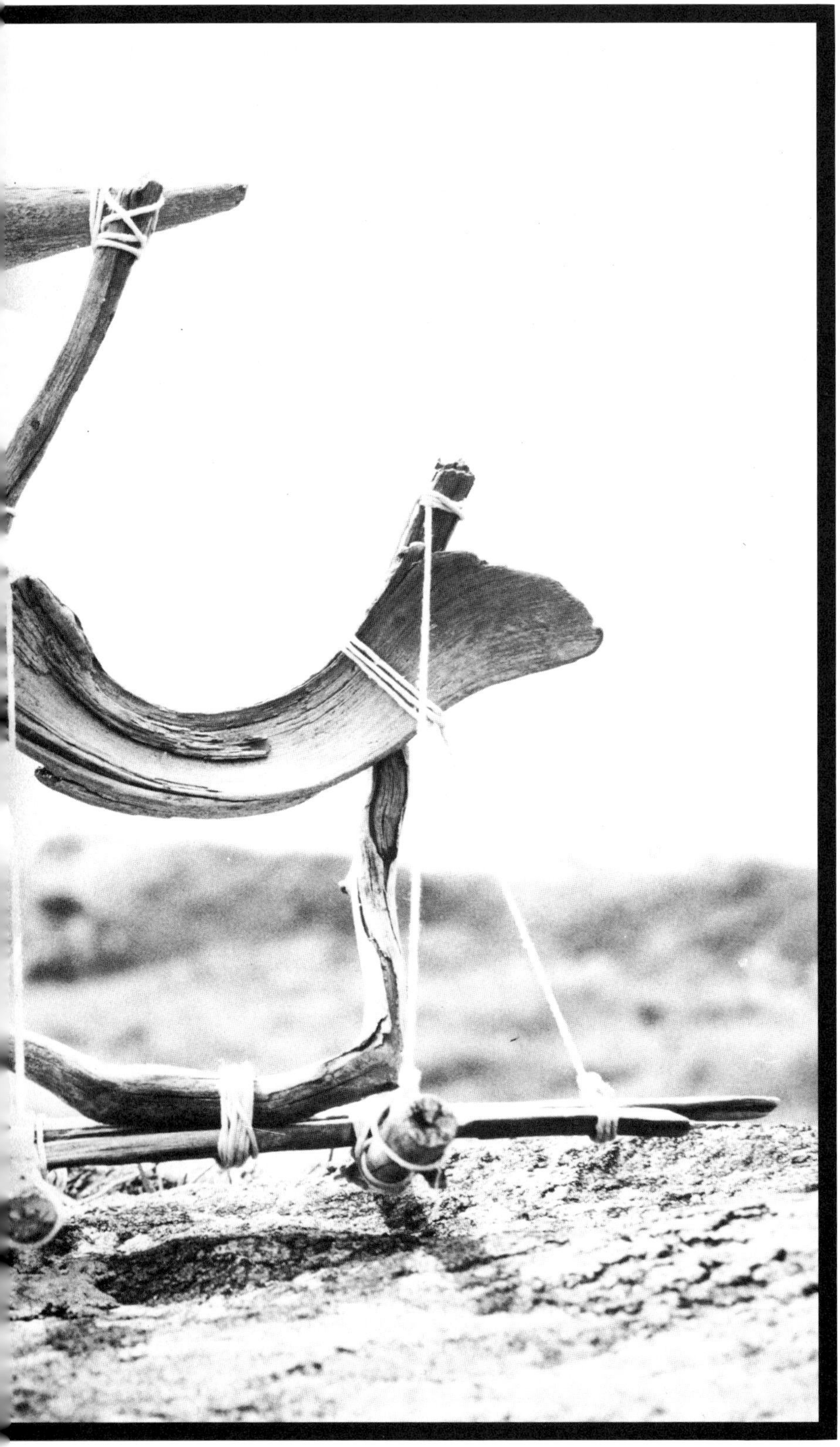

Another subject for which the viewer has no preconceived ideas or information, because it was made by the photographer. Again, the viewer must assess the composition strictly on its merits and without any foreknowledge of the subject.

This in turn leads to two consequences for you and your work. First, when you look at photographs, whether they are your own or not, and when you take pictures, you should never think about composition solely in terms of lines, planes, compositional movement, etc. Through the examples given in this part of the book and their interpretations I have tried to show the close connections and interrelationships between these formal aspects of composition and their meaning. If you have really grasped that the formal aspects of composition constitute the meaning of the photograph and that the compositional elements are nothing but the vocabulary and grammar of the photographic language, which you can and must use to express yourself or to realise your visions, then you are on the way to a real mastery of composition and all its elements.

The second consequence is that it is not enough to have a language and to know how to apply it. If you have nothing to say in the language all your exertions will be to no avail and learning about composition will not help you at all. You may feel that I could have said so earlier, but I have found that many people, once they have grasped the principle of the thing, have seen some examples of the possibilities open to them, and have mastered the intricacies of the photographic language, suddenly develop interesting ideas which they can express in their pictures.

11 Cropping

In newspaper-work and in all kinds of action- and life-photography it is often necessary to crop pictures when enlarging them. This is quite obviously so because in many situations getting the shot is more important than composing it. When this happens there is no other choice than to improve the photograph by cropping it. But in the kind of photography with which we are dealing in this book there is no excuse for cropping. Apart from two or three valid reasons for cropping which we will discuss in this chapter, it usually is nothing but an indication of sloppy technique and laziness when taking a photograph.

In 35 mm photography you have nothing to give away as far as the sharpness and graininess of your negatives are concerned and if you employ a bigger format you want to use all of it and not throw away the additional qualities gained by its use. So, if you find yourself needing to crop your negatives very often, you should check your picture-taking technique and your use of interchangeable lenses (see Chapter 5).

On the other hand you might resort to cropping because of one of the very few adequate and proper reasons. The first and most important of these is the choice of picture format. Although it is, in my opinion, perfectly possible to compose any subject matter in one of the formats provided by the camera manufacturers, there are many instances where you would like to have quite a different format. Photographs 79 and 80 show examples of this kind of choice. Both shots were taken on 35 mm film, but when I took them I already had in mind the very elongated format which I later used for the enlargement. If you are going to do something like that you should always keep in mind the desired format when taking the picture. If you do not do this carefully you will find more often than not that the enlargement does not work in the way you had intended.

On the other hand, if you do not want a picture format which is as out-of-the-way as these two, you should use, if at all possible, the film format which comes closest to your intentions.

In this context a word about the format of enlarging-papers seems necessary. Some people lament that the formats of

78

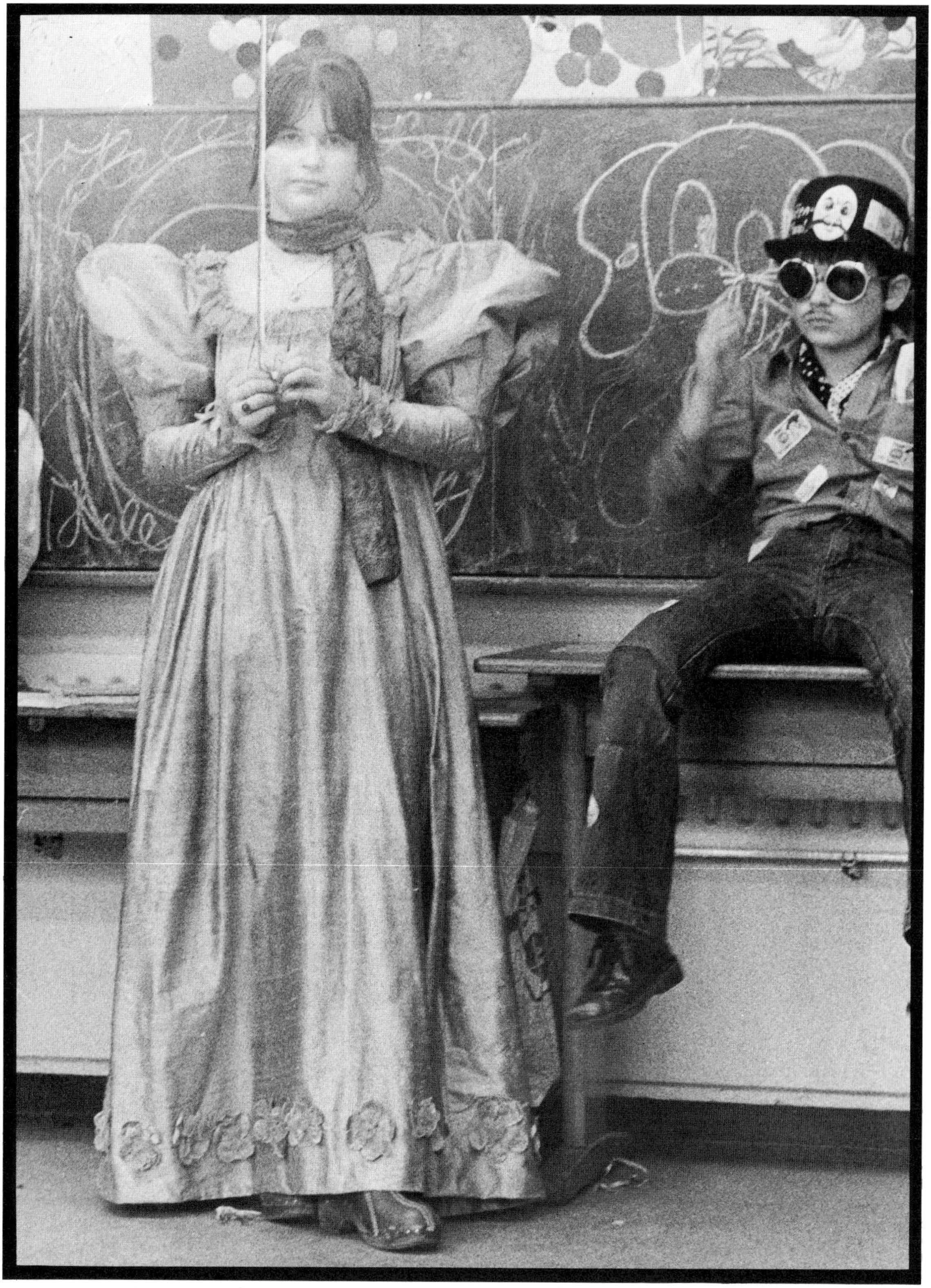

As far as their composition is concerned, snapshots are always very difficult to realise because usually there is no time to change the lens, the viewpoint or anything else. But experience will help you recognize the possibilities of a scene or an event immediately and make the best use of the technical means available. On the other hand, in order to preserve the spontaneity and casual air of the moment, a snapshot should not always look, or even be, as carefully composed as another photograph. The informal impression is enhanced here by the way the picture frame cuts off parts of the people shown.

enlarging-papers and films are different. In my opinion this is unimportant. I never use the full sheet of paper anyway because I prefer to choose the exact size and format of the enlargement myself. I think that this is far too important a decision, from the point of view of the composition, for it to be left to chance, which in this case is represented by the manufactured sizes and formats.

Of course you may not necessarily agree with me on this, but I strongly advise you at least to think about it carefully. Photographic paper is not very expensive and there really is no reason to develop a phobia which forces you to use every available square inch of your paper. Contrary to the conditions concerning the use of negatives, there is no technical reason for sticking to the full size of the paper.

On the other hand everything can be done quite differently if you find a reason for doing so. Although it is generally desirable to use all, or at least as much as possible, of the negative, the reverse is equally possible and sometimes leads to the desired results. Illustrations 81 and 82 are examples of extreme enlargements using only very small portions of 35 mm negatives. The reason for these proceedings is, of course, that the grain is an integral part of the pictures. In the case of the sea gulls the grain provides some kind of transparency which enhances the impression of light and effortless motion. In the second photograph it strengthens the strangeness of the scene depicted.

If you want to make the grain part of your composition there are two easy ways to do so. First of all you can photograph your subject from a greater distance or you can use a lens of shorter focal length than you would normally choose. In both cases you should photograph on high-speed film (at least 400 ASA) and develop for the grain (how to do this is explained in most of the available darkroom manuals). If this is not possible, for example if you do not have a high-speed film or because you did not think about it when taking your picture, you can make a normal enlargement and re-photograph it on high-speed film, to cover only a part of the negative. (There are, of course, other ways to do this, but the method described here is the easiest if you only want to do it occasionally and without having to learn the necessary darkroom techniques.)

Regardless of the technique used, it is always advisable to shoot some frames where the subject is recorded in different scales, because it requires a lot of experience to know beforehand what size of grain you will get and which is most suitable for your intentions.

79

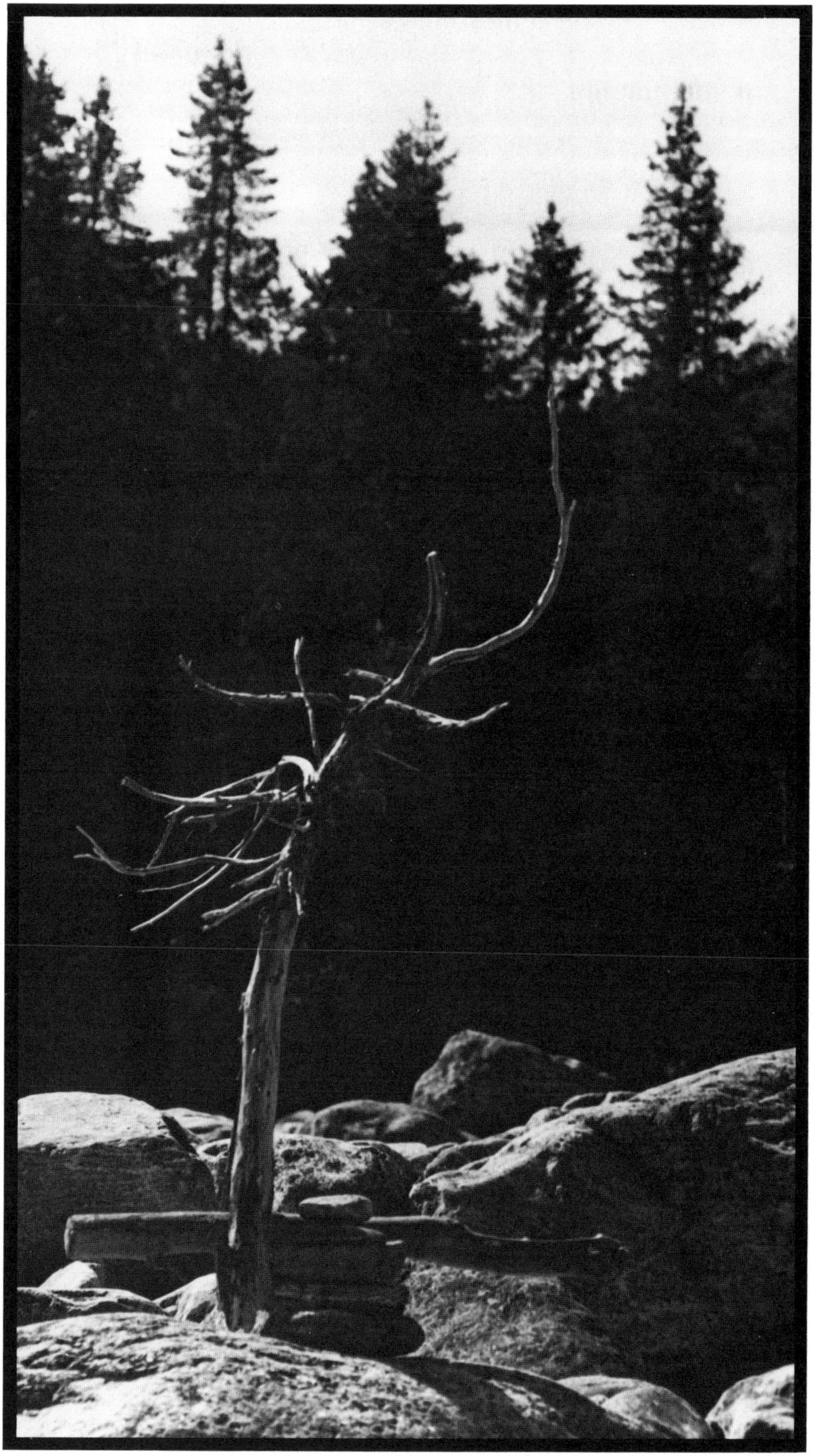

Left and opposite
Sometimes you will want to use unusual formats, either because the distribution of the compositional elements requires it (79) or because you want to crop the subject very closely (80). But you should really decide if you are going to do this before taking your picture in order not to lose too much definition and tonal value by excessive cropping.

80

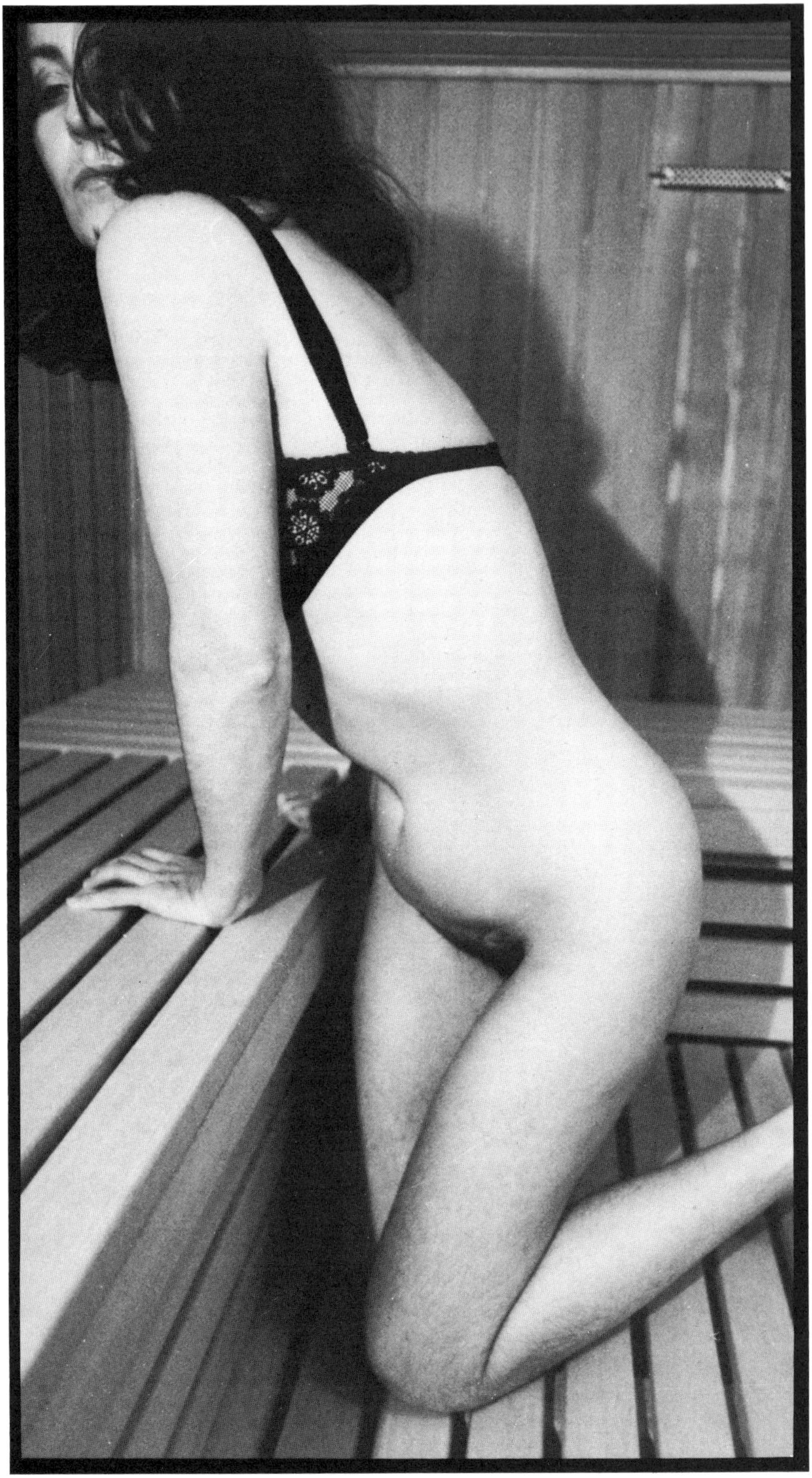

81

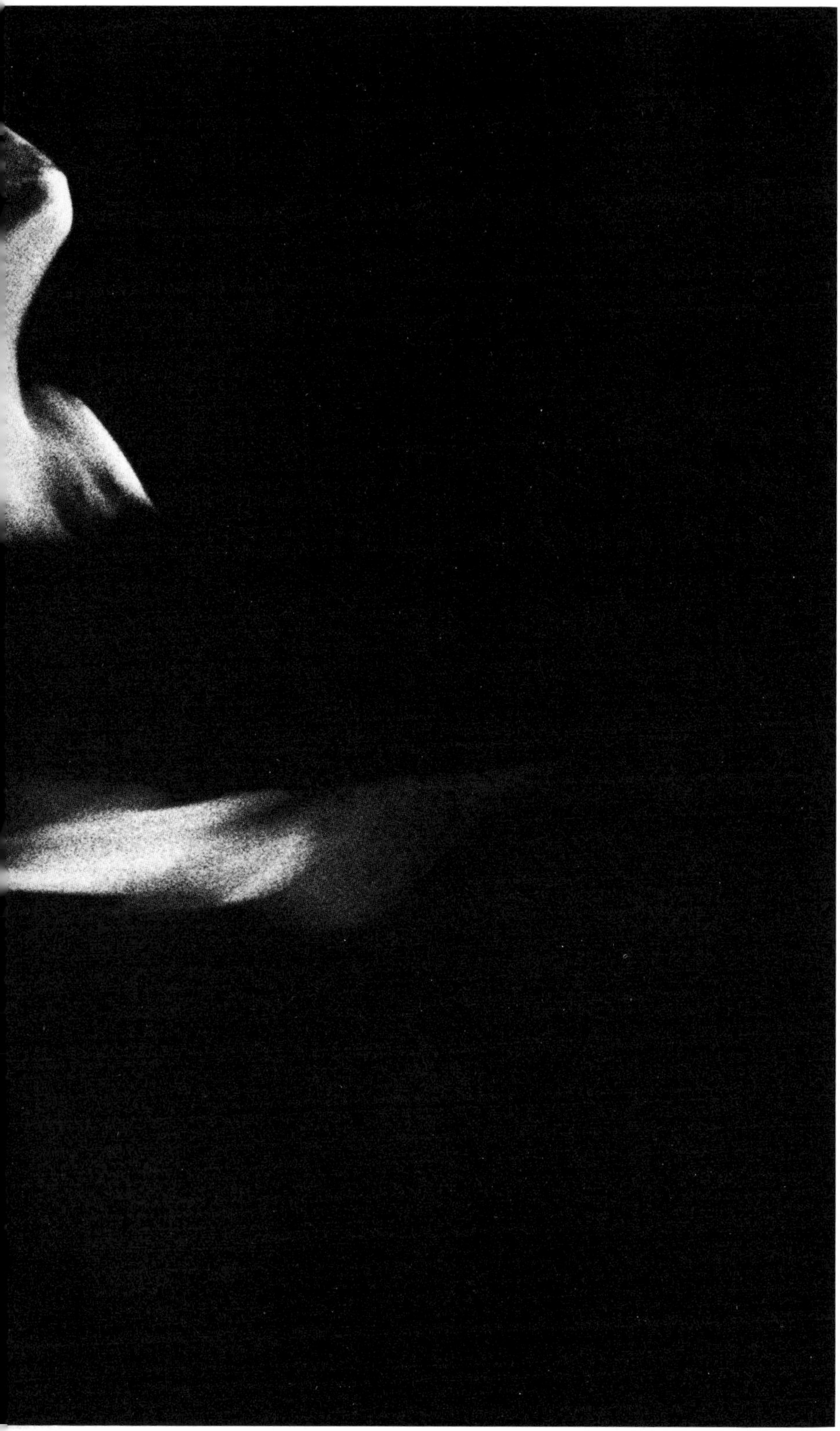

Left
Some subjects look best if they are made to look grainy. Apart from using high-speed film and developing it for grain, it will often be necessary to use only a small fraction of the negative. (For this picture I used less than a quarter of the 35 mm negative!) To make this possible, you will have to frame the scene accordingly, for example by using short focal lengths.

Overleaf left
An extreme example of cropping, using less than 1/8 of a 35 mm negative, so stressing the grain.

Overleaf right
The perspective rendering of an object depends on its placing in the picture frame. This is immediately apparent with wide-angle lenses. That is why very interesting perspective effects can be achieved by enlarging only part of a negative. (Compare with 15 which uses the whole of the negative.)

82

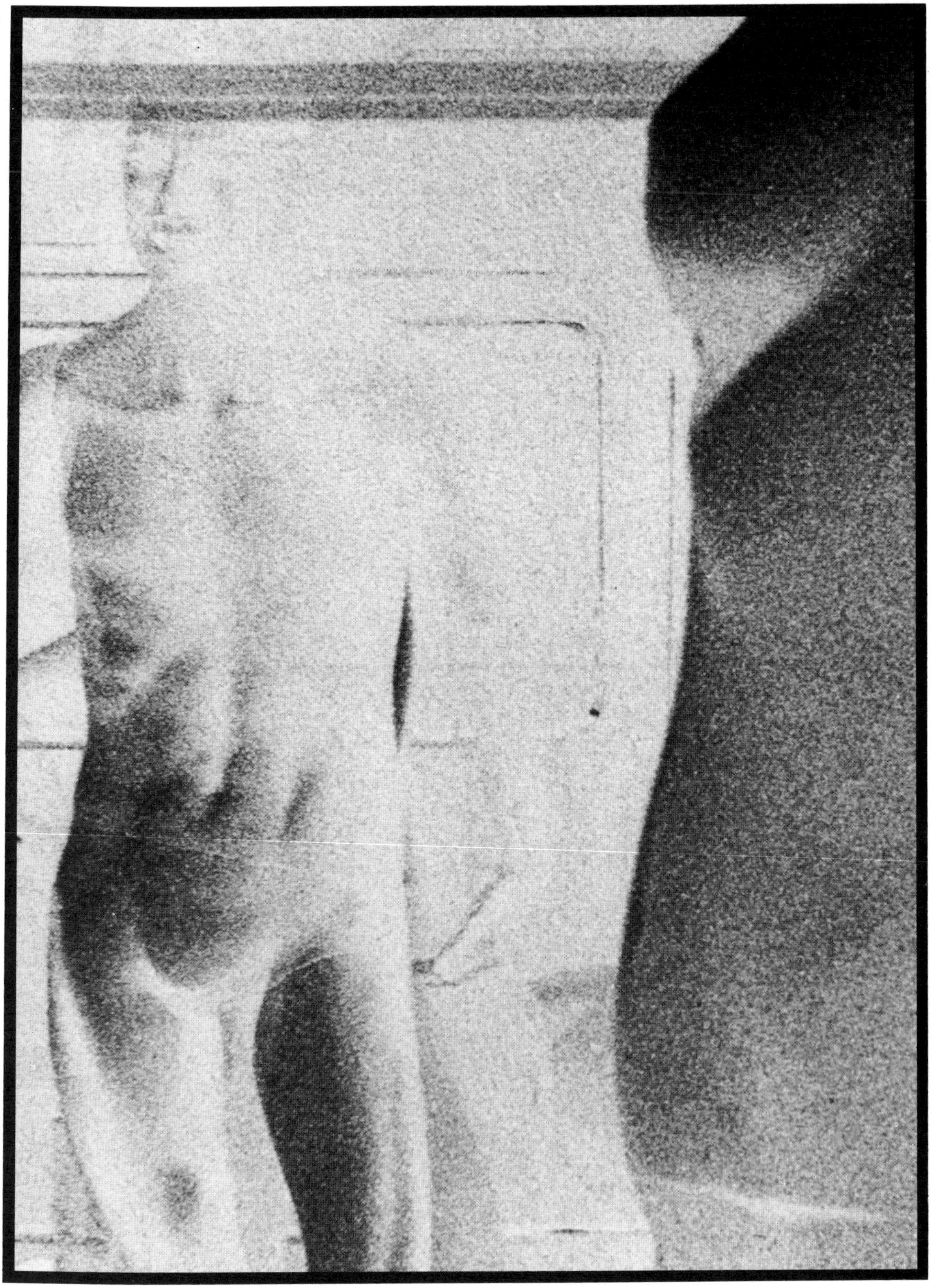

83

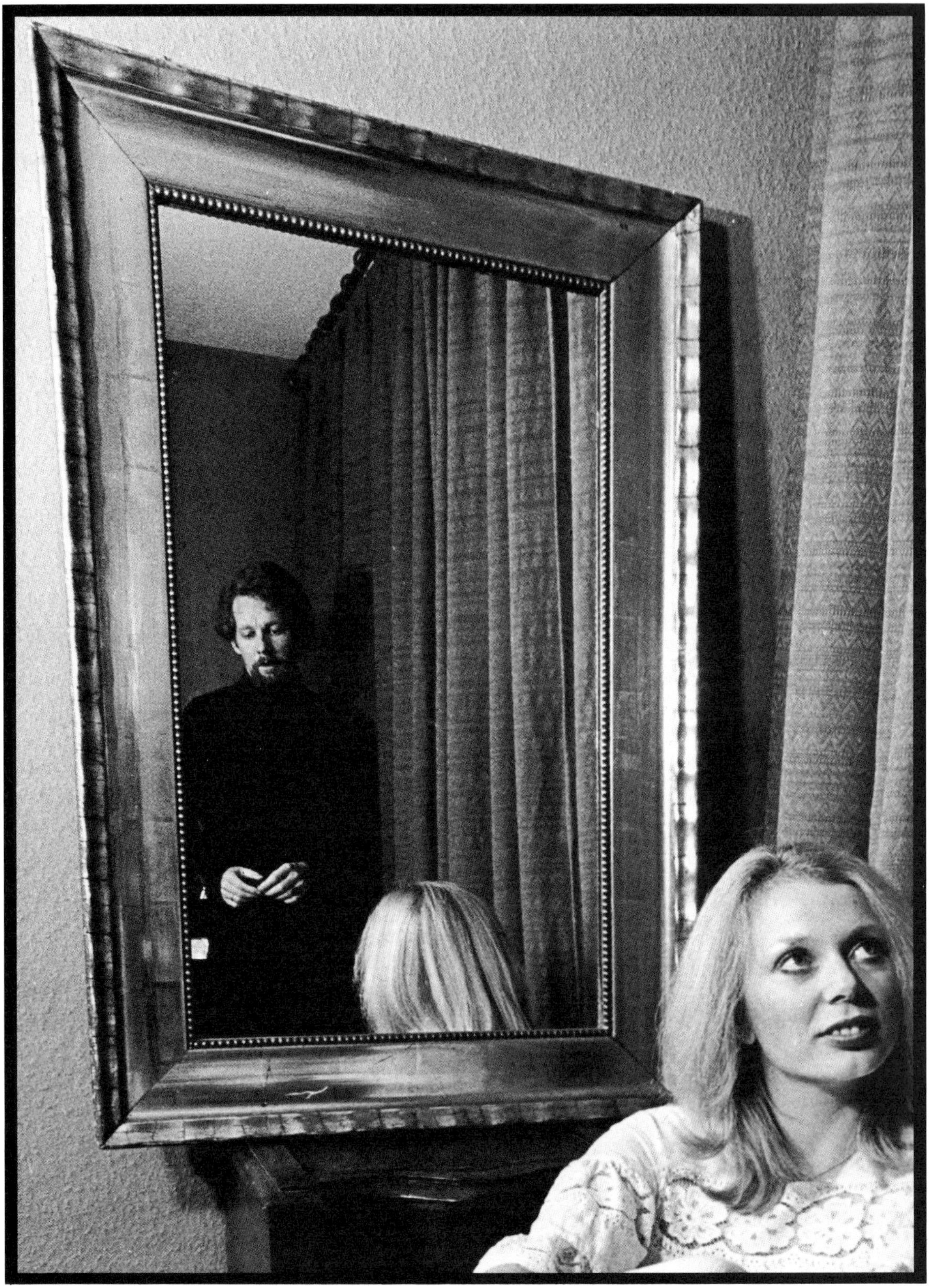

84

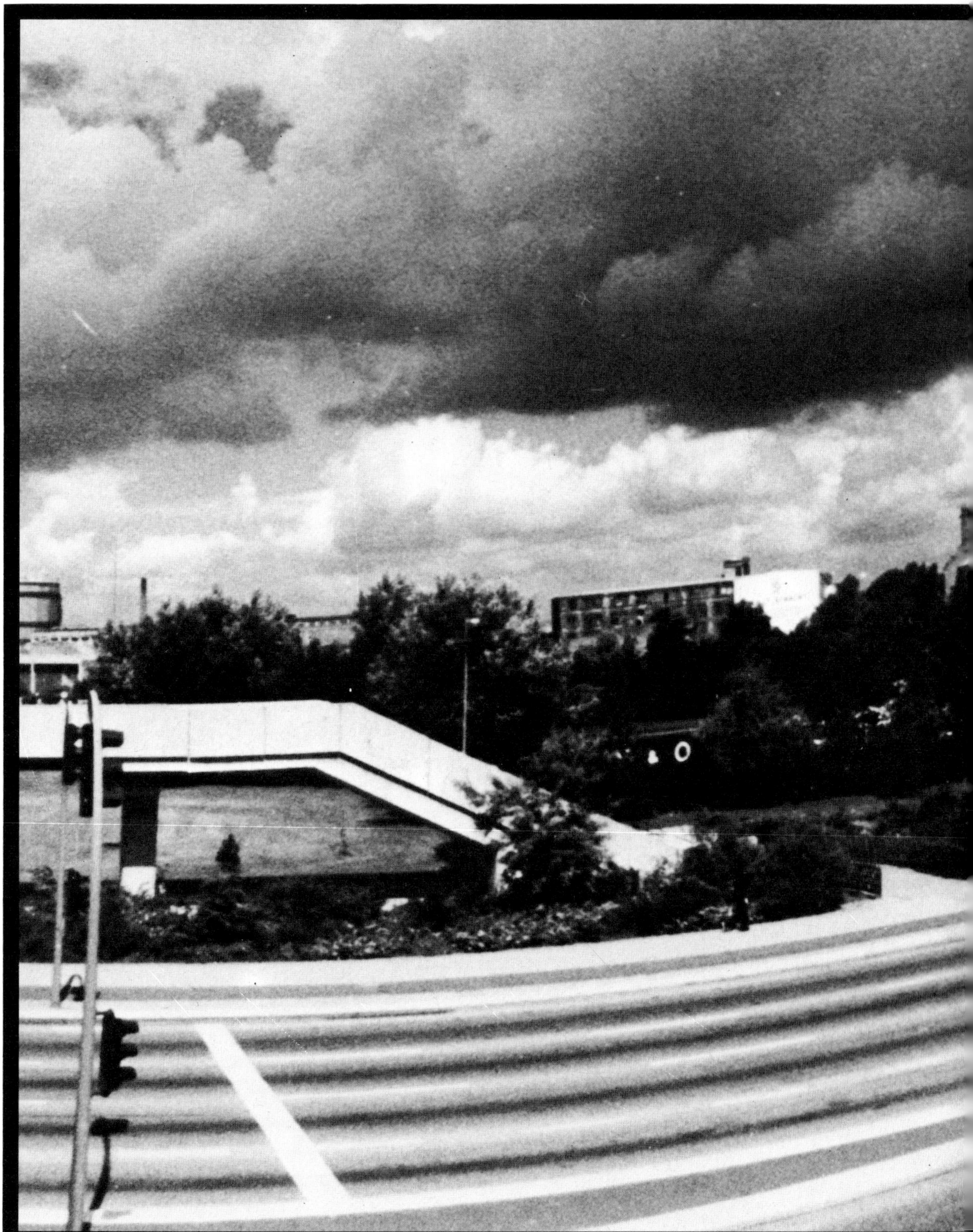

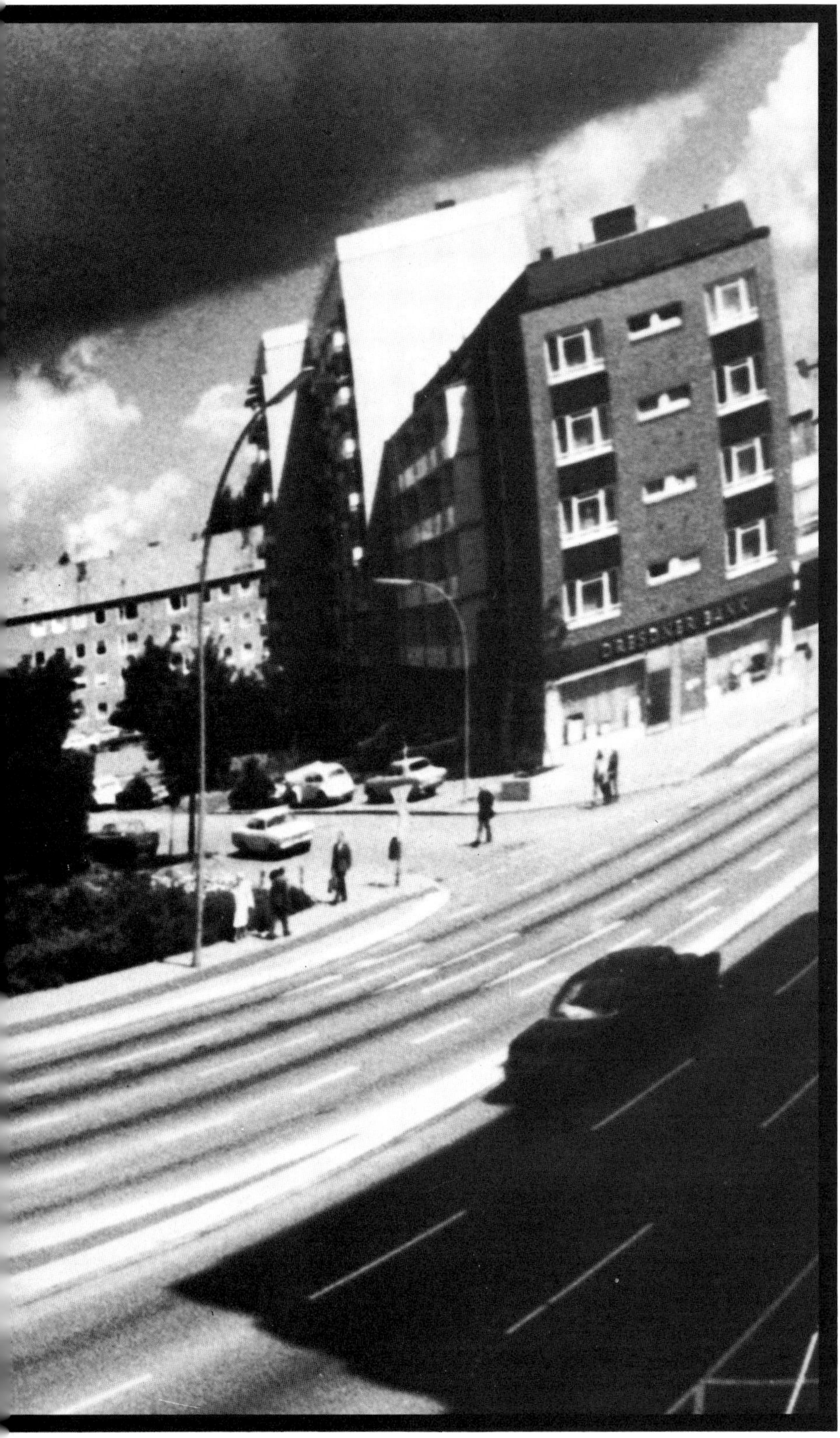

When using fish-eye lenses, the curvature of the lines depicted depends on their position in the picture frame. (They are straight when running through the centre and become more curved the greater the distance from the centre of the picture plane.) That is why it can be very rewarding to devise fish-eye compositions using only a small part of the negative.

The third and, in my opinion, the last reason for cropping is concerned with perspective and is mainly applicable to photographs taken with lenses of very short focal lengths or fish-eye lenses. If you use a wide-angle lens, an object will look noticeably different according to its position in the picture-frame. This fact can be used to change the rendering of space to something quite unusual if you enlarge only the left- or right-hand part of a negative. The next two illustrations show what pictures treated in this way look like. Illustration 83 was taken with a 17 mm wide-angle lens (compare with picture 15), while illustration 84 was photographed with a fish-eye lens. The effect is strongest in the fish-eye photograph, because you can see only part of the curved lines which are characteristic of such photographs (compare picture 66).

It is quite obvious that this kind of enlargement must be planned in advance, because you will have to decide the position of your subject matter when taking the picture, although you are, of course, free to reverse your negative, if this enables you to realise your intentions. If you do so you should remember that the impression provided by your photograph might change when you reverse it (compare pictures 3, 4 and 5).

This really covers the uses of cropping as far as I am concerned. There might, of course, be other ways of using this technique which I have overlooked, but they will probably be similar to those described above. But let me repeat again: cropping is no substitute for careful framing and the choice of the proper focal length when taking a picture. If you use it as such you will not only end up with enlargements which are technically worse than they should be, but you will never learn the importance of framing for the composition of your photographs.

12 Instant Photography

This chapter leads directly out of the preceding one because photographic accuracy plays an important part in it. In instant photography, for example, you have practically no chance to crop if you have made a mistake or if your first decision does not please you. But let us stick to the right sequence of things. In taking a photograph you will have to deal with three factors. First is the subject matter; second your vision, that is, the idea of the finished photograph which you have formed while looking at the subject; third is the finished photograph itself. If I were fond of platitudes I would say that the art of photography lies in reaching complete harmony between the second and third factors – and I would be quite right.

The importance of instant photography

The usual procedure in taking pictures is this: you walk around looking for things to photograph or you just might find an interesting subject by chance. When you see it and take a picture of it, you do so for a particular reason, therefore you should have an idea of what the finished picture will look like. Then, perhaps, you take other photographs and some time may elapse before you see the finished picture. The question then is: Does the finished picture work, or are you discontented with it? If so, why does it not work? Is it because you overlooked some properties of the subject or is it because your techniques were wrong for the realisation of your idea? Anyway, can you really remember down to the last detail what you intended to do and why you took that particular picture? Most people cannot remember and are then at a loss when trying to find out why a particular picture did or did not work. But this is quite obviously very important if you want to learn about composition, or if you want to generally improve your photographic technique.

The answer to this problem, of course, is instant photography. In my opinion it cannot be overrated as a way of teaching oneself and, although you may not at first believe this, it is also a means of photographic expression in its own right.

85

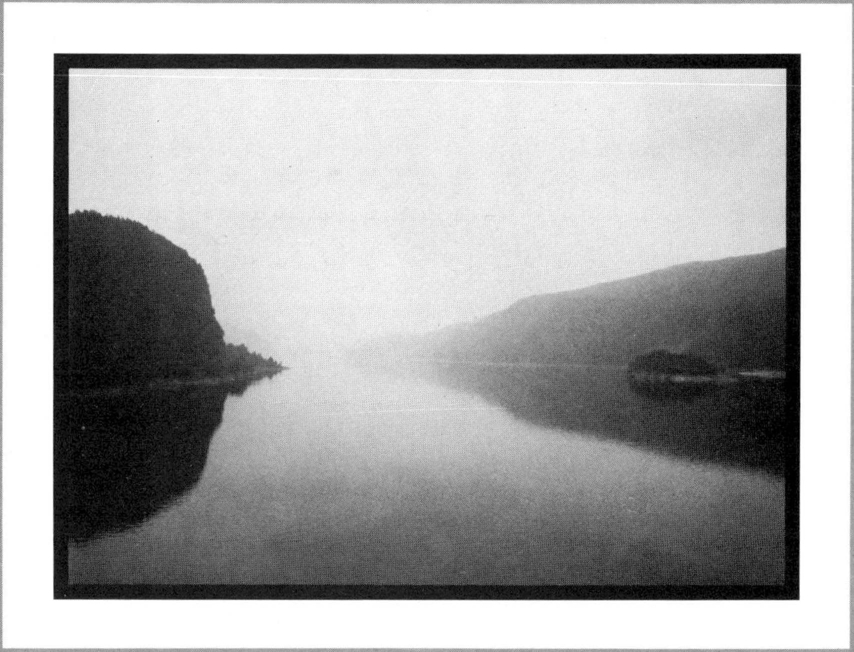

86

Left
Instant photographs are very small, therefore their composition should rely on simple forms and 'generalised' statements and not on detail and structure. This, of course, is especially true for panoramic views of landscapes, as in these two examples.

Overleaf
It is always more difficult to get a viewer's interest centred on a small print. You are usually much better off with bold and simple visualisations, because in this size of print complicated and detailed compositions would not be recognisable even at relatively short viewing distances.

The problems of instant photography

If you are used to 'normal' photography, the first time you use 'instant' photography you are likely to receive quite a surprise. You will probably think that the camera or film is defective or that you cannot take photographs at all. Both impressions are quite wrong. As you can see from the illustrations in this chapter, it is perfectly possible to make instant pictures which are quite up to one's usual standard. If you intend to do so, there are two things to remember: instant photography must be treated seriously and there are no negatives which can be adjusted during the printing.

It is most important to take instant photography seriously. Many people regard it as an amusing toy for snapshots of the family and the like and they do not work as hard at it as at their 'usual' photography. I do not have to tell you that this attitude will get you nowhere. But if you take it seriously there are other things to be considered. In 'normal' black-and-white photographs there are negatives and therefore many ways to amend, or at least to hide, mistakes which you made when taking the picture. In instant photography there is no such possibility.

Even if your 'métier' is the taking of colour-transparencies which cannot be changed afterwards by ordinary and easily available means, there still is an enormous difference with instant photography. Usually your slides are not ready for viewing until some time after you took them and it is easy to be mistaken, or even self-deluded, as far as your original ideas and intentions at the moment of the picture-taking were concerned. In instant photography this cannot occur. You take a photograph and you are confronted with the result after a few seconds. That is why you can immediately compare the photograph with your subject and – what is infinitely more important – with your 'vision', your 'previsualisation', or, if you do not like fancy words, with what was in your mind a few seconds ago – provided there was anything in it, of course!

When I took up instant photography I was surprised at the number of really bad pictures which at first I turned out. Although there were some technical reasons for this, which we will discuss next, the main reason was that my 'vision' was much less precise than I suspected or cared to believe. Something like that is immediately revealed in instant photography. But the really great thing about instant photography – and the main reason why I have included it in this book – is that you have the chance of a second try (and more if necessary).

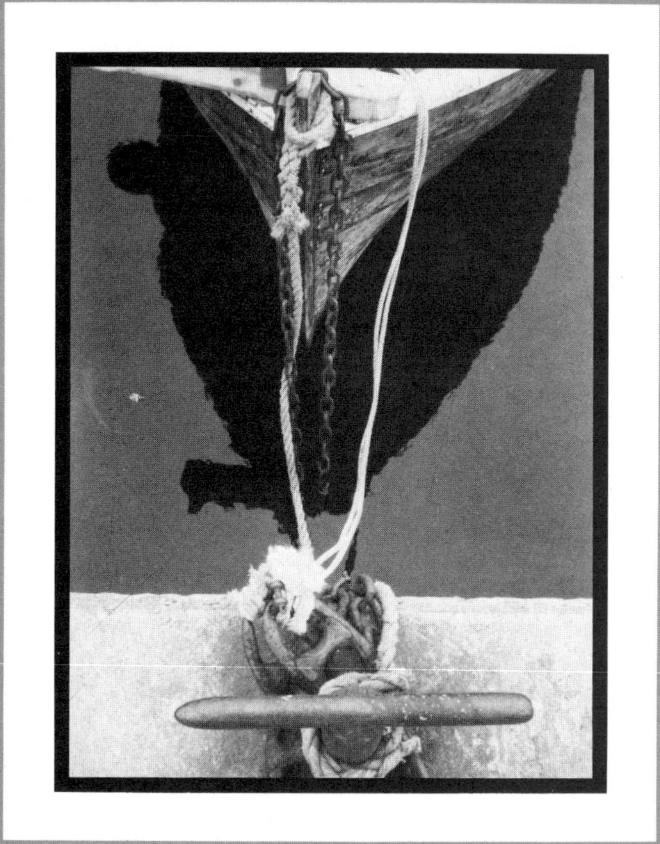

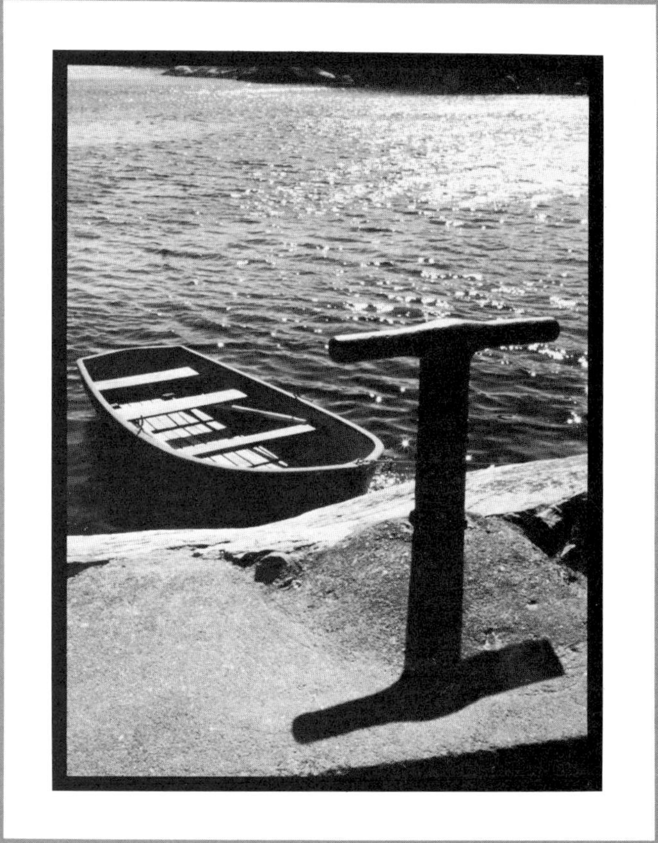

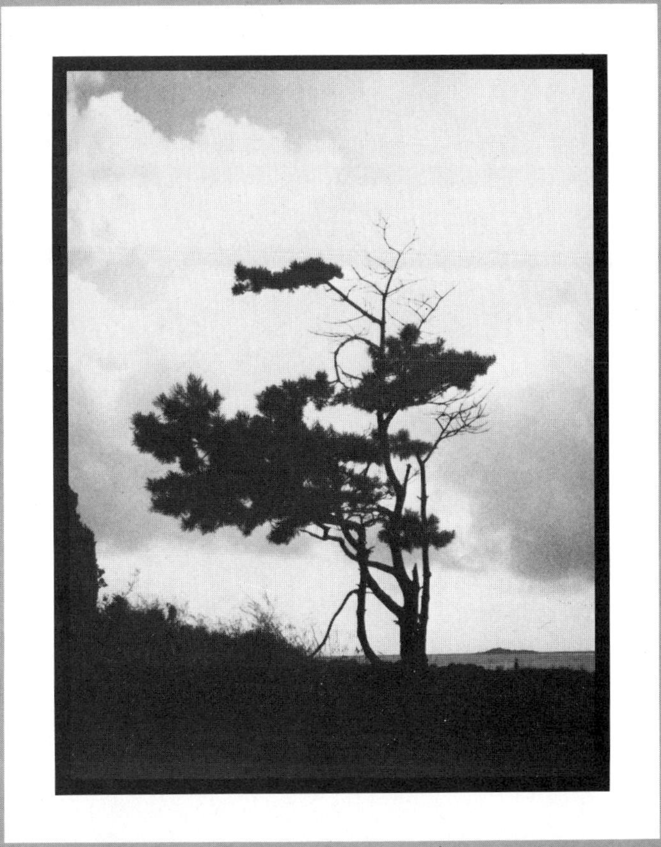

89

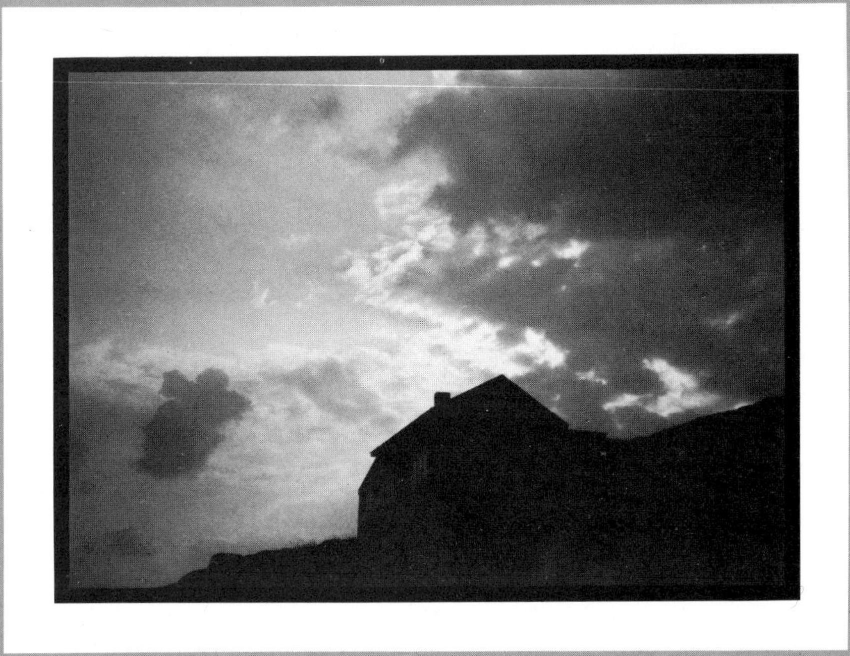

90

Left
Especially in difficult lighting situations (like contre jour), the determination of exposure for instant pictures is critical, because you cannot hide your mistakes later on in the darkroom. But once you get the hang of it, you will be amazed at the technical qualities of today's instant materials.

Overleaf
These four photographs were taken with one of the cheapest and most unsophisticated instant cameras available. This is especially noticeable in (94). The very curious and interesting reflections caused by the setting sun are due to the simple plastic lens of this camera and cannot be achieved in any other way.

In normal photography you either succeed with your photograph or you do not. There is usually no going back for a second try, either because your subject is far away or because the situation or your mood have changed. With instant photography you are on the spot and can repeat your picture until it satisfies you. You also have the opportunity to find out why your intentions did not work out properly. You might even use it to improve and sharpen your vision.

That all this is a valuable aid when you are working at composition (and other photographic techniques) goes without saying, but as I have already stated, instant photography is also an interesting means of expression in itself. If you want to use it in this way you will, of course, have to put a lot of effort into it. First of all you are restricted to a very small size and specific format for your pictures. Generally speaking there must be some relation between the picture-size and the amount of detail which the viewer is supposed to see. For example, you obviously cannot render on a Polaroid film-pack of 8.3 by 10 cm a subject which would normally require a 50 by 60 cm enlargement, or you will at least have to photograph it differently. This does not mean that you cannot photograph landscapes on Polaroid film. As the illustrations in this chapter show, this can be done if the viewer's interest is concentrated on the foreground, or if the landspace consists of many similar elements, some of which are clearly shown in the foreground, or if the landscape is built up of some simple and clear forms without great detail. (This, of course, is not only interesting for instant photography, in general landscape photography these principles lead to bold and impressive results, irrespective of image size.)

Exposure problems

Another thing which you will have to take into account is the exposure of the picture. All the illustrations shown here have been selected from a portfolio of about 180 photographs taken with a simple Polaroid-Land camera with a limited 'lighten-darken' control. It sometimes required a second exposure to get the picture exactly right – so do not be disappointed if you do not always succeed with your first try.

Special effects

Incidentally, the simpler models of the Polaroid-Land cameras are equipped with plastic lenses that can be used to achieve some very special effects, which I have been unable to duplicate with any other equipment. The last photograph in this chapter (*94*) shows you what will happen when you point it directly

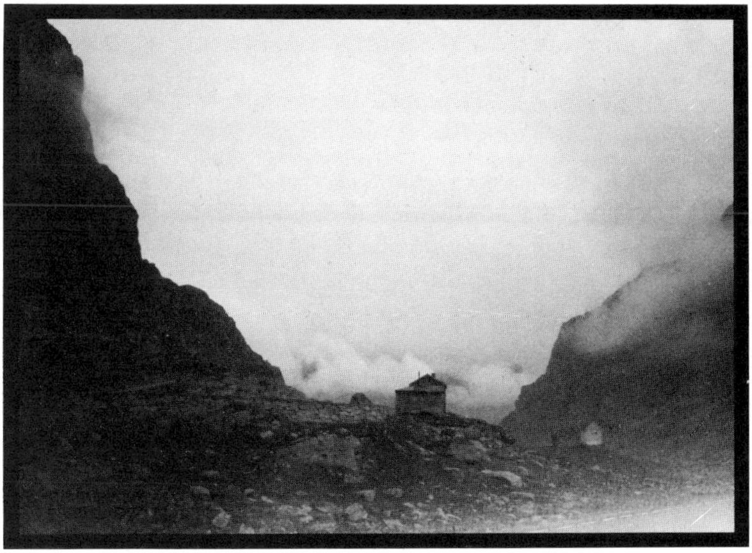

91

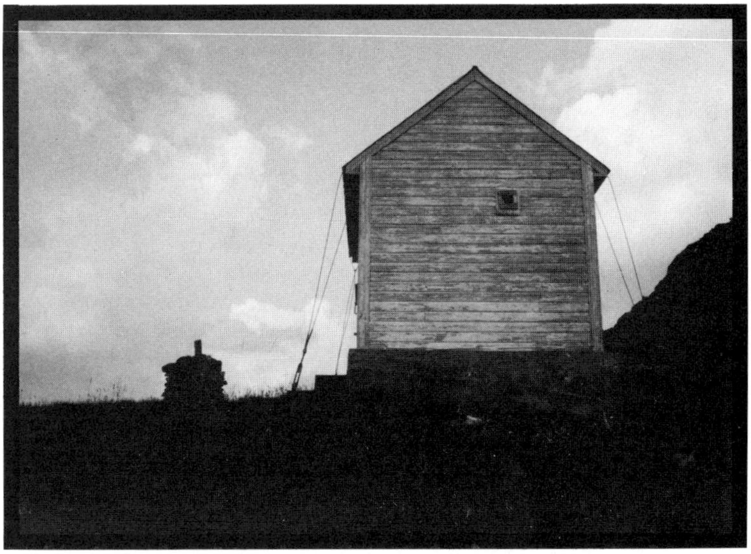

92

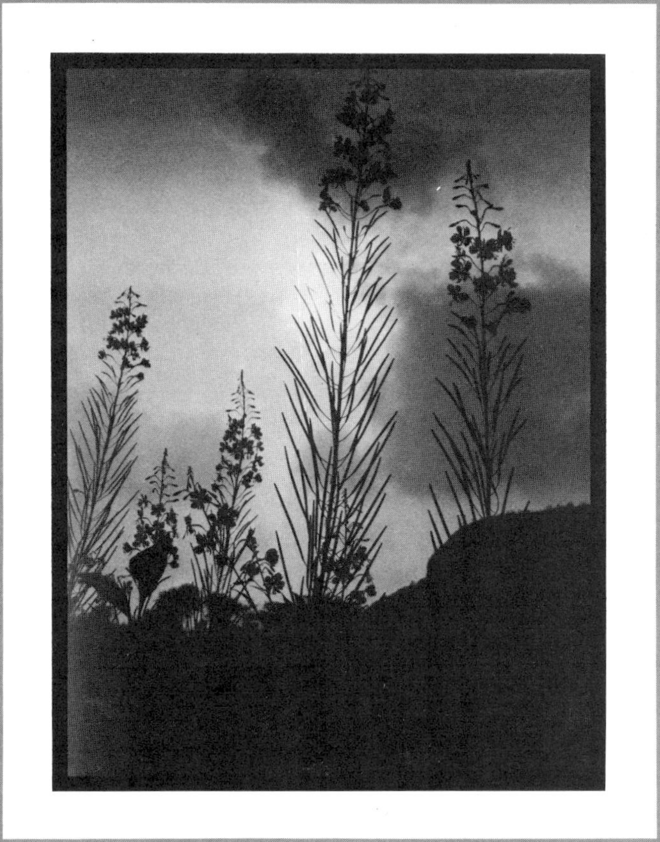

93

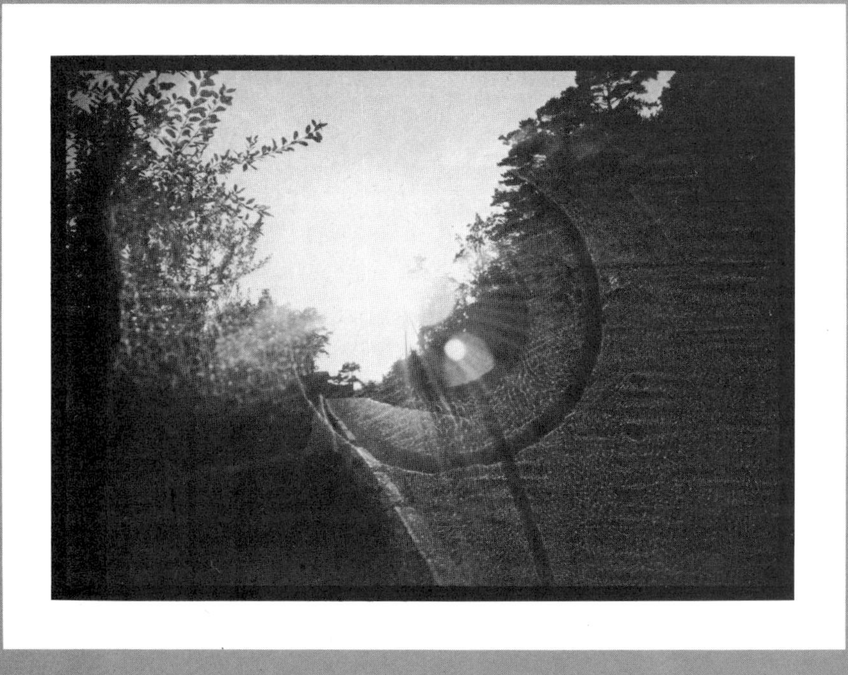

94

into the sun. After I discovered these effects by accident I experimented with them and have now collected quite an interesting portfolio of 'plastic against-the-sun' Polaroids.

A useful aid

Apart from these more out-of-the-way experiments, the fact remains that instant photography is worth exploring as a medium by itself and as a valuable aid to learning about composition (and general photographic problems). In addition to this, of course, you can use it as most professional photographers do: as a 'dry run' test to material for important and unrepeatable shots.

The best way to get involved in Polaroid photography, in my opinion, is to start doing it. Apart from framing your shot, the simpler Polaroid cameras offer only two ways of influencing the final picture: by the use of the lighten-darken control and by the timing of development. You will very soon find out what these manipulations do to your pictures. I am deliberately not giving you information on this, because I believe that by trial and error you will achieve personal and satisfying results sooner than by sticking to some rule or other. But always remember that instant photography means that you need never be satisfied with the second best result. You can always try again, although it may cost you something in the way of films. And even if you do not want to get deeply involved in instant photography you should at least consider its value for checking the composition of your photographs. The experience of immediately comparing the picture you thought you took with the one you actually took is quite sobering and helps to show up defects and possible ways to improve your compositions.

13 Theoretical and Practical Aspects of Composition

Overleaf left
Sometimes even tiny details can make or mar a composition. In this case the small, almost white piece of wastepaper in the foreground is very important because it acts as a counterweight to the light-grey turrets in the background.

Overleaf right
The wheel-marks in this photograph serve a function similar to that of the piece of paper in 95. The proportions have been exaggerated by using the movements of a view camera.

So far we have equally, or at least almost equally, divided our attention between photographic composition, its description and interpretation on the one hand and the more practical considerations of how to create photographs on the other. Now the time has come to look more closely at the connections and differences between these two aspects of our subject in order to come to some final conclusions. Final, I must hasten to add, only in the context of this book, for generally speaking we have barely scratched the surface, although we have done so hard enough to provide some data for our practical work. I will now review this data to see whether there are other ways in which it can be used.

Creating and interpreting pictures

In order to do this, we must distinguish between two entirely different approaches: the aesthetic and the practical. Obviously, these activities are completely different from each other and cannot be easily or successfully intermingled, although it is necessary to know about both if you really want to make the most of all compositional possibilities.

Historically speaking, composition has two main sources, which roughly correspond to this distinction. Some schools of artists tried to develop well-defined rules of composition. This allowed the construction (and interpretation) of pictures (and other works of art) in a rigid and predictable framework of points of reference. But these attempts always failed in the long run for a variety of reasons, so that no generally approved agreement upon any one set of rules could ever be reached. (And that was all to the good, because art otherwise would be extinct by now!)

The second source is provided by historians, psychologists and other people who in their turn have tried time and again to create sets of compositional rules as tools for the description and interpretation of pictures. Again these attempts have failed as generalisations for a diversity of technical reasons. (An example is described in the next chapter.)

Today's theories of composition for or in photography are

95

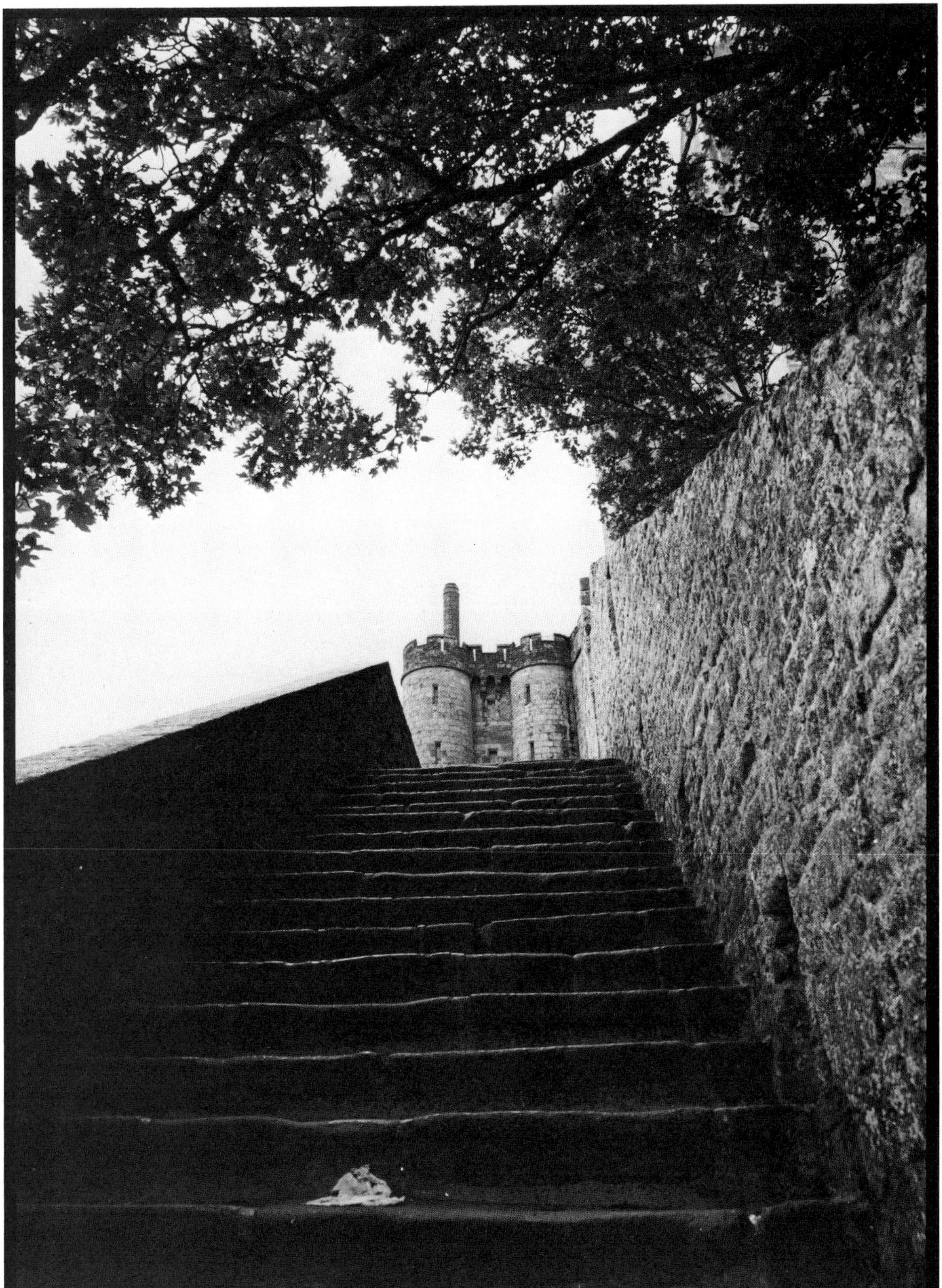

96

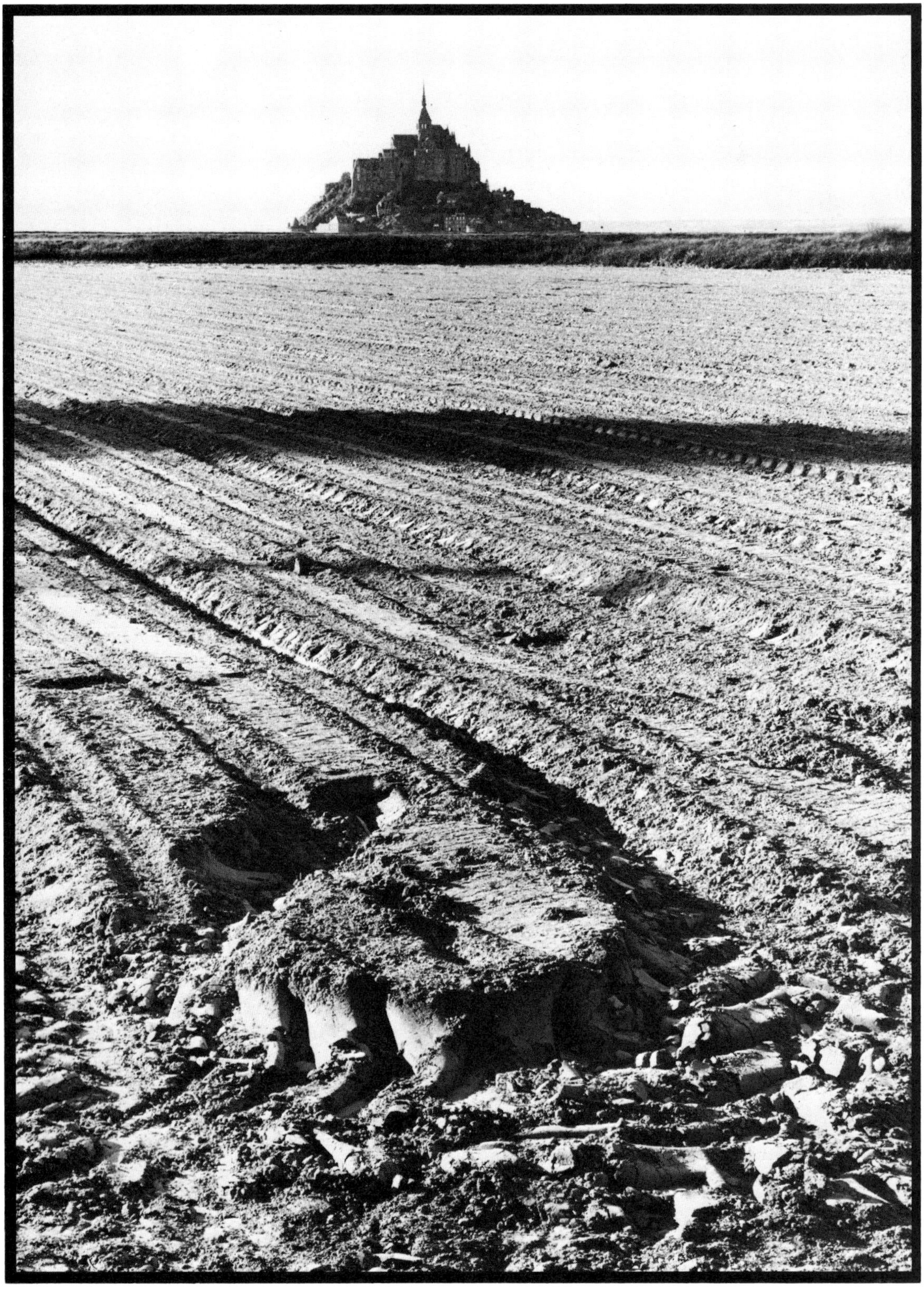

generally nothing more than an attempt to salvage something or other from these historical ruins. We have met this difficulty at almost every turn in this book and we have tried to overcome it (I hope successfully) once and for all. But because the situation is as it is – both imprecise and subjective – we have had to walk very carefully and our conclusions were not as comprehensive, far-reaching and applicable as you probably wished them to be. Let us, however, summarise our exertions.

First of all, I hope I have succeeded in making you very suspicious of rules relating to any kind of creative activity. Second, I have shown that the conventional rules of composition – or what you might have imagined them to be – do not exist. And third, I have suggested some substitutes, not in the way of rules, which after all is an impossible thing to do, but in the form of ideas and suggestions which you can adapt to your own ideas and methods. I hope I have convincingly demonstrated that the perception of pictures depends at least partially on physiological patterns and so can be objectively described and predicted to some degree. It is, of course, important to know this, because it implies that you have to reckon with these structures if you want to communicate something with your photographs. On the other hand it would have been very unwise to pursue this possibility further for two reasons. First, the whole matter is exceedingly complicated and science has barely touched these phenomena, so that the practical application of these concepts to your daily work is almost nil. Second, a set of rules – whatever it may be – does nothing to further your creativity.

Nevertheless you need to know about the principles of these things in order to be able to incorporate them into your own photographic language. To be more precise: it is absolutely no use to learn that, for example, a diagonal line of a certain kind will give this or that impact to your photograph if you then try to apply this 'rule' rigidly to your picture-making. Instead, a statement like this should simply make you more aware of your reactions to photographs (be they your own or those of other people) and should lead you to discover why and how you yourself react to a given photograph. This will lead to a sharpening and deepening of your sensitivity, which is what all teaching is about, as far as the creative process is concerned. You cannot teach rules because there are none, and you cannot teach patterns of behaviour because this would hamper or restrict creativity; but you can show people how to develop their sensitivity.

On the other hand an entirely different set of factors permits

Right
Most photographers try to arrange the composition of their pictures as consistently as possible. While this works out quite well in most cases, sometimes the breaking up of a composition heightens its impact. In this picture the shadow on the left-hand side is a very disturbing element, partly because you cannot see the object responsible for it and partly because it does not fit into the very quiet and static overall impression of the composition. But, paradoxically, this is exactly what gives the picture its disturbing and appealing quality.

Overleaf left
Usually you are advised to place the main part of the subject in the middle of the photograph. But very often the opposite works quite as well, because by doing it the unusual or unconventional way you can force the viewer to look more closely than he would otherwise do. That is why this composition has a much more disturbing and moving quality than a normal still-life of the same subject would have.

Overleaf right
Stones generally have interesting textures and structures. But this is very seldom enough to form a convincing composition. Therefore, you should always be on the lookout for additional components. In this picture the strange feature of the composition is the very marked and unusual distribution of light and dark areas.

97

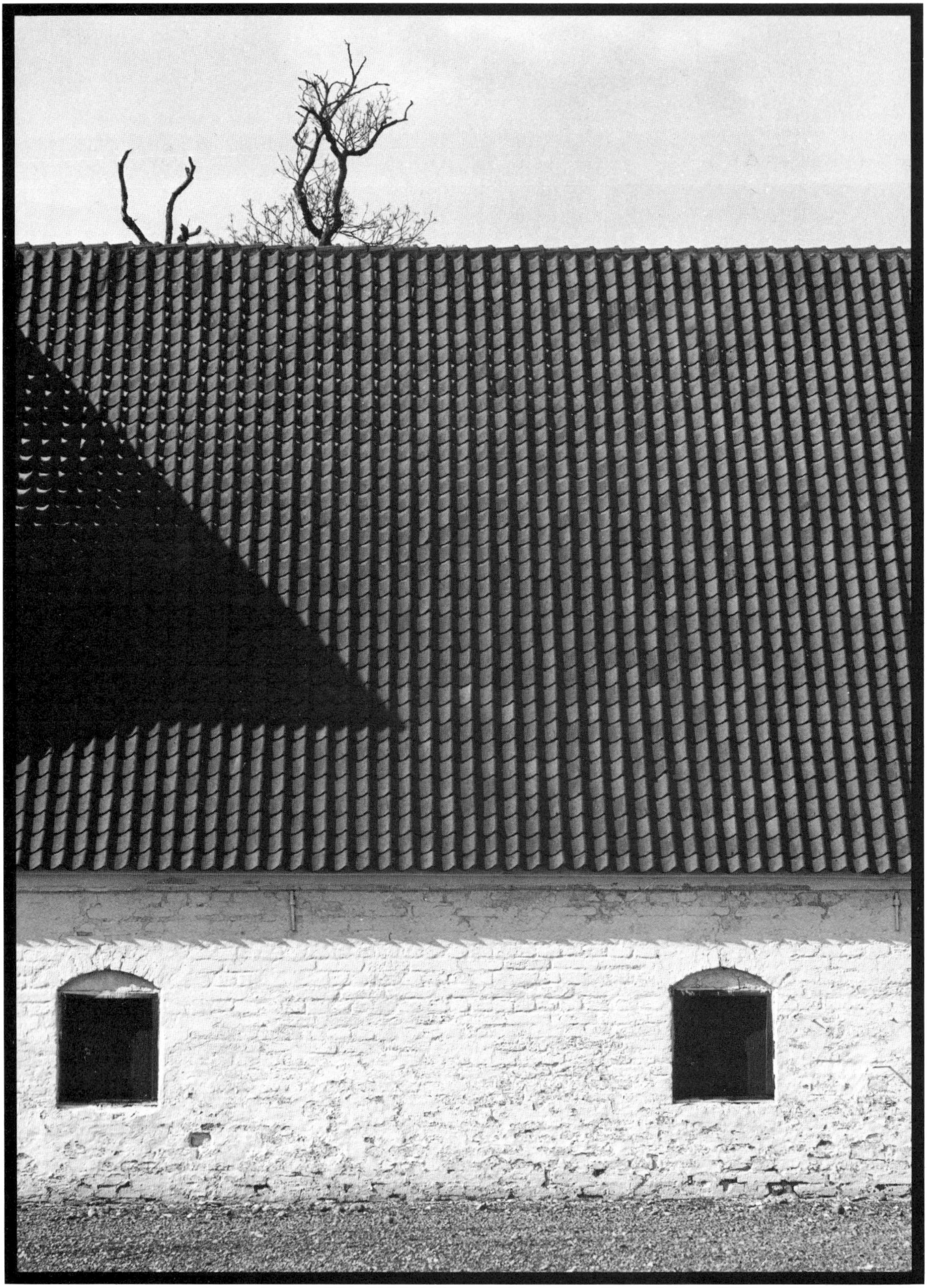

98

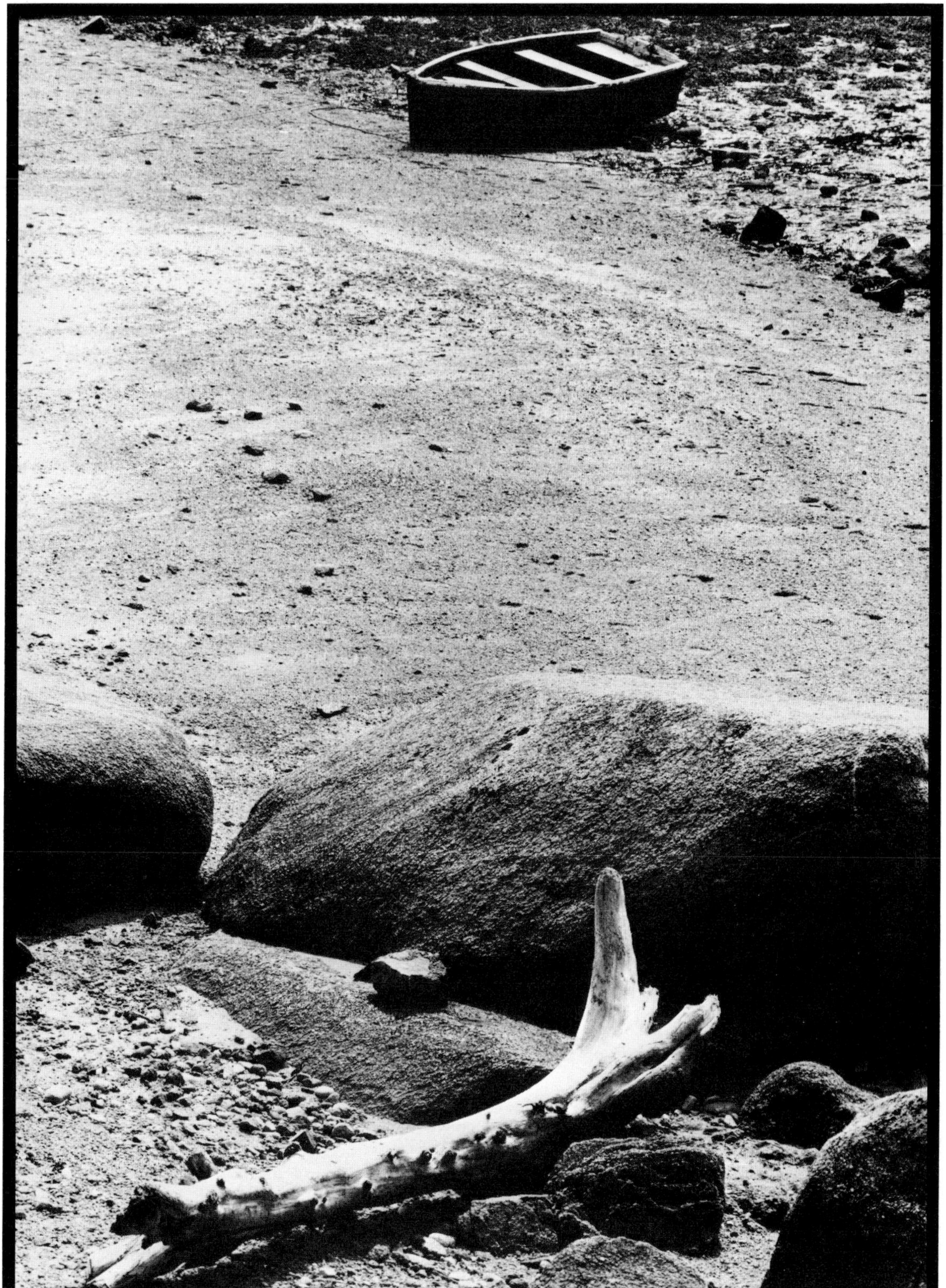

99

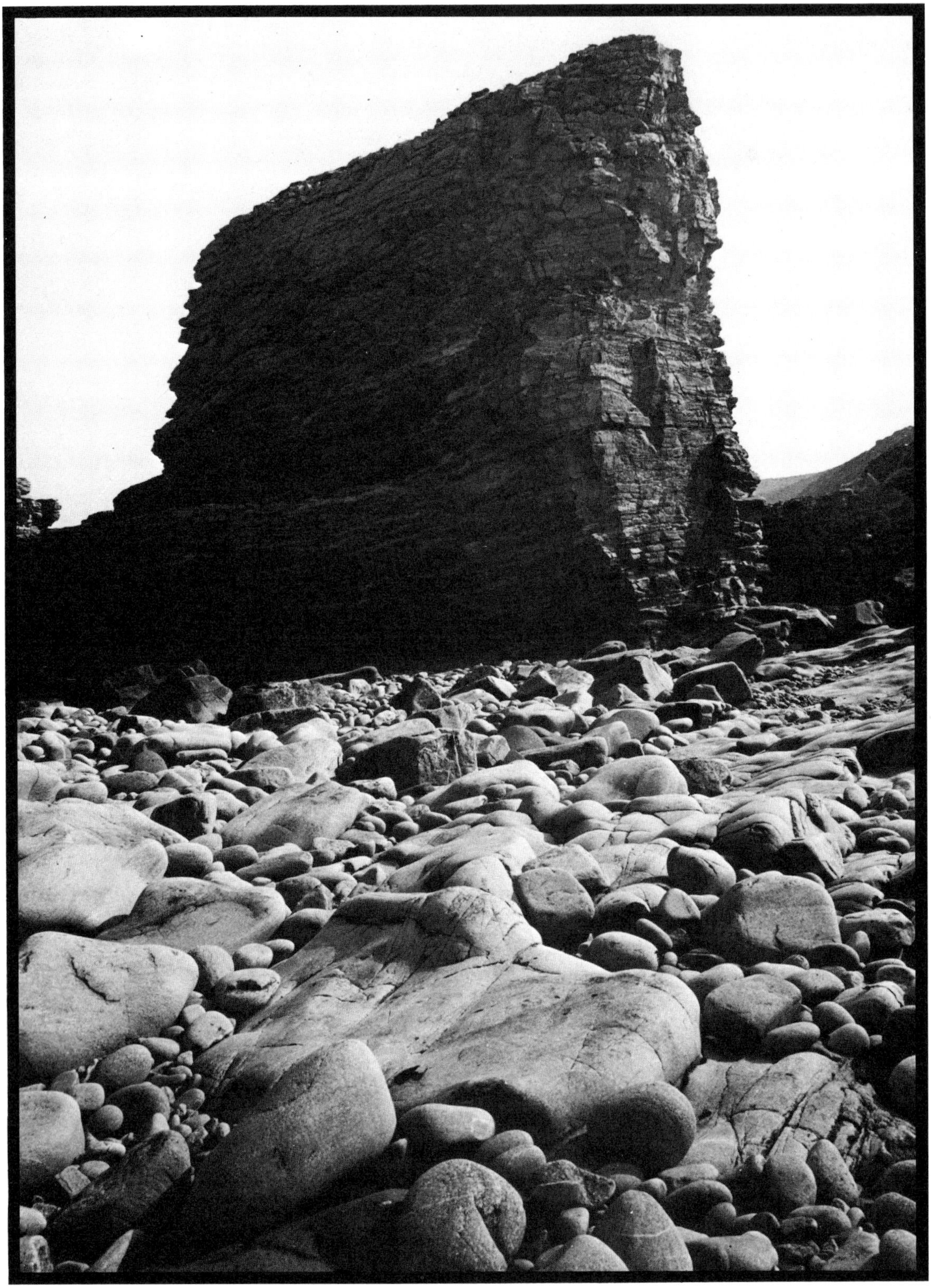

a very sure and verifiable approach. The use of technical means (be it a piece of equipment or a working method) can influence the composition of a picture enormously and we can state with some precision what the use of a particular technique will do to the appearance of a photograph. This is the basis of the language of photography, which everyone must learn (and can learn) if he wants to express himself in it. As an example of this we discussed the use of interchangeable lenses and their influence on the composition of a photograph. Remember that this was nothing but an example – *everything* you do when taking a photograph influences the final appearance of the picture, which in turn allows you to influence the viewer.

If all this seems clear cut and obvious, remember that much of this book has dealt with the difficulties and intricacies of this process. The peculiarities of perception on the one hand and the technical manipulations on the other hand both work together to form the response of the viewer. And this, finally, is what everything is about. Practically speaking, composition is the photographer's way of conveying his meaning (mood, feelings, information, etc) to the viewer and doing so in a way which ensures (with certain instability factors, which we have discussed) that at least some viewers will see it in a way which comes close to the photographer's intentions.

Very low viewpoints stress the monumentality of objects, even of very small subjects like this plant. By placing the camera on the ground I created the ambiguous effect of this composition. On the one hand this plant looks quite big, on the other hand your knowledge tells you that it actually must be very small.

Composition and meaning

Two different abilities, the practical and the creative, are involved in producing a (good) photograph. Without knowing what technical possibilities exist and what results they will yield you will not be able to handle the language of photography properly. But fortunately the basics of the technical side of photography can be taught and tested and improved by practice.

Composition, which enables you to employ your technical skills significantly, is quite another matter. As I have already stated and demonstrated, the creative processes involved in composition cannot be taught, although the results (the photographs) are open to analysis. The examples of my photographs, however, and my comments about them should provide you with starting-points for your own excursions into this field. And also why I have repeatedly stated, and do so again now (for the final time!), that you cannot learn about composition by reading a book alone – neither this one, nor any other. You will have to do your own work in order to gain the necessary experience and to expand your sensibility.

This has led me to the very personal view, that this is indeed

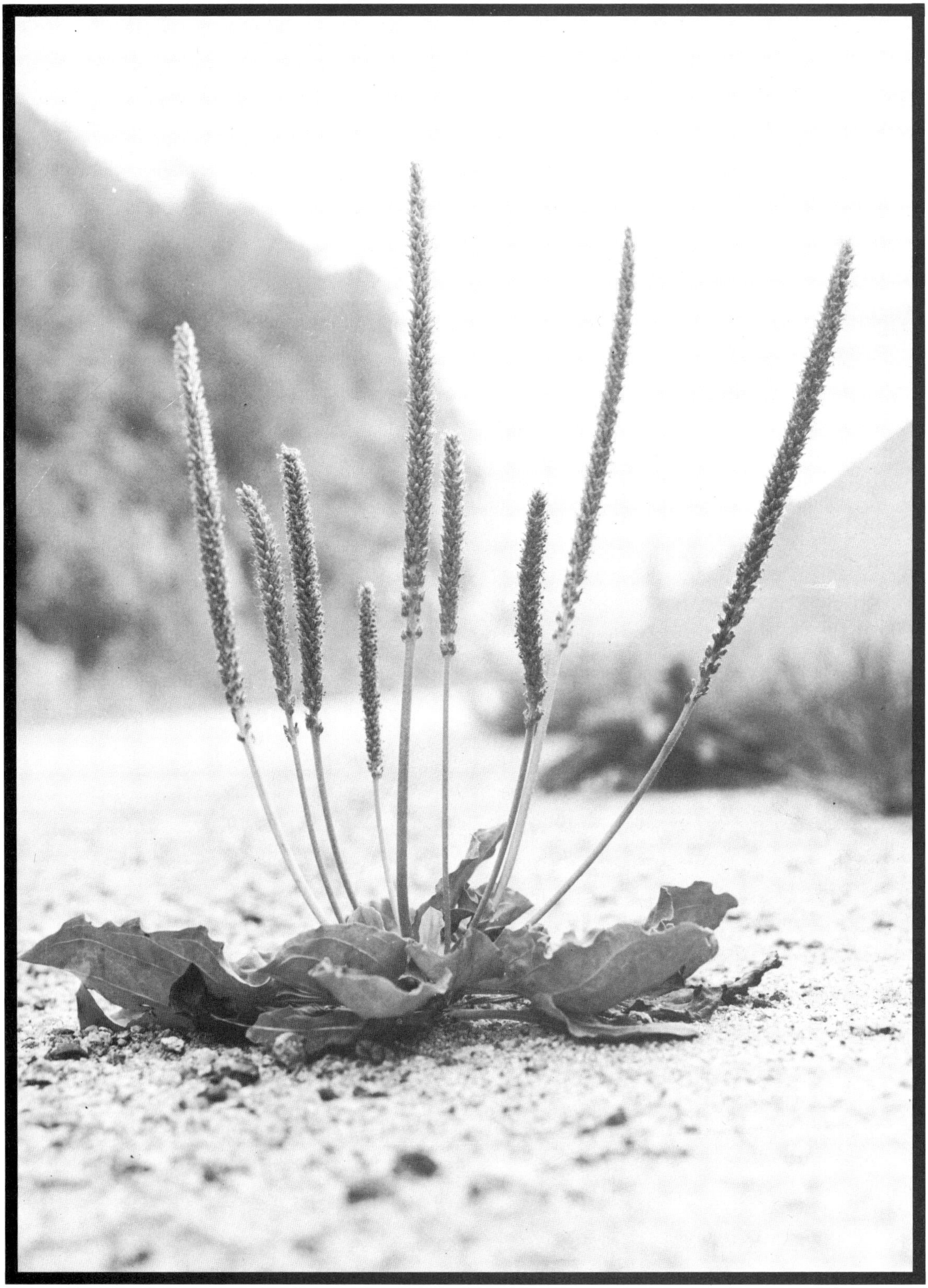

101

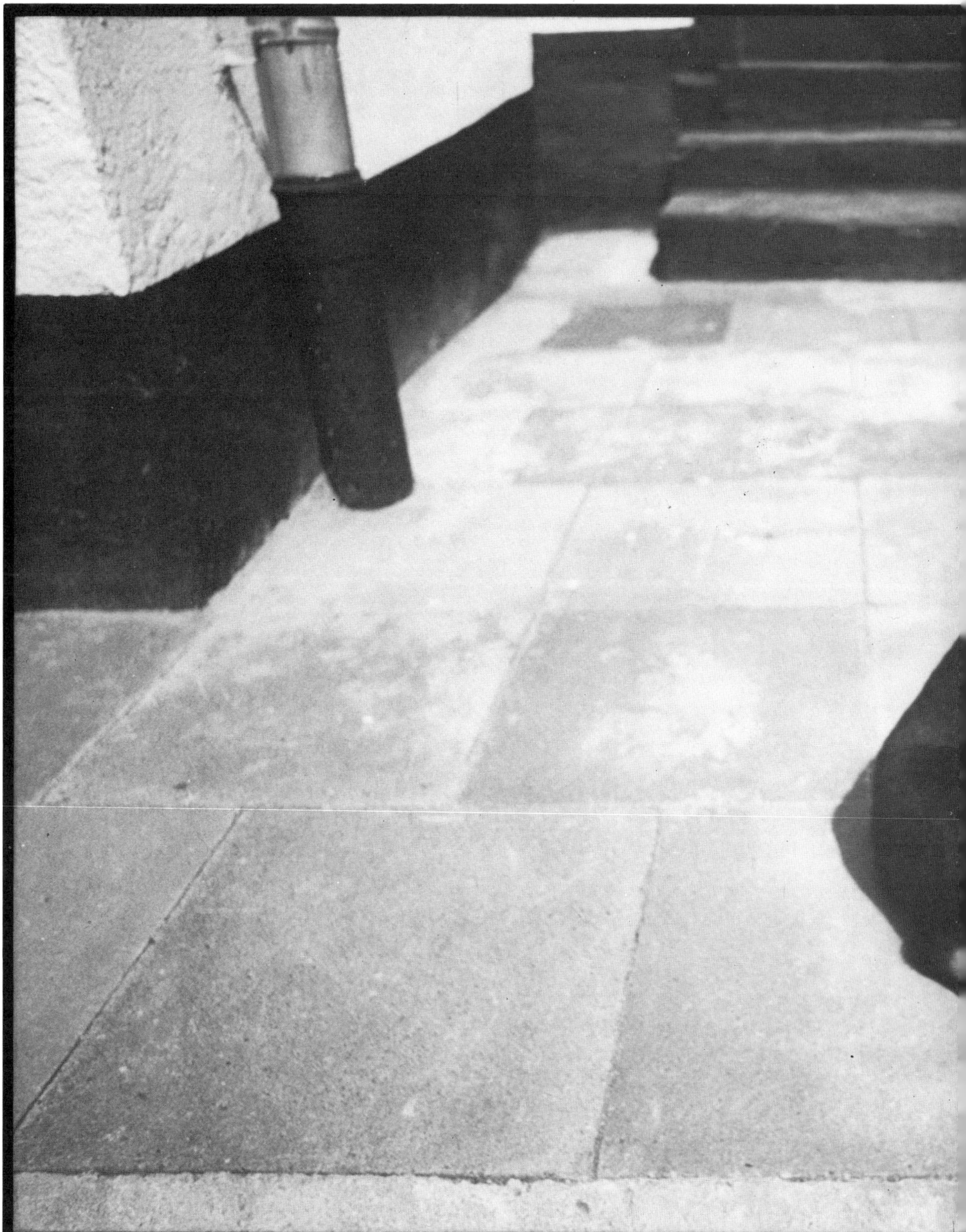

the most important single step in learning about composition: to realise that you are entirely free in your creative work, but that each of your decisions has its effect on the intended viewer of your work – and so to act accordingly. This in turn implies that you might be playing around with your creative photography, but that if you intend anyone else to see it, you assume some responsibility, because your personality influences the viewer through your work. And if you have really accepted this as your personal responsibility, you will at the same time probably have achieved what you set out to do when you started reading this book.

But this is my personal view and if you find it overly sombre when all you wanted was to have some fun, well, why not? I must admit (and do so gladly) that I had my share of pleasure when I took the photographs for this book. It is no mean thing to do, to show what you like and enjoy and to do so in a way which allows the viewer of your photographs to recognise and share your joy and pleasure, the world is not only made up of deep thoughts and serious problems. If you do what interests you most, you will find enough people who are eager to share your photographs with you.

103

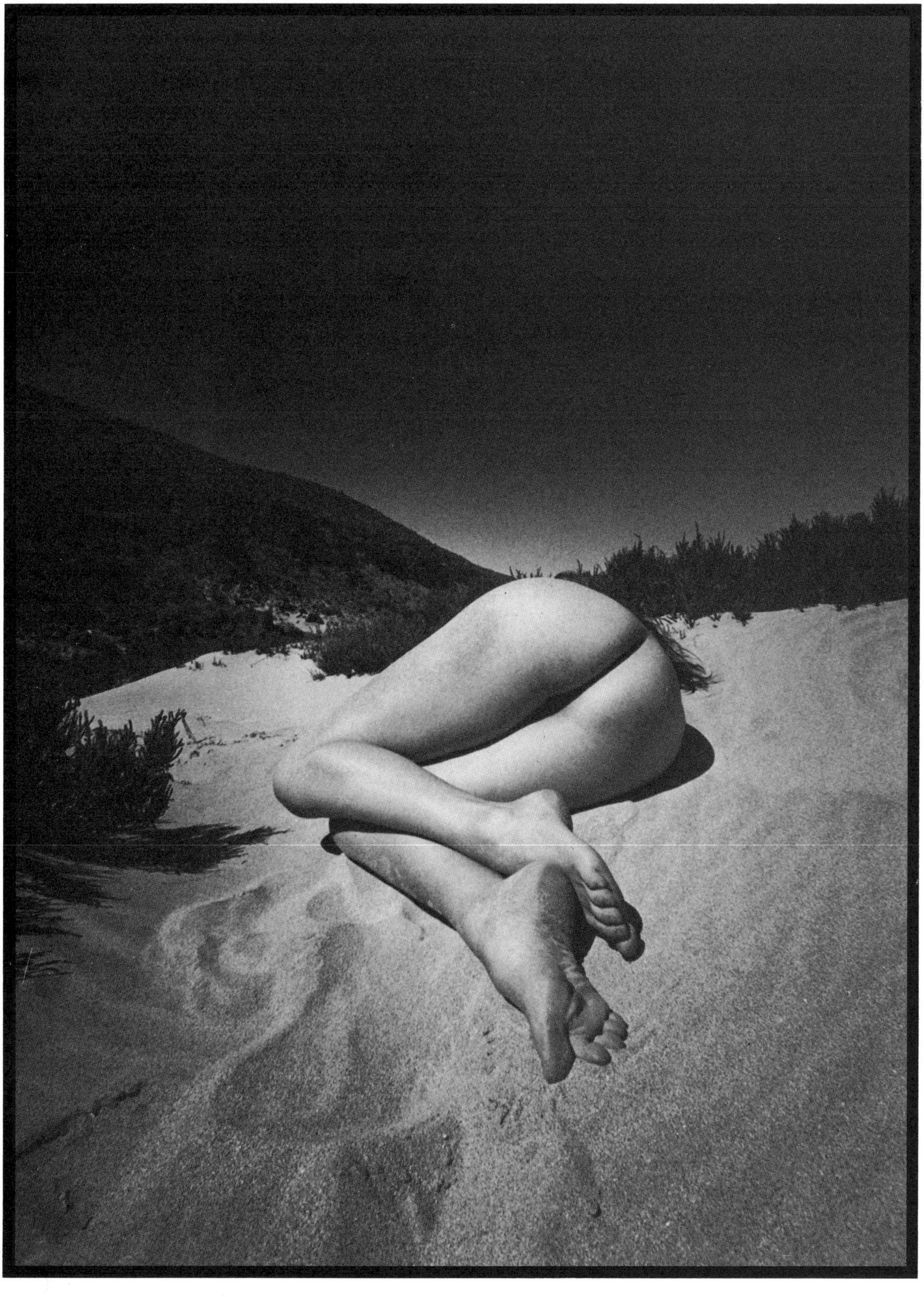

102

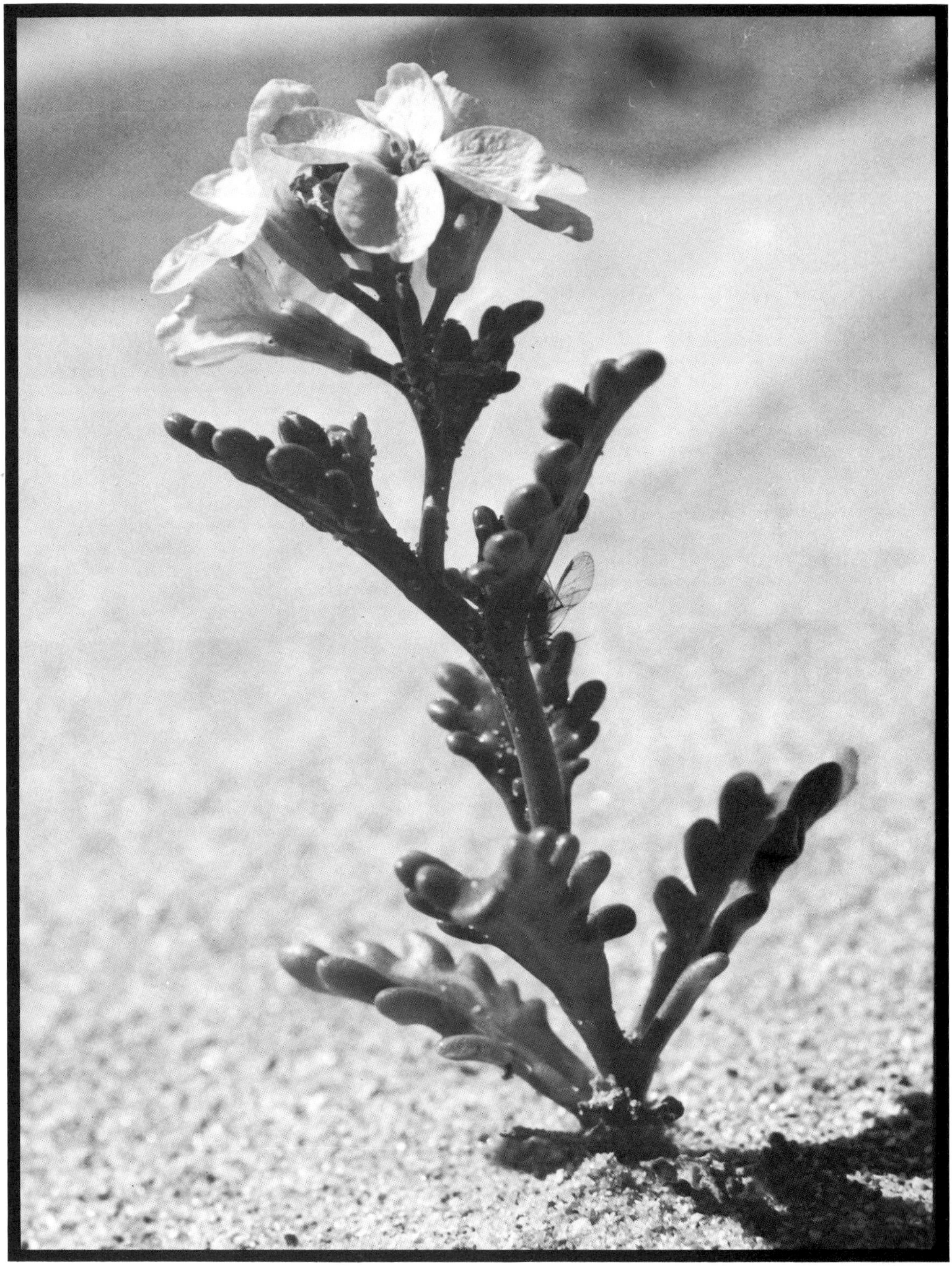

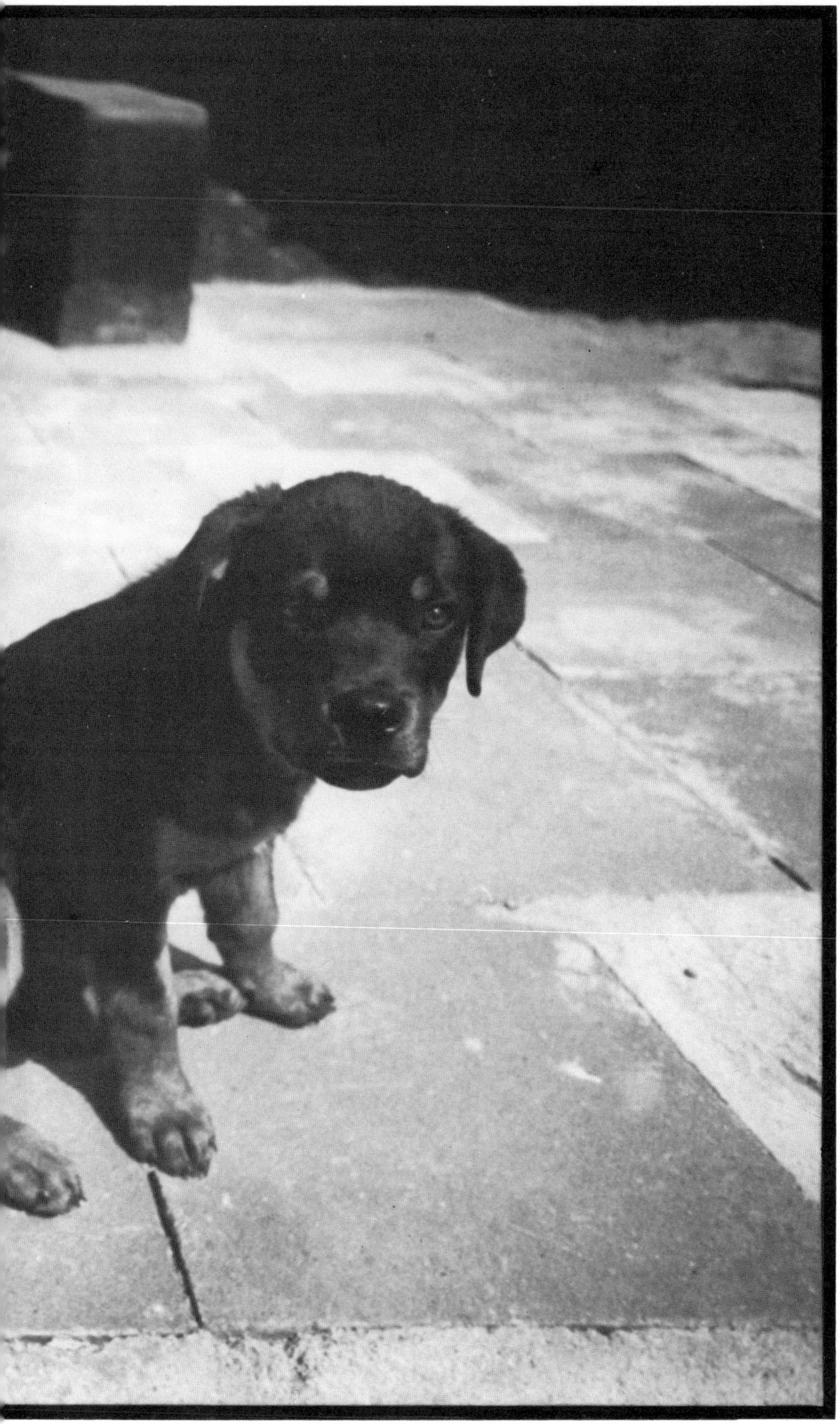

Left
Puppies have the knack of looking very lonely and sad if they want to be cuddled. This impression is heightened here by the composition of the photograph. The puppy sits isolated (and consequently lonely) on the light grey tiles, while the black band in the upper part of the picture exudes oppressiveness. This distribution of the compositional elements was made possible by the use of a 17 mm wide-angle lens, which allowed me to get very close to the puppy.

Overleaf left
One of the big compositional problems of black and white close-ups is the separation of the subject from its background. The only way to overcome this problem is to select your subject most carefully. Although the plant shown here is very common where I took the photograph in Norway it was virtually the only one on a mile of beach which grew in front of the right background.

Overleaf right
Dark skies look very unnatural indeed. But in this age of infra-red films and dark red filters we have become so accustomed to them that we often scarcely seem to notice anything out of the ordinary in a photograph of this sort. This is why you should not hesitate to darken a sky by one of these means or by burning it in in the darkroom if you feel that it will enhance other parts of the scene.

14 Composition and the Golden Mean

You do not have to read this chapter. I just wanted to give you a closer look at a so-called 'rule of composition', what it is supposed to be and what it really is. Unfortunately this requires some dry and slightly mathematical theorising. Although understanding this is not essential for your photographic work, I have included it in this book because it affords interesting insights into old-fashioned ideas on composition and modern reactions to it.

The golden mean

It is interesting to note that the golden mean or medial section is still accepted as an important means of composition. Even in a book like *Principles of Composition in Photography* by A. Feininger (1973) the medial section is dealt with at some length, although the author states in Chapter III of his book that it is one of the oldest clichés in composition and has become almost unusable through too much wear and tear. However, it seems to die exceedingly slowly because it is easy to comprehend, can be neatly expressed in numbers without too much mathematical exertion and is supposed to be venerably old. On the other hand, it does not work.

Before we go into that, however, let us first try to find out what the golden mean really is or is supposed to be. If you look for this term in a good dictionary or encyclopedia you might receive your first shock. According to one such dictionary, published in 1966, it says: 'The areas covered by the medial section . . . are relatively small. It has been used . . . in antique and Roman architecture, the Italian renaissance and . . . it has been used in arts and crafts. But it cannot be talked of in a general way as the medial section, because the cases where there is a direct connection between the qualitative and the quantitative in art are not a rule, but the exception.' The quoted article continues like this, but the upshot is that the medial section is known to have been used in the history of art and architecture, but that no special importance or general applicability can be attached to it. We could, of course, leave it at that, but the golden mean has been so deeply and widely

accepted in popular notions of composition that I have chosen it for this study.

To begin at the beginning, what is this golden mean? Mathematically speaking, the rule of the golden mean says that a line can be divided into two unequal parts (a and b), so that the relation between these two parts (a : b) is the same as that between the bigger of these two parts (b) and the whole line (a + b). Thus

$$a : b = b : (a + b)$$

(Compare diagram 104 for this and for a demonstration for the geometrical construction of the golden mean.) This suggests that planes and lines which are divided according to these proportions are especially aesthetically pleasing and harmonious.

In the past some authors have tried to prove this assumption by carrying out a test on representative groups of people in the following way. Members of these groups were shown rectangles of different proportions (black drawings on white ground) and were asked which they liked best. One of these tests was conducted by Borissavlievitch (*The Golden Number*, London, 1958). Its results seem to prove the validity of the medial section without the least doubt. Diagram 105 shows on its x-axis the proportions of the rectangles which were tested by Borissavlievitch, while the y-axis shows the preferences expressed by the test groups as percentages. The result seems to be conclusive because the curve has a very pronounced peak at rectangles with the proportions of 1 : 1.6 (this being with tolerable exactitude the medial section).

However, if we look elsewhere, we will find 'Birkhoff's Law', which says:

$$M = O : C$$

Without going into this in great detail I will just state that Birkhoff tries to show, with an impressive array of mathematical tools and empirical results, that the square is actually aesthetically the most pleasing and harmonious rectangle, while all others are of a lesser order.

Well, what does this show? Absolutely and positively nothing because both views are entirely wrong. I conclusively proved this in a previous, more scientific, non-photographic book (A. Brück, *Vasarely-Analysen*, Hamburg, 1969). I am not going to repeat it here, but I will just give you the main point, as far as it concerns the golden mean.

First of all there is a basic difference in the perception of an 'empty rectangle' and a 'filled rectangle'. The former term means a rectangular plane (usually white), which is bordered

104

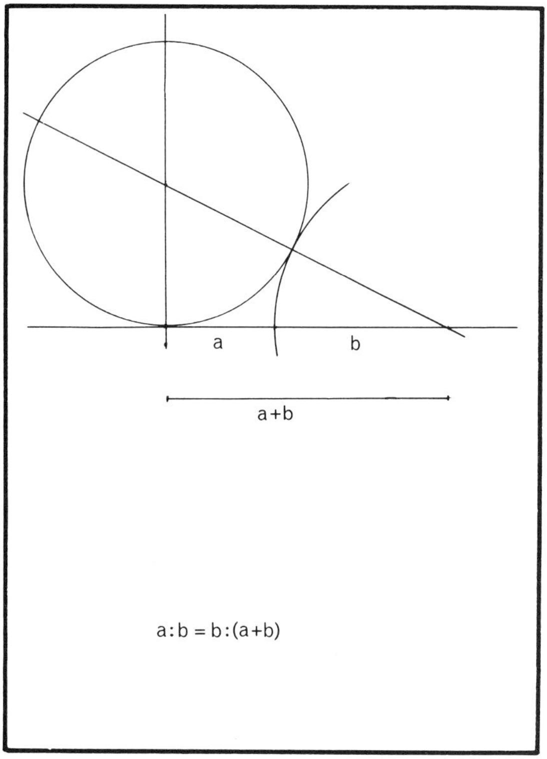

105

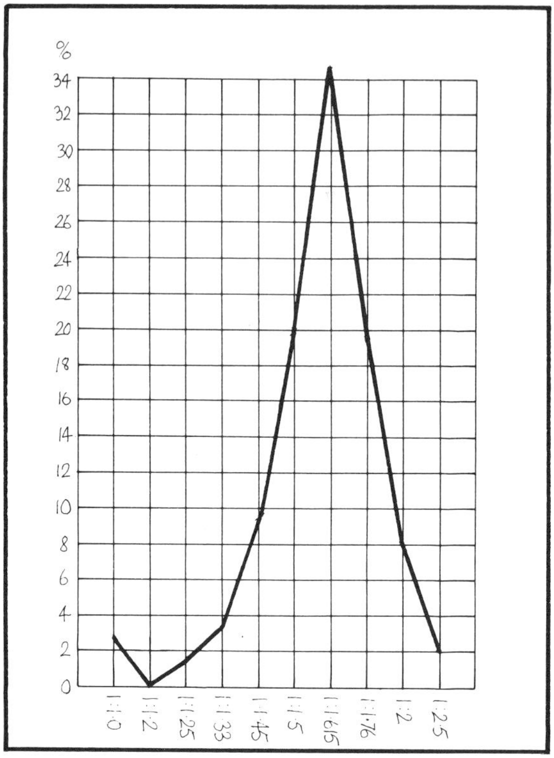

The construction of the Golden Mean (left) and the alleged preferences for the Golden Mean (right).

and set off against its surroundings by four lines (usually black). The second term means a rectangle, which is structured – in our case a picture.

As a result of Borissavlievitch's test (page 180) it can now be shown empirically that most people do prefer a rectangle of the proportions of the medial section to all others. But this result is only valid for empty rectangles as defined above.

The role of the golden mean in composition

In order to find out about 'filled rectangles' (ie, pictures), I calculated the proportions of about 1200 randomly 'selected' paintings – about half of them created before and half of them created after 1900, so as to take into account both 'old masters' and 'modern art'. The result is shown in diagram 106. The dotted line is the same as that shown in diagram 105 and serves as a point of reference because we now know that it shows the conditions concerning 'empty rectangles'. The other line shows the use of the proportions as far as pictures are concerned. It shows that most painters preferred rectangles which came relatively close to the square but, figuratively speaking, they avoided the medial section like the plague. To show that this is not a result of the breaking of rules in modern times, the breakdown of the results between 'old masters' and 'modern

106

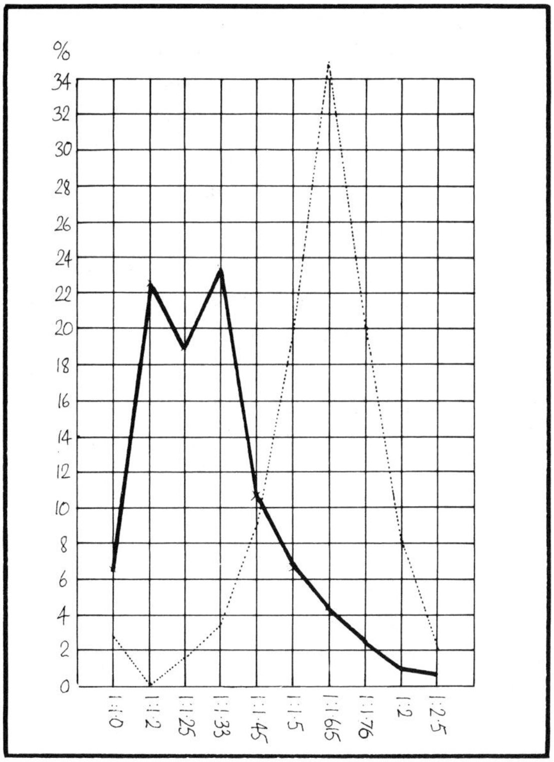

Real preferences for proportions (see text page 181).

art' is interesting. Only 5.13 per cent of the old masters used the medial section for the proportions of their pictures as opposed to 6.0 per cent of twentieth-century artists.

Of course much more could be said about this, but as far as we are concerned the result is conclusive. The medial section is an abstract concept, which only applies to 'empty rectangles'. But because photography is not concerned with 'empty rectangles', it simply cannot exist as a rule of composition. As a rule of composition the whole concept is fictitious.

This, of course, is why I have refrained from really digging into the concepts of classical 'rules of composition'. But if I had done so the conclusions would have been similar, showing that there is absolutely nothing behind them. They have only survived so long because everyone has taken them for granted, and accepted them unquestioningly.

Another interpretation

But before concluding this chapter, I must warn you not to fall into another trap which I prepared for the unwary. If you have another look at diagram 106, you will notice that although the golden mean is not what it was made out to be, there seems to be a substitute for it. The curve of the proportions of rectangles actually used for pictures shows a very pronounced peak at

another section of the x-axis, which might lead you to conclude that a preference (or some aesthetically superior quality) could be attributed to rectangles with the proportions thus indicated. But that is not so. First of all we have to assume that the paintings used for this survey qualify as 'art'. We do not know what that is or how the term is defined, but the assumption is that they are 'good' (without specifying the point of reference for this judgement). In consequence we must accept that they are of equal quality as far as the choice of a certain proportion for the picture plane is concerned – regardless of what this proportion might be.

The inevitable conclusion is that this curve requires a different interpretation from that concerned with the golden mean. The latter implies that the rectangle with the proportions of the golden mean is the best in its aesthetic category, while all others are less good in varying degrees. But the preference for certain proportions as used in paintings cannot be construed to mean the same thing. It merely shows that in a given number of cases one proportion worked best, while in others the use of different proportions led to qualitatively equivalent solutions. Because of this we cannot draw the conclusion that any one proportion, be it the golden mean or not, works better than another. We can only state with confidence that the proportions of the picture-plane are an integral part of the whole composition. In this it is on an equal footing with all other elements of composition.

The use of proportions

Fortunately at least one generalisation is possible. There is one interpretation of diagram 106 which is permissible. If you are concerned with a variety of subjects and if you realise each part in the appropriate composition, you are likely to use all the proportions shown in the diagram at one time or another. But there is a strong probability that you will use most often those which feature prominently in the diagram – that is, rectangles with the proportions 1 : 1.2 – 1 : 1.33).

If you now look back at what I said about cropping in Chapter 11, you might find this fact useful in order to decide what kind of camera-format to use, if you have to make do with just one.

In this chapter, illustrations 107, 108 and 109 are enlargements which show the whole negative of three different formats. They are 6 × 6, 6 × 7 and 35 mm (24 × 36 mm), which are the ones commonly used today. If you care to compute their proportions you can fit them into the diagram.

107

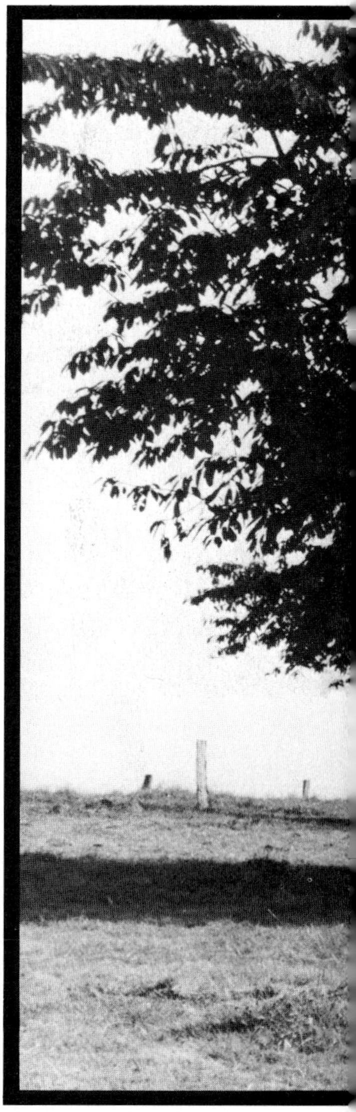

But I have done it for you anyway. They are 6×6, proportions 1 : 1; 6×7, proportions 1 : 1.167; 24×36 mm, proportions 1 : 1.5.

From this it is easy to see that the 6×7 format comes closest to the range of proportions which you are likely to use most often. So, for a given final image size, if you use this format you will have the smallest possible loss of technical quality by cropping. (By now I hardly need to stress the fact that this is, of course, only one of the factors which must be taken into account in a decision of this kind.) But remember, this is a statistical probability, nothing more. It might fit your needs or it might be completely wrong for them. This you will – as usual – have to find out yourself, which leaves us exactly where we started. Except, perhaps, for one thing: if you still believed in the golden mean as a 'rule of composition', you would be even worse off.

An enlargement showing the proportions of the 35 mm negative.

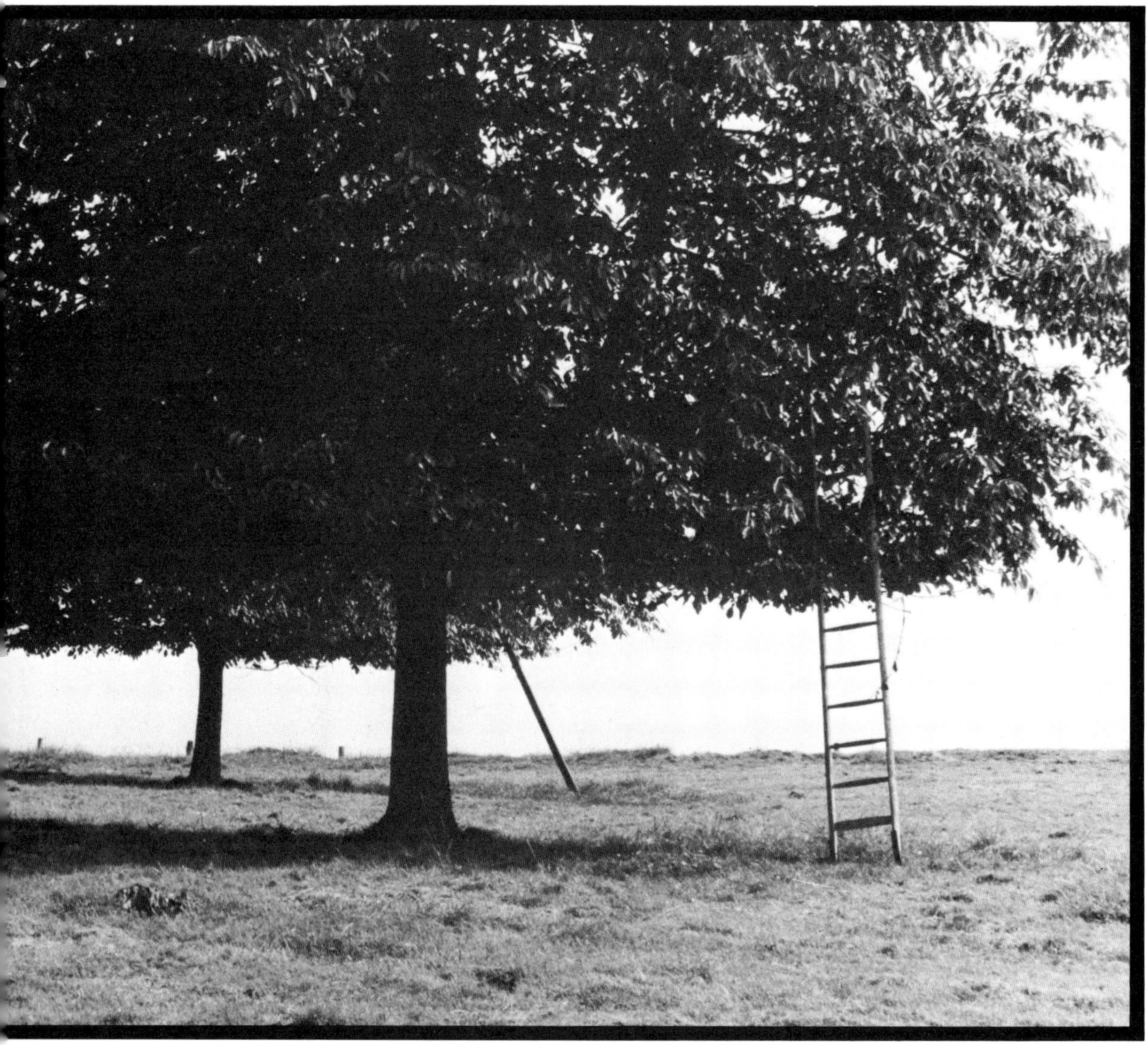

108

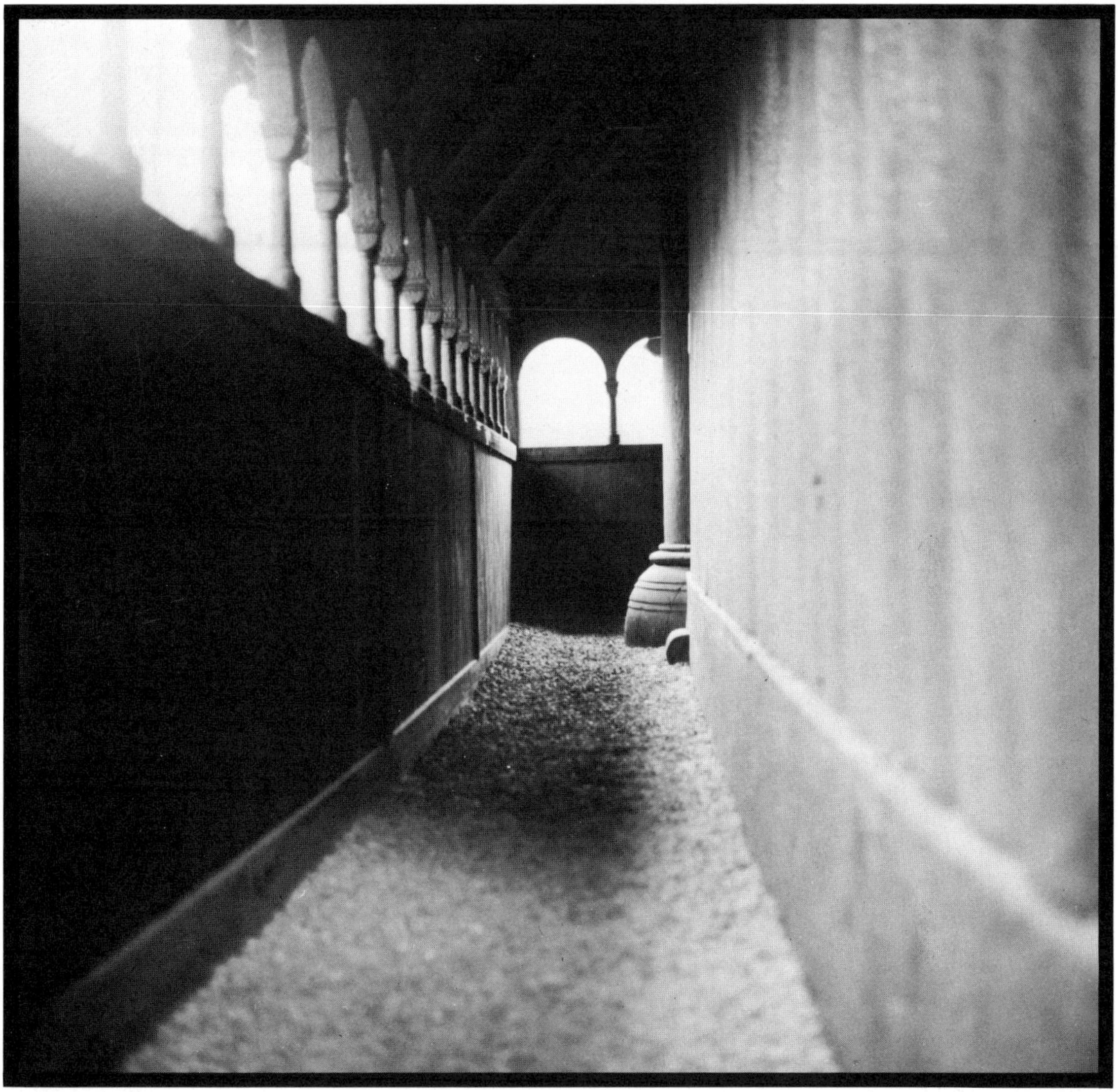

Enlargement showing the proportions of 6 × 6 cm ($2\frac{1}{4} \times 2\frac{1}{4}$) negative.

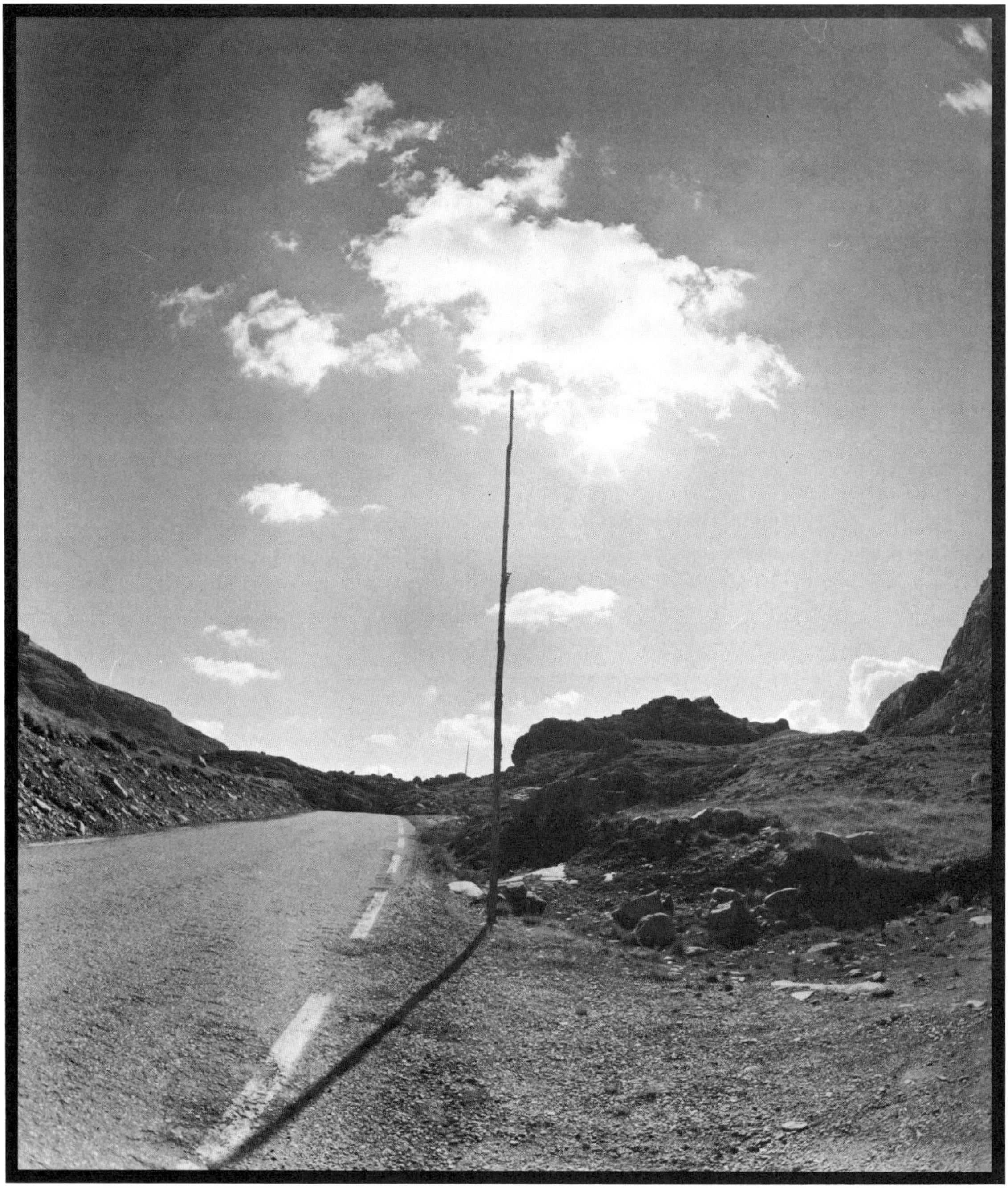

Enlargement showing the proportions of a 6 × 7 cm negative.

15 Epilogue

Sometimes, especially at the beginning of this book, we might have seemed to be at cross-purposes: you set out to learn something about composition, I set out to show that this cannot be done. Generally, such a situation is very unprofitable for both parties concerned. But I hope that our case proves to be the exception to the rule, because I believe that I have had some interesting things to offer as a substitute. An insight into what makes photographs tick – or to state it more properly, an insight into the determining factors in the relationship between the photographer, his work and the viewer – is not what I would call a poor compensation for the mindless application of rules which do not work anyway.

I have tried to show that this network of relationships between artist/art/viewer presents a different appearance with each change in the point of view. If you look at it from the outside with what might be termed the 'scientific eye' your intention would be to describe what is there. The difficulty then is that the person who wants to describe the network (the 'experimenter') is at the same time part of it (as the viewer), so that he has to react to and thus change the situation which he/she only wanted to describe.

Fortunately, we are not concerned with this methodological difficulty at all because we occupy an entirely different position in the network. As photographers we want to change it anyway, in order to accommodate it to our own purposes. By working through this book you will have found out that this can be done and how to go about it, which is quite a different prospect from learning some rules of doubtful quality and then applying them to some picture or other. For once you are not working to a set of foregone conclusions. In this relationship between photographer/work/viewer you are the prime mover, not just an industrious artisan who tries to match his output to an ominous set of rules.

This in turn implies that every deficiency in you or me (be it in the power of vision or in the ability to realise it in the form of a picture) will be reflected in this relationship. And because nobody is perfect, as the saying goes, we will have to work constantly on improvements and new approaches. If I have succeeded in convincing you of this necessity and in showing you some lines along which you can work, we can both be content with our efforts, I with writing this book and you with working through it.

110

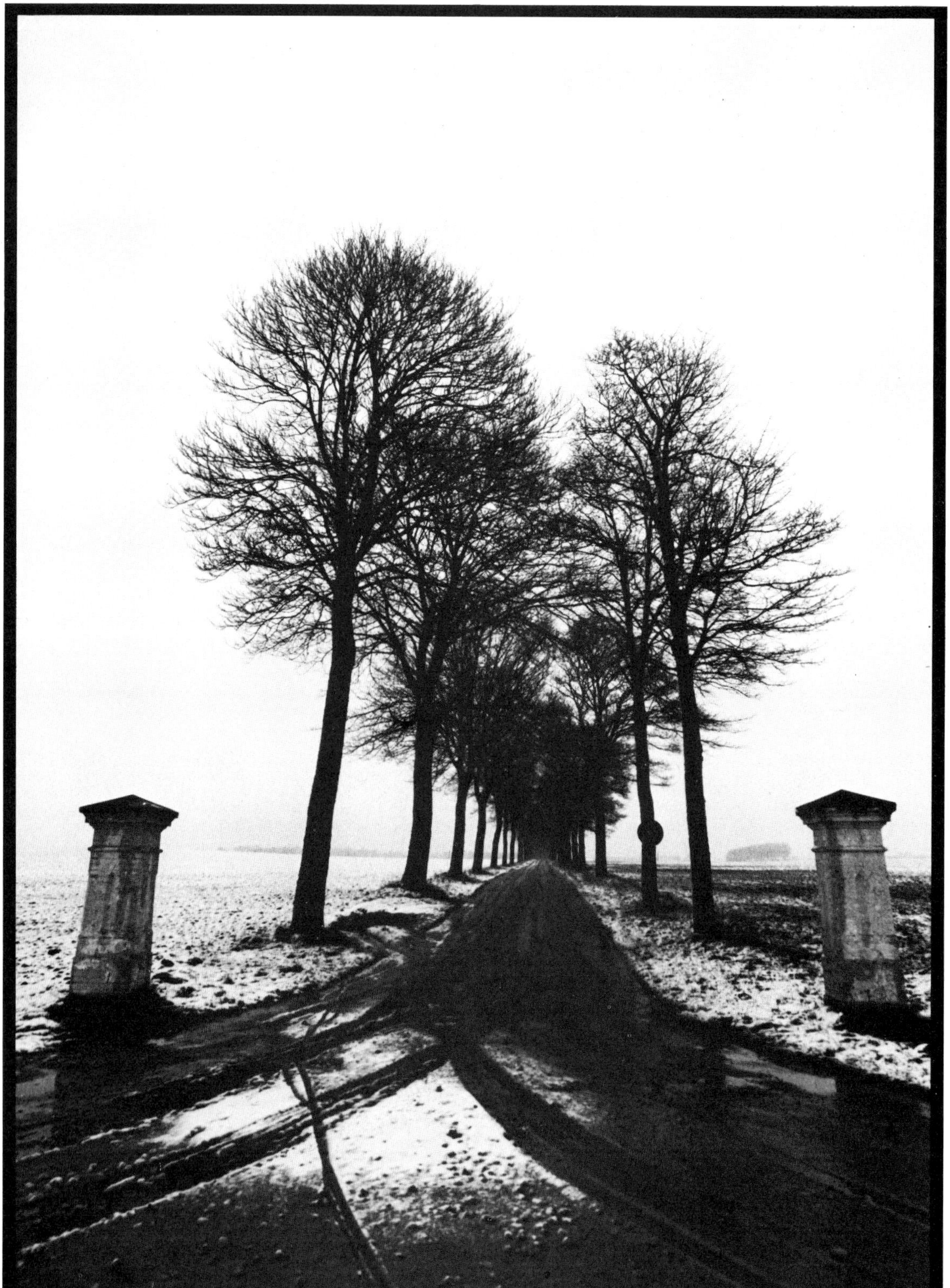

INDEX

Entries in italic are the main ones of a particular subject